ENGLISH HERITAGE

London

IN THE FOOTSTEPS OF
THE FAMOUS

Nicholas Best

D1472401

Bradt Trav
The Globe Pequot Press Inc, USA

Published in 2002 by Bradt Travel Guides Ltd,
19 High Street, Chalfont St Peter, Bucks SL9 9QE, England
Published in the USA by The Globe Pequot Press Inc,
246 Goose Lane, PO Box 480, Guilford, Connecticut 06437-0480

British Library Cataloguing in Publication Data
A catalogue record for this book is available from the British Library

ISBN 1 84162 043 2

Library of Congress Cataloging-in-Publication Data applied for

Cover
Designed by Concise Artisans. *Cartoon* Dave Colton.
Photograph White Tower, Tower of London, Crown copyright: Historic Royal Palaces

Line drawings Carole Vincer
Cartoons Dave Colton
Maps Steve Munns

Typeset from the author's disc by Wakewing, High Wycombe

Author/Acknowledgements

AUTHOR

Nicholas Best grew up in Kenya and first discovered London when he was an officer in the Grenadier Guards, patrolling the Tower of London in the middle of the night. His novels have been praised as 'wickedly funny' (*Daily Mail*), 'the funniest book of the year' (*Daily Telegraph*), and 'in places as sharp as Waugh and sometimes better' (*Times Literary Supplement*). He lives in Cambridge.

ACKNOWLEDGEMENTS

I should like to thank the following for their help: Donald Rumbelow, Christopher Jones, Marion Colthorpe, Norman Hammond and Jean Wilson; Mark Fox of the Theatre Royal; Val Horsler of English Heritage; Hugh Roberts and Caroline De Guitaut of the Royal Collection; and Anne Bailey, Iain MacKenzie and Miss J M Wraight of the Admiralty.

Thanks also to HM the Queen Mother for allowing me to quote from a wartime letter; to Nigel Nicolson for permission to quote from his father's diary; to A P Watt on behalf of the National Trust for permission to quote from Rudyard Kipling's autobiography *Something of Myself*; to Palgrave, for permission to quote from Sadie Anderson's 1936 translation of *The Letters of Mozart and his Family*; and to Andre Deutsch for allowing me to quote from *84 Charing Cross Road*, Helene Hanff's entertaining correspondence with her English bookseller, first published in 1971.

DEDICATION

For my daughters Kit and Evie – a reminder of where they were born

Contents

Introduction   VIII

Walk 1   **Westminster and St James'**   I
               (including the Abbey and Buckingham Palace)
               Walk at a glance 1, St James' Palace 4,
               Horse Guards Parade 8, 10 Downing Street 9,
               The Old Admiralty Building 10, Banqueting House 11,
               Houses of Parliament 12, Westminster Hall 13,
               Old Palace Yard 15, The Sanctuary 17,
               Jerusalem Chamber 17, Westminster Abbey 18,
               Cabinet War Rooms 29, St James' Park 29,
               Buckingham Palace 31, White's Club 33,
               16 St James' Square 34, Schomberg House 35,
               The Athenaeum Club 36, Duke of York's steps 37,
               Royal Opera Arcade 37, Haymarket 39,
               Trafalgar Square 40, Charing Cross 41, What now? 43,
               Where to eat 43

Walk 2   **The Tower of London**   44
               Walk at a glance 44, Traitors' Gate 46, Bloody Tower 49,
               Wakefield Tower 52, White Tower 53, Martin Tower 60,
               Bowyer Tower 62, Waterloo Block 63, Tower Green 64,
               Devereux Tower 70, Beauchamp Tower 72,
               Bell Tower 72, Queen's House 73, Queen's Stair 76,
               The Middle Tower 78, Tower Hill Scaffold 79,
               Tower Hill Underground 82, What now? 82,
               Where to eat 83

Walk 3   **St Paul's Cathedral and the Temple**   84
               Walk at a glance 84, St Paul's Cathedral 85,
               British Telecom 92, St Bartholomew-the-Great church 93,
               The Charterhouse 95, St John's Gate 96,
               37a Clerkenwell Green 97, Central Criminal Court 98,
               17 Gough Square 101, Ye Olde Cheshire Cheese 102,
               St Dunstan-in-the-West church 103,
               Middle Temple Hall 104, Middle Temple Garden 105,
               What now? 106, Where to eat 106

Walk 4   **Covent Garden and Somerset House**   107
Walk at a glance 107, Royal Opera House 108,
Theatre Royal 110, 8 Russell Street 111, Covent Garden
Market 112, St Paul's church, Covent Garden 113,
10 Henrietta Street 114, 35 Maiden Lane 115,
27 Southampton Street 116, 36 Tavistock Street 117,
26 Wellington Street 118, Somerset House 119,
12 Buckingham Street 121, 43 Villiers Street 122,
Craven Street 123, What now? 125, Where to eat 126

Walk 5   **Soho**   127
Walk at a glance 127, 33 Wardour Street 128,
Gerrard Street 129, 84 Charing Cross Road 132,
Old Compton Street 133, 4 Denmark Street 135,
Frith Street 137, 28 Dean Street 139, 15 Poland Street 140,
Carnaby Street 142, 41 Beak Street 142, Café Royal, 68
Regent Street 143, What now? 144, Where to eat 145

Walk 6   **Mayfair**   146
Walk at a glance 146, 37 Dover Street 147, 50 Albemarle
Street 148, Burlington House 149, Savile Row 151,
103 and 147 New Bond Street 154, Brook Street 155,
21 Hanover Square 157, 7 Stratford Place 158,
45 Berkeley Square 159, 3 Bolton Street 160,
What now? 161, Where to eat 161

Walk 7   **Belgravia**   162
Walk at a glance 162, Ebury Street 162, Eaton Square 165,
99 Eaton Place 167, Cadogan Place 167, Cadogan Hotel,
Sloane Street 169, What now? 170, Where to eat 171

Walk 8   **Bloomsbury and the British Museum**   172
Walk at a glance 172, 44 Bedford Square 173, 3 Gower
Street 174, British Museum 175, 24 Russell Square 178,
Gordon Square 179, 5 Woburn Walk 182, 183 North
Gower Street 183, What now? 184, Where to eat 185

Walk 9   **The City**   186
Walk at a glance 186, Guildhall 186, Mansion House 188,
Royal Exchange 190, 32 Cornhill 191,
The George & Vulture, George Yard 192, Monument 193,
What now? 196, Where to eat 197

Walk 10   **Jack the Ripper**   198
Walk at a glance 198, 1st murder 200, 2nd murder 201,
3rd murder 202, 4th murder 203, 5th murder 206,
So who *was* Jack the Ripper? 208, What now? 209,
Where to eat 209

Index   213

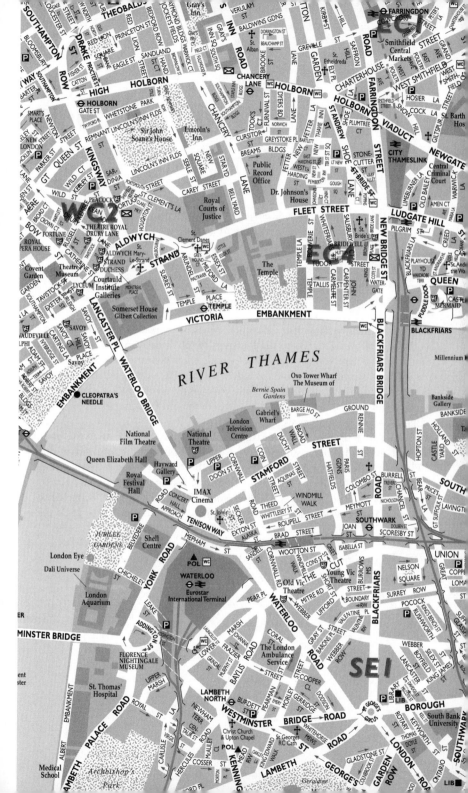

Introduction

'I went through a door Shakespeare once went through, and into a pub he knew. We sat at a table against the back wall and I leaned my head back, against a wall Shakespeare's head once touched, and it was indescribable.'

Helene Hanff
84 Charing Cross Road

This is a guidebook with a difference. It takes you on short walks around London, following always in the footsteps of the famous. At every point you will stand where somebody famous stood, often centuries earlier, and will learn from eyewitness accounts exactly what they were doing when they stood there. If you follow the guide carefully you will see all of London that is worth seeing and you will see it through the eyes of the most distinguished people in English – and sometimes world – history.

There are ten walks to choose from, each with a list of contents at the front. Everybody is in here somewhere, from **William the Conqueror** and **Thomas à Becket** to **Anne Boleyn**, **Elizabeth I**, **Sir Isaac Newton**, **Jane Austen**, **Lord Nelson** and **Charles Dickens**. **Wolfgang Amadeus Mozart** is here too, and so are **Felix Mendelssohn**, **Richard Wagner**, **Karl Marx**, **Fyodor Dostoevsky** and hundreds of others, including of course **Jack the Ripper**. No London guide would be complete without him.

Have a look at the contents page of each walk. The Westminster walk alone is worth the price of the book. Read the summary on pages 1 to 3 and see if you agree.

Westminster and St James'

WALK AT A GLANCE

Features This is the single most historic walk in the world.
Time Allow several hours.
Length 2 miles, in several easy stages.
⊖ Green Park, Piccadilly Circus

1 **St James' Palace**
- Queen Mary barricades the gate
- Queen Elizabeth I emerges to fight the Spanish
- Charles I sets off for execution
- Casanova calls for his sedan chair
- America's first ambassador has an awkward meeting with George III.

2 **Horse Guards Parade**
- the Americans win at Yorktown
- the Prime Minister takes it very badly.

3 **10 Downing Street**
- Sir Robert Walpole moves in
- Lloyd George hears the guns in France
- Neville Chamberlain announces World War II
- Winston Churchill is bombed at dinner.

4 **The old Admiralty**
- Captain Cook returns from the South Seas
- Lord Nelson's death is announced by a muddy lieutenant.

5 **The Banqueting House**
- Samuel Pepys witnesses the execution of Charles I
- his son Charles II enjoys a food fight.

6 **Houses of Parliament**
- Winston Churchill offers blood, toil, tears and sweat.

7 Westminster Hall
- a mounted knight throws down the gauntlet
- the Duke of York attempts a coup
- William Wallace, Sir Thomas More and Charles I are sentenced to death
- Oliver Cromwell's head is displayed on a pike.

8 Old Palace Yard
- William Caxton sets up England's first printing press
- Sir Walter Ralegh is beheaded.

9 The Sanctuary
- Richard III promises to spare his nieces from rape.

10 Jerusalem Chamber
- Henry IV dies
- William Shakespeare puts it in a play.

11 Westminster Abbey
- William the Conqueror is crowned in 1066 (and later Richard III, Henry VIII and Anne Boleyn on the same spot)
- St Thomas à Becket attends the reburial of Edward the Confessor
- England's first Parliament meets in the Chapter House
- a mob murders a gaoler during the Peasants' Revolt
- Henry V is buried by a grieving nation
- the poet Edmund Spenser is buried near Geoffrey Chaucer
- the two little princes, Elizabeth I, Sir Isaac Newton, Charles Dickens and Charles Darwin are buried too, as is the Unknown Warrior of World War I.

12 Cabinet War Rooms
- Winston Churchill goes underground during the Blitz.

13 St James' Park
- James Boswell picks up girls.

14 Buckingham Palace
- George III waves to Mozart
- Queen Victoria sees the troops off to the Crimean War
- Kaiser Wilhelm and Archduke Ferdinand attend the funeral of Edward VII
- George VI and Queen Elizabeth are bombed by the Luftwaffe
- Eleanor Roosevelt rations her bathwater.

15 White's Club
- William Pitt is attacked by a mob
- Beau Brummell holds court in the bow window.

16 St James' Square
- George IV receives good news from Waterloo
- Dwight Eisenhower and Bernard Montgomery have a little parking problem.

17 Schomberg House
- Lady Hamilton poses nude
- Johann Christian Bach calls on Thomas Gainsborough.

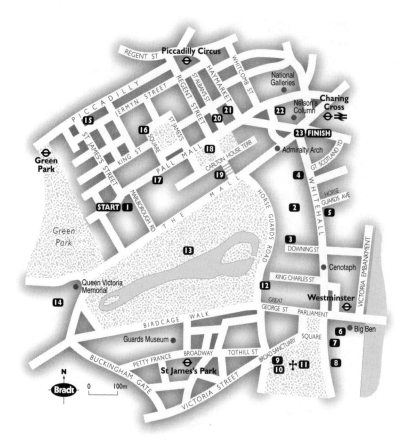

18 The Athenaeum
• Charles Dickens and William Makepeace Thackeray patch up their quarrel.

19 Duke of York's steps
• William Gladstone offers to reform a prostitute.

20 Royal Opera Arcade
• Harriette Wilson sells her memoirs
• the Duke of Wellington says 'Publish and be damned'.

21 Haymarket
• Giuseppe Verdi conducts his own opera
• Oscar Wilde is accosted by a rentboy
• Fyodor Dostoevsky is appalled by child prostitution.

22 Trafalgar Square
• Londoners celebrate the end of World War II.

23 Charles I statue
• Samuel Pepys sees a Parliamentary general hanged
• Daniel Defoe reflects on the significance of it all.

ST JAMES' PALACE
Elizabeth I

1

Main gate

St James' has been a palace since the 1530s. In August 1588, **Queen Elizabeth I** set up her command post here to fight the Spanish Armada, which was sailing up the Channel to invade England and restore a Catholic monarch to the throne.

The Armada's progress was reported every few hours. The queen fretted increasingly as the danger drew closer. Eventually, she could wait no more. On the morning of Thursday, August 8, she emerged from St James' to join her army at Tilbury Fort, where the Spanish were expected to land. She was dressed for battle in a red wig, a white velvet dress and a silver breastplate 'like some Amazonian empress'.

Elizabeth travelled downriver from Whitehall Steps. At Tilbury, she made a famous speech, rallying the army: 'I know I have the body of a weak and feeble woman, but I have the heart and stomach of a king.' Her words were greeted with a roar of approval by the troops.

The queen hurried back to St James' on August 10. Invasion was expected at any moment. Church bells rang as she arrived and the streets were hung with blue cloth in her honour. The crowds cheering her coach 'did nothing but talk of the great queen she was and how they would die for her'.

Elizabeth remained at the palace for the rest of the month, masterminding the operations against the Spanish. Their Armada had already been dispersed and their troops massed in Holland never came ashore. It was one of the greatest triumphs of her reign... and of English history.

Did you know?

? St James' Palace was a traditional rallying point in times of crisis. In February 1554, **Sir Thomas Wyatt** led a march on London aimed at preventing **Queen Mary** from marrying the King of Spain. The queen promptly withdrew into the palace and barricaded the gate. The rebels were defeated on February 7 but the battle was fierce on both sides, particularly for one unfortunate rebel: 'In this conflyct one pikeman, setting his backe to the wall at sainct James, kept xvij. horsemen of him a great tyme, and at last was slayne.'

? St James' was a leper hospital for women until 1531, when **Henry VIII** bought the land for a new palace. The gatehouse, the Chapel Royal (large window right of the gate) and a few surrounding walls are all that now remain of his original design.

George IV
Chapel Royal and Cleveland Row

The Chapel Royal has seen many royal marriages, none more disastrous than that of the future **George IV** and Princess Caroline of Brunswick on April 8 1795. 'I am not well,' said George, when he first saw his bride. 'Pray get me a glass of brandy.'

They spent their wedding night at the palace, but George was outraged to discover that his bride's manners 'were not those of a novice. In taking those liberties natural on these occasions, she said: "Ah, mon Dieu, qu'il est gros!" and how should she know this without a previous means of comparison?'

George was so upset he spent the night drunk in front of the fireplace. Caroline left him there.

Did you know?

? George's brother, the **Duke of Cumberland**, had an apartment overlooking Cleveland Row. A bizarre incident occurred in his rooms in the early hours of May 31 1810, when he claimed to have been attacked by an intruder with a sword. Someone had certainly been attacked, because Cumberland's valet lay dead in another room. A jury later concluded that the man had committed suicide after failing to murder his employer. But he was left-handed and his throat had been cut by a right hand... A more plausible explanation is that the duke was a practising homosexual – his rooms were fitted with mirrors in unusual places – and had murdered the valet rather than have his secret betrayed.

John Adams, Giacomo Casanova
Friary Court, Marlborough Road

Although the monarch hasn't lived here for more than 200 years, foreign ambassadors are still accredited to the Court of St James', rather than Buckingham Palace. It was here, on June 1 1785, that **John Adams** (later US President) presented his credentials to **George III** as the first American ambassador from the newly independent colonies.

The meeting was deeply embarrassing for both men. Adams had helped draft the Declaration of Independence and during the war that followed had been proscribed as an outlaw by the British. His appointment as ambassador was a deliberate provocation, to show King George that the Americans would appoint whoever they pleased. Adams' name was mud with the king, so it was debatable which of them was more nervous as the American arrived for their fateful first meeting.

He was taken to the Foreign Secretary's office in Cleveland Row to begin with, and then by coach for the few yards to the palace. His wig was newly dressed and powdered, he wore black breeches, silk stockings and buckled shoes, and he fiddled nervously with his sword and gloves as he was ushered into the royal presence. Adams bowed three times – once in the doorway, once halfway into the room, and once directly in front of the king – and then launched into a speech he had learned by heart.

> The appointment of a public minister from the United States to Your Majesty's court will form an epoch in the history of England and of America

he told George, adding that his purpose was to restore

> the old good nature and good humour between people who, though separated by the ocean and under different governments, have the same language, a similar religion, and kindred blood.

George responded with a tremor in his voice:

> I will be very frank with you. I was the last to consent to the separation, but the separation having been made and having become inevitable, I have always said that I would be the first to meet the friendship of the United States as an independent power.

Adams then withdrew, walking backwards out of the room, and the audience was over – to everyone's relief. It had gone much better than he had anticipated, as he later reported to Thomas Jefferson:

> The Mission was treated by His Majesty with all the Respect, and the Person with all the Kindness, which could have been expected or reasonably desired, and with much more, I confess, than was in fact expected by me.

Did you know?

? It was not only ambassadors who were presented at Court. Wearing his best rings, and with an order hanging round his neck on a red ribbon, the Italian adventurer **Giacomo Casanova** had an audience with the king in the spring of 1763: 'On Sunday morning I made an elegant toilette and went to Court about 11, and met the Comte de Guerchi in the last antechamber, as we had arranged. He presented me to George III, who spoke to me, but in such a low voice that I could not understand him and had to reply with a bow ... After the presentation was over I got into my sedan chair and went to Soho Square. A man in court dress cannot walk the streets of London without being pelted with mud by the mob, while gentlemen look on and laugh.'

? Friary Court is where the death of a monarch is traditionally announced by the Garter King of Arms. Flanked by the Earl Marshal and two serjeants-at-arms, he stands on the brick balcony and declares to the crowd below: 'The king is dead. Long live the king!' The ceremony is then repeated at three other places in London, as well as Windsor, Edinburgh and York.

Charles I
The Mall

Charles I spent much of his early life at St James', so it was appropriate that he should be held here in January 1649, after the victorious Parliamentary army sentenced him to death for his part in the English Civil War.

The execution was set for January 30. Charles slept only four hours the night before and was awake two hours before dawn. He dressed in black for the occasion, wearing two shirts instead of one in case he shivered with cold on the scaffold and was mistaken for a coward. Then he knelt down and prayed until it was time to go to Whitehall.

The call came at ten. Charles' people ignored the first knock on the door, but when it came again he led the way outside and was taken through the palace gardens to St James' Park, where troops were waiting to escort him to Whitehall.

The royal apartments have burned down since Charles' time. They overlooked the garden where the southern range of Friary Court now stands (neither Marlborough Road nor the Mall existed then). Just beyond the garden:

> the Park had several Companies of Foot drawn up, who made a Guard
> on either side as the King passed, and a Guard of Halberdiers in
> company went some before, and othersome followed; and drums beat,
> and the noise was so great as one could hardly hear what another spoke.

They set off for Horse Guards Parade. With them went Charles' dog, Rogue, gambolling playfully at his master's heels, delighted that they were all going for a walk in the park. It was the last walk he and his master would ever have together.

Did you know?

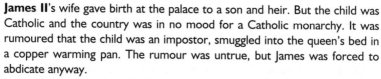

? During the English Civil War, Charles' younger son (later **James II**) was a Parliamentary prisoner at the palace. He escaped in 1648, disguised as a woman.

? On June 10 1688, **James II**'s wife gave birth at the palace to a son and heir. But the child was Catholic and the country was in no mood for a Catholic monarchy. It was rumoured that the child was an impostor, smuggled into the queen's bed in a copper warming pan. The rumour was untrue, but James was forced to abdicate anyway.

? James was replaced by his Protestant son-in-law, **William III** (Prince of Orange), whose people arrived from Holland and swiftly took over the palace. **John Evelyn** saw them on December 18 1688: 'All the world go to see the Prince at St James' where is a greate Court, there I saw him and severall of my Acquaintance that come over with him. He is very stately, serious, and reserved.'

HORSE GUARDS PARADE
Lord North, Duke of Wellington

2

Central archway, leading to Whitehall

Horse Guards Parade marks the official entrance to Whitehall, once a royal palace but now the heart of British Government. As you face the central archway, the rear of Downing Street is on your right, and the old Admiralty buildings are on your left, across the parade ground.

Just before noon on Sunday, November 25 1781, the Admiralty was dozing peacefully in the winter sunshine when a messenger arrived from the port of Falmouth, on the Cornish coast. He brought dreadful news from the American colonies. Lord Cornwallis and his army had surrendered to the rebels at a placed called ... Yorktown.

Oh dear! The news was rushed across to the Prime Minister in Downing Street (No 10 is on the right of the white Treasury building). **Lord North** took it very badly,

> as he would have taken a ball in his breast... He opened his arms,
> exclaiming wildly, as he paced up and down the apartment during a
> few minutes, 'O God! it is all over!' – words which he repeated many
> times under emotions of the deepest consternation and distress.

The game was up and the colonies were lost. North resigned soon afterwards.

Did you know?

? The Horse Guards building itself dates from the 1750s and was the headquarters of the British army for more than a century. The parade ground has been used by the army since medieval times. **George III** reviewed his Foot Guards here on February 25 1793 before sending them to the Napoleonic Wars. Today, those same regiments celebrate the monarch's birthday here every year at the ceremony of Trooping the Colour.

? In the 1840s, the **Duke of Wellington** was commander-in-chief of the British army and occupied the room above the central archway. 'The Duke generally proceeded to his office at the Horse Guards on foot or on horseback. If on horseback he usually rode through the Park, if on foot he came by the streets, and always alone. Everybody knew him; and everybody, high and low, rich and poor, saluted him as he passed.' The duke's desk is still in the room, still in everyday use.

? In earlier times, the southeast corner of the parade ground was Whitehall's tilt yard, where medieval knights used to joust. A young courtier spotted **Elizabeth I** here on May 3 1578: 'In the morning, about eight o'clock, I happened to walk in the Tiltyard, under the gallery where Her Majesty useth to stand to see the running at tilt; where by chance she was, and, looking out of the window, my eye was full towards her; she shewed to be greatly ashamed thereof, for that she was unready and in her nightstuff.'

? It was via the tilt yard steps (since demolished) that **Charles I** crossed to Whitehall on his way to execution.

10 DOWNING STREET
Sir Robert Walpole, Winston Churchill
Rear view, from Horse Guards Parade. Not the front door

Although he didn't realise it, Britain's first Prime Minister made a momentous move on September 22 1735.

> Yesterday the Right Hon **Sir Robert Walpole** with his Lady and
> Family removed from their House in St James' Square, to his new
> House adjoining to the Treasury in St James' Park.

The house was 10 Downing Street. It has been the Prime Minister's official residence ever since.

Before Walpole's alterations, the house (on the right of the white Treasury building) faced Horse Guards Parade rather than Downing Street. Walpole turned it around and moved the front door to Downing Street because it was closer to the House of Commons. The rear exit is still used by outgoing Prime Ministers hoping to avoid the cameras after an election defeat.

No 10 has often been at the centre of world events, never more so than at the time when the ultimatum was given to Germany on August 4 1914 to provide a guarantee of Belgian neutrality by midnight. As the deadline approached, **Margot Asquith**, the Prime Minister's wife, joined him in the Cabinet Room (ground floor rear, overlooking the garden):

> The clock on the mantelpiece hammered out the hour and when the
> last beat of midnight struck it was as silent as dawn. We were at war. I
> left to go to bed, and, as I was passing at the foot of the staircase, I saw
> Winston Churchill with a happy face striding towards the double
> doors of the Cabinet Room.

Halfway through World War I, Asquith was succeeded as Prime Minister by **Lloyd George**. On still summer evenings, when Lloyd George took time off from chasing his secretary round her desk, it was sometimes possible to hear the rumble of guns in France as British troops braced themselves for another big push.

Britain went to war again on Sunday, September 3 1939. Prime Minister **Neville Chamberlain** broadcast to the nation at 11.15am:

> I am speaking to you from the Cabinet Room at 10 Downing Street.
> This morning the British Ambassador in Berlin handed the German
> government a final note, stating that unless we heard from them by
> 11 o'clock that they were prepared at once to withdraw their troops
> from Poland, a state of war would exist between us. I have to tell you
> now that no such undertaking has been received, and that
> consequently this country is at war with Germany.

Chamberlain was swiftly replaced by **Winston Churchill**. On October 14

1940, Churchill was hosting a dinner in the Garden Rooms at the rear of No 10 when it was interrupted by an air raid.

> The butler and parlourmaid continued to serve the dinner with complete detachment... The cook and the kitchen-maid, never turning a hair, were at work. I got up abruptly, went into the kitchen, told the butler to put the dinner on the hot plate in the dining-room, and ordered the cook and the other servants into the shelter, such as it was. I had been seated again at the table only about three minutes when a really loud crash, close at hand, and a violent shock showed that the house had been struck...

> We went into the kitchen to view the scene. The devastation was complete... the blast had smitten the large, tidy kitchen, with all its bright saucepans and crockery, into a heap of black dust and rubble.

Did you know?

? Other occupants of No 10 have included: **William Pitt**, the **Duke of Wellington**, **Benjamin Disraeli**, **William Gladstone** and **Margaret Thatcher**.

THE OLD ADMIRALTY BUILDING
Captain Cook, Lord Nelson
Whitehall, turn left through Horse Guards archway

There was intense excitement in the Admiralty boardroom (upstairs left, rear of building) on the morning of August 1 1775. **Captain James Cook** had returned from his second voyage of discovery and was on his way to London to report to their Lordships.

> Two o'clock Monday – This Moment Capt Cook is arrived. I have not yet had an opportunity of conversing with him, as he is still in the boardroom – giving an account of himself & Co... He has some Birds for (Sir Joseph Banks) that he would have wrote to you himself about, if he had not been kept too long at the Admiralty and at the same time wishing to see his wife.

Cook had been away three years exploring the Antarctic and South Pacific (104 days out of sight of land), and disproving the myth of a great southern continent.

In all that time he had lost only one man to disease, establishing beyond doubt that the way to defeat scurvy and fever was through hygiene and diet.

Did you know?

? **Horatio Nelson** reported regularly to the Admiralty when in London. His mistress, **Lady Hamilton**, sometimes dropped him off on her way to do some shopping. Other women wondered what she saw in Nelson: 'The first time I saw him was in the drawing-room of the Admiralty, and a most uncouth creature I thought him. He was just returned from Teneriffe, after losing his arm. He looked so sickly, it was painful to see him, and his general appearance was that of an Idiot.'

? News of Nelson's death at Trafalgar was delivered to the boardroom at 1am on November 6 1805. A mud-stained lieutenant raced upstairs and burst in on the Secretary of the Admiralty: 'Sir, we have gained a great victory, but we have lost Lord Nelson!' The admiral's body was brought here (window, ground floor, left of pillars) on January 8 1806, before its burial next day in St Paul's Cathedral (see page 85).

THE BANQUETING HOUSE
Charles I

5

Whitehall, across the road from Horse Guards Parade

This is where **Charles I** was executed just after 2pm on January 30 1649. There was a delay of several hours after his arrival from St James' while Parliament hastily passed a bill preventing his son's succession as king. Then Charles was brought through the Banqueting House and led out onto the scaffold, either through a window or a hole in the wall constructed for the purpose above the door to the left.

A crowd of thousands was held well back by troops afraid of a rescue attempt. The lower part of the scaffold was shielded by black cloth, so that spectators could see the axe rise but not fall. The mood was sombre because few people wanted the king to die. They did not like what Parliament was doing in their name.

Charles made a rambling speech, interrupted by somebody thoughtlessly reaching down to feel the sharpness of the axe. The crowd was so far away that only the people on the scaffold could hear what he was saying.

> I never did begin the war with the two Houses of Parliament, and I
> call God to witness (to whom I must shortly make an account) that I
> never did intend to incroach upon their privileges.

When he was ready, Charles turned to one of his guards: 'Take care that they do not put me to pain.' He tucked his hair into a nightcap and took off his cloak and decorations. 'Remember!' he told his priest. Lying down (the block was too low to kneel), he paused for a moment, then gave the signal by stretching out his hands.

He was beheaded with one blow, to a groan of disgust from the crowd – 'such a groan as I never heard before, and desire I may never hear again.' Then everybody pressed forward to dip their handkerchiefs in the blood.

Did you know?

? The official axeman refused to execute the king, as did many others. His eventual replacement was heavily masked and never revealed his identity.

? Among the onlookers was 15-year-old **Samuel Pepys**. Years later, after the monarchy had been restored, the diarist met an old schoolfriend. 'He did remember that I was a great Roundhead (Parliamentarian) when I was a boy, and I was much afeared that he would have remembered the words that I said the day that the King was beheaded (that were I to preach upon him, my text should be: "The memory of the wicked shall rot").'

? The Banqueting House is all that now remains of Whitehall Palace. It is open to the public and has a magnificent ceiling painted by **Peter Paul Rubens**. On April 4 1667, after he had been restored to his father's throne following long years of Puritan repression, **Charles II** enjoyed a convivial banquet there: 'The King sate on an elevated Throne at the upper end, at a Table alone. The Knights at a Table on the right-hand reaching all the length of the roome; over against them a cuppord of rich gilded Plate &c...on the balusters above Wind musique, Trumpets & kettle drumms... At the banquet came in the Queene & stood by the Kings left hand, but did not sit. Then was the banqueting Stuff flung about the roome profusely... I now staied no longer than this sport began for feare of disorder. The Cheere was extraordinary, each knight having 40 dishes to his messe, piled up 5 or 6 high. The roome hung with the richest Tapissry in the World &c.'

HOUSES OF PARLIAMENT
Winston Churchill

6

Big Ben end

On June 4 1940, the German army was sweeping across Europe. The British army had fled from Dunkirk and the Battle of Britain was about to begin – the most serious threat to the island since the Norman invasion of 1066.

In the House of Commons, the Prime Minister rose to his feet. **Winston Churchill** had already told Parliament that he had nothing to offer but blood, toil, tears and sweat. Now he spoke again.

> We shall not flag or fail. We shall go on to the end. We shall fight in
> France, we shall fight on the seas and oceans, we shall fight with

growing confidence and growing strength in the air, we shall defend our island, whatever the cost may be. We shall fight on the beaches, we shall fight on the landing grounds, we shall fight in the fields and in the streets, we shall fight in the hills. We shall never surrender.

Did you know?

? In private, Churchill is said to have added: 'We will hit them over the head with beer bottles. It's all we have to fight them with.'

? There has been a palace at Westminster at least since **Edward the Confessor** moved here in the 1040s. Two centuries later, **Henry III**'s barons held the first 'Parliament' (French for 'speaking') in one of the palace halls. Westminster has remained a 'palace' ever since, even though the last monarch moved out in the 1530s. Unfortunately, the ancient palace burnt down in 1834. The only building to escape was Westminster Hall (next stop). The present Houses of Parliament were completed in 1851.

WESTMINSTER HALL
William Wallace, Sir Thomas More, Charles I, Oliver Cromwell

7

In front of the Houses of Parliament, by the statue of Oliver Cromwell

On October 10 1460, during the Wars of the Roses, a band of men came down the road from Charing Cross. There were 500 of them, heavily armed, advancing on Westminster Hall. At their head rode the royal Duke of York, his sword carried upright in front of him in the manner of a king.

To a fanfare of trumpets, the duke dismounted and strode into Westminster Hall. His intention was to seize the throne from **Henry VI**, who was mentally disturbed.

> He went straight through the great hall until he came to the chamber where the king, with the commons, was accustomed to hold his parliament. There he strode up to the throne and put his hand on its cushion just as though he were a man about to take possession of what was rightfully his. He kept it there for a while then, withdrawing it, he turned to the people and, standing quietly under the canopy of state, waited expectantly for their applause.

None came. After a frosty silence, the Archbishop of Canterbury asked if he wanted to see the king. The duke replied that he had as good a claim to the kingship as any. To show that he meant business, he broke into the royal apartments and occupied them for several days before being persuaded to leave. Far from winning the crown, he was killed in battle a few weeks later.

Westminster Hall is all that now remains of the original palace. Built in 1097 and remodelled in the 1390s, it was used for all sorts of state occasions, among them the coronation feasts after a new monarch had been crowned in the Abbey.

Henry IV's feast of October 13 1399 was chronicled by **Jean Froissart**.

> When dinner was half over, a knight of the name of Dymock entered the Hall fully armed and mounted on a handsome steed, richly barbed with crimson housings. The knight was armed for wager of battle, and was preceded by another knight bearing his lance. The knight presented the king with a written paper, the contents of which were, that if any knight or gentleman should dare to maintain that king Henry was not a lawful sovereign, he was ready to offer him combat in the presence of the king, when and where he should be pleased to appoint.

For 600 years, until the opening of new law courts in 1882, Westminster Hall was also the seat of royal justice. The courts of the King's Bench occupied different corners of the Hall, establishing a legal system now widespread in the English-speaking world.

Among the famous trials held here were those of:

Sir William Wallace This Scottish patriot was tried on August 23 1305 with a laurel crown on his head, in mockery of his boast that he would one day wear a crown at Westminster. The judges showed him no mercy:

> You shall be carried from Westminster to the Tower... hanged and drawn, and as an outlaw beheaded... your heart, liver, lungs, and entrails from which your wicked thoughts come shall be burned... your head shall be placed on London Bridge... your quarters hung on gibbets at New Castle, Berwick, Stirling, and Perth...

Sir Thomas More Objected to **Henry VIII** divorcing the first of his six wives. 'I am the King's good servant, but God's first.' Tried for high treason on July 1 1535. Sentenced to be hanged, castrated and disembowelled while still alive, but was actually beheaded, his head boiled and displayed on London Bridge. He is now a Catholic saint.

Guy Fawkes Attempted to blow up king and Parliament in 1605 (an event still commemorated every November 5 with bonfires and fireworks). Tried January 27 1606. 'The Queen and Prince were in a secret place by to hear and some say the King in another'. Tortured at the Tower, then executed in Old Palace Yard (see page 16), opposite the scene of his crime.

Charles I Tried January 20 1649, but refused to recognise the Parliamentary court. 'I would know by what power I am called hither... I am not suffered for to speak. Expect what justice other people will have.' Taken away in a sedan chair, he was beheaded at the Banqueting House (see page 11).

Did you know?

? Parliament's leader was **Oliver Cromwell**. After the restoration of the monarchy, Cromwell's body was exhumed in 1661 and his head stuck on a pole above the southern end of Westminster Hall. It stayed there until 1684, when a storm blew it down. The head passed through various hands until 1960, when it was reburied at a secret location in the chapel of Cromwell's old college at Cambridge.

? The office of king's champion has been held by the Dymoke family since 1377. The head of the family still attends modern coronations, but no longer has to wear armour or throw down a gauntlet!

OLD PALACE YARD
Sir Walter Ralegh
Far end of Parliament, opposite the Abbey

Old Palace Yard has changed since **Sir Walter Ralegh** was beheaded on October 29 1618. There was no road then – just a quiet little yard attached to the palace where the Houses of Parliament now stand. But Westminster Hall, the Abbey, and the Jewel House across the green were all here in Ralegh's time. They were the last buildings he saw as he laid his head on the block.

Ralegh was executed by **James I**, ostensibly for an attack on the Spanish. He spent his last night in the gatehouse prison (now demolished) at the other end of the Abbey. There he bade a tearful farewell to his wife before sitting up most of the night writing poetry to her.

He arrived for his execution at eight o'clock next morning, out of breath after being pushed through the crowd.

> All preparations that are terrible were presented to his eye. Guards and officers were about him, the scaffold and the executioner, the axe and the more cruel expectations of his enemies.

Ralegh wore grey silk stockings, black taffeta breeches, a brown doublet and a nightcap under his hat which he gave to a bald onlooker who needed it more than he did. After a lengthy speech, he shook hands with his friends and knelt on the executioner's cloak, facing west towards the Chapter House of the Abbey.

The crowd called for him to face east, towards his Redeemer. Ralegh obliged, under protest: 'What matter it which way the head lie, so the heart be right?'

The axeman hesitated. 'What dost thou fear?' demanded Ralegh. 'Strike, man, strike!' The first blow killed him. The second severed his head from his body.

Did you know?

? Ralegh was the driving force behind the English colonisation of North America. It was from Virginia that his people introduced tobacco to England.

? After Ralegh's death, his severed head was given to his wife. She had it embalmed and kept it in a red leather bag for the rest of her life.

? Among the onlookers outraged at Ralegh's execution were **John Hampden** and **John Pym**, later prominent in the struggle for Parliament against the powers of the king.

? **Guy Fawkes** was executed here too, a few yards from the Houses of Parliament that he had tried to blow up. On January 31 1606, the chief villain of the Gunpowder Plot was dragged from the Tower of London on a hurdle, then hanged by the neck before being quartered. He was so weak from torture when he arrived that he couldn't climb the ladder to the gallows. He had to be helped by the hangman.

Just beyond the railings, close to the Chapter House of the Abbey, **William Caxton** set up Britain's first printing press in 1476. It was an immediate sensation. As he explained, of an earlier book printed in Bruges,

> It is not wreton with penne and ynke as other bokes ben, to thende that every man may have them attones (at once), ffor all the bookes of this storye named *the recule of the historyes of troyes* thus empryntid as ye here see were begonne in oon day, and also fynysshid in oon day.

Caxton chose his premises carefully. Between the king's palace, the Abbey, and the Chapter House (where parliament met), he was bound to have some important custom. He published in English, rather than Latin, producing books on chess and fishing for a wide audience. One of his earliest successes was *The Canterbury Tales*, by **Geoffrey Chaucer**, probably published in 1478.

Caxton enjoyed the patronage of three successive monarchs, including **Edward IV**, who gave him £20. But he never got any printing business from the Abbey. The monks preferred quill pens to word processors.

Did you know?

? Caxton died a rich man, no doubt from underpaying his writers.

? Geoffrey Chaucer lived near by and is buried in the Abbey.

? Just beyond the Chapter House stands the Jewel Tower, built in 1365 as part of the royal palace. It was surrounded by a moat, and was used by monarchs from Edward III onwards as a strong room for their personal valuables. Today it houses an exhibition about Parliament and a small display, including a sword dating from AD800 which was found near by.

? A long way past the Jewel Tower, the next bridge across the river leads to Lambeth Palace, the London residence of the Archbishops of Canterbury since 1197. The palace was a great centre of power and intrigue during the Middle Ages, when the 'Cardinal of Canterbury' was the Pope's representative in England. It's a long walk to go and see it, two miles there and back.

THE SANCTUARY
Richard III

9

West end of Westminster Abbey

When **Edward IV** died in 1483, his brother, the Duke of Gloucester (later **Richard III**), moved swiftly to seize the throne. He captured the elder of Edward's two sons and hurried to London to capture the other, who was at Westminster with his mother, Queen Elizabeth.

On May 1, she fled to the safety of the Abbey.

> The Quene, in great flight and heaviness… gat herself in all the haste possible with her younger son and her daughters out of the palace of Westminster, in which she then lay, into the Sanctuary, lodging herself and her company there in the Abbot's place.

The Archbishop of York arrived before dawn.

> He found much heaviness, rumble, haste and business, carriage and conveyance of her stuff into Sanctuary, chests, coffers, packs, fardels, trusses, all on men's backs, no man unoccupied, some lading, some going, some discharging… The Quene herself sat alone, alow on the rushes, all desolate and dismayed.

Richard's troops surrounded the Abbey, but were unable to invade the Sanctuary (the area immediately around the Abbey). Instead, he persuaded the queen to surrender her son, adding that if she gave up her five daughters as well:

> I shalle see that they shalbe in suertie of their lyffes and also not suffre any maner hurt by any maner persone or persones to theim or any of theim in their bodies and persones to be done by wey of Ravisshement or defouling contrarie their willes.

None of the girls was raped. But the little prince joined his brother in the Tower of London and was never seen again.

Did you know?

? The medieval idea of Sanctuary – a holy place not to be violated – was abandoned after it was abused by criminals fleeing the law.

? One of Queen Elizabeth's daughters later married **Henry VII** and became the queen depicted on playing cards. She is an ancestor of the present monarch.

? The skeletons of the two little princes were discovered at the Tower in 1674 and reburied in Westminster Abbey.

JERUSALEM CHAMBER
Henry IV

10

West end of Westminster Abbey, behind the bookshop

The crenellated building behind the bookshop is the Jerusalem Chamber, once a part of the Abbot's house. It is the setting for a famous scene in **William Shakespeare**'s play *Henry IV*.

A fortune-teller had prophesied that **Henry IV** would die in Jerusalem. In March 1413, near to death, he came to the Abbey to pray at Edward the Confessor's shrine before setting out for the Holy Land.

> While he was making his prayers at St Edward's Shrine to take there his leave and so speed him on his journey, he became so sick that such as were about him feared that he would have died right there. Wherefore they, for his comfort, bore him into the Abbot's place and laid him down before the fire in this chamber.
>
> On coming to himself and learning that he was in the chamber named Hierusalem, then said the King, 'Laud be to the Father of Heaven! for now I know that I shall die in this chamber, according to the prophecy made of me beforesaid, that I should die in Hierusalem,' and so he made himself ready, and died shortly after.

Did you know?

? In Shakespeare's play, the king's son (later **Henry V**) takes the crown while his father is still alive. Unfortunately, there is no historical evidence for this.

? The Jerusalem Chamber was used in 1611 by the committee translating the Bible into English. King James' Authorized Version is rivalled only by Shakespeare as the greatest work in the English language.

? There is so much history in the Abbey and its surroundings that the whole area has been designated a World Heritage site by the United Nations.

WESTMINSTER ABBEY
The Nave

11

Henry V was one of England's greatest monarchs, a fine military commander – his archers beat the French at Agincourt – and an outstanding statesman as well. The English were devastated when he died suddenly in 1422, aged only 35.

He was buried in the Abbey on November 7. All of London lined the streets as his body was brought to the main door. The soldiers in the procession wore black and carried their weapons in reverse as a sign of mourning. Among the nobles,

> an Erle armed complet hys horse trapped and garnysshed whyth the Kyngs armes rode bare hedyd... in hys hande a batylax borne wt the poynte downwarde.

Flying the banner of St George, the coffin was escorted into the Abbey and taken up the nave towards the choir. It was accompanied by horses bearing the arms of the King of England and of France. There was straw on the floor to prevent the horses slipping. They were ridden by armed men, one of them a knight wearing a crown and the king's coat armour.

At the entry to the choir, Henry's coffin was transferred to a hearse for the funeral service. The way was lit by 60 men in black hoods, carrying wax torches around the king's body.

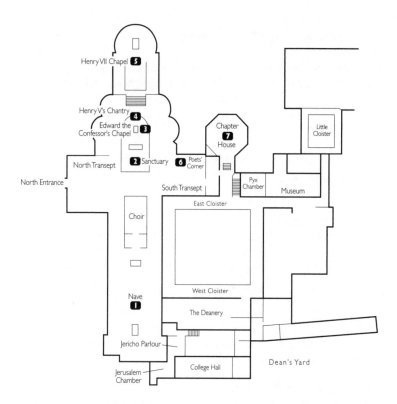

He was buried with suche solempne ceremonies, suche mournyng of
lordes, such prayer of pryestes, such lamentynge of commons as
never was before that daye sene in the Realme of Englande.

After the service, the king's corpse was interred at the far end of Edward the
Confessor's chapel (behind the altar). A small chantry was then built over the
coffin in the shape of a giant 'H'. For many years a shield and saddle used at
the funeral hung from the bar above the coffin. They are kept now in the
Undercroft museum, together with a sword and helmet popularly supposed to
have been Henry's.

Did you know?

? The first Westminster Abbey was completed by **Edward the Confessor** in
1065, replacing a Saxon church on the same spot. Edward's abbey in turn was
rebuilt between the 13th and 15th centuries. The nave was still not finished
at the time of Henry V's funeral.

? At the beginning of the nave lies the tomb of the Unknown Warrior, a British
serviceman killed on the Western Front during World War I. British deaths in

SOME OF THE ABBEY'S GRAVES

Nave
Richard II (first contemporary portrait of an English monarch, painted for Abbey c1398), the Unknown Warrior, Ben Jonson (16th-century dramatist), David Livingstone (19th-century missionary/explorer), Ernest Rutherford (atomic physicist), Sir Isaac Newton, Charles Darwin

Chapel of Edward the Confessor (Coronation Chair)
Edward I, Henry III, St Edward (the Confessor), Henry V, Edward III, Richard II

Henry VII Chapel
George II, Edward VI, Henry VII, James I (nothing visible), Elizabeth I, Mary I, Edward V (and the Duke of York, the little princes in the Tower), Anne, William III and Mary, Charles II, Mary Queen of Scots

North Transept
Prime Ministers: William Gladstone, Lord Palmerston, George Canning, William Pitt the elder (Earl of Chatham), William Pitt the younger
Statesmen: Henry Grattan (Irish patriot), Charles James Fox, William Wilberforce (anti-slavery)

South Transept (Poets' Corner)
Poets: John Dryden, Robert Browning, Alfred Lord Tennyson, Geoffrey Chaucer, Edmund Spenser
Literary men: Dr Johnson, David Garrick (actor), Richard Brinsley Sheridan, Lord Macaulay, Charles Dickens, William Makepeace Thackeray, Rudyard Kipling, Thomas Hardy
Composers: George Frederick Handel

the war reached three quarters of a million, with an equivalent number of women dying unmarried because there were no husbands for them – a calamity which affected almost every family in the land. So many soldiers, sailors and airmen had no known graves that a single unidentified body was reburied in the Abbey in remembrance of them all. Many Britons still observe two minutes' silence at 11am on November 11 (or the nearest Sunday) in memory of the moment in 1918 when the guns at last fell silent.

The Sanctuary
Nothing visible remains, but this is where **William the Conqueror** was crowned on December 25 1066, two months after the battle of Hastings. Never could he have imagined that 900 years later his would be one of the most enduring royal dynasties of all time.

William's claim to the throne was precarious. Although his rival, **King Harold**, had been killed at Hastings, the English had been very reluctant to pay William homage. It was only by ravaging the countryside around London that he had forced them into offering him the crown. He needed the coronation to make him legitimate.

Unfortunately, the ceremony did not go well.

When Archbishop Ealdred asked the English, and Geoffrey bishop of Coutences asked the Normans, if they would accept William as their king, all of them gladly shouted out with one voice, if not in one language, that they would.

The armed guard outside (William's Norman troops), hearing the tumult of the joyful crowd in the church and the harsh accents of a foreign tongue, imagined that some treachery was afoot, and foolishly set fire to some of the buildings. The fire spread rapidly from house to house. The crowd who had been rejoicing in the church took fright and throngs of men and women of every rank and condition rushed out of the church in frantic haste.

Only the bishops and a few clergy and monks remained, terrified, in the Sanctuary, and with difficulty completed the consecration of the king, who was trembling from head to foot.

Did you know?

? William I was crowned at the central crossing of the original Abbey, directly above the grave of Edward the Confessor. Every monarch since then has been a descendant of William's. All but two of them – **Edward V** (one of the little princes murdered in the Tower in 1483) and **Edward VIII** (abdicated 1936 to marry an American divorcee) – have been crowned here, the most historic spot in all England.

? The original Sanctuary was completely rebuilt by **Henry III** in the 13th century. He opened it up and enlarged it to provide a suitable 'theatre' for future coronations. The work was completed by 1259 and the present pavement dates from ten years later. It has been the setting for all the coronations ever since.

? A picture of the original abbey can be seen in France's Bayeux tapestry, which tells the story of the Norman Conquest.

One of the first monarchs to be crowned in the new Sanctuary was **Edward II**. The ceremony on February 25 1308 was dominated by his flamboyant boyfriend **Piers Gaveston**, 'seeking his own glory rather than the king's'.

WARNING

When **William III** was crowned in Westminster Abbey in 1689, his purse was stolen during the ceremony. He reached for it at the end to put some money in the offertory, and found to his great embarrassment that it had been taken without him even noticing.

British pickpockets are the finest in the world. If they can steal the king's purse while he's being crowned, what chance does a tourist have who goes into the Abbey with all his credit cards in a shoulder bag or an outside pocket?

Keep your money in two different places, both of them zipped up and out of sight, preferably underneath your clothes. Otherwise, you will be jostled in the Abbey, you will feel the money go, and when you turn round, the only person there will be... Oliver Twist.

YOU HAVE BEEN WARNED!

Piers wore an outfit of royal purple for the occasion, trimmed with pearls. He looked lovely – 'none was near to Piers in bravery of apparell or delicacie of fashion' – but purple really wasn't his colour. It was the king's, and he shouldn't have worn it.

Nor should he have walked second last in the procession, just in front of the king. Nor should he have carried St Edward's crown, or fastened a gilt spur to Edward's left foot. The barons were so annoyed at his presumption that they talked of killing him on the spot. Piers was indeed murdered later, and Edward too.

Richard III's coronation on July 6 1483 was just as fraught as his predecessors'. The coronation preparations had been made for the elder of the two little princes, but it was their uncle Richard who turned up to be crowned, having declared his nephews illegitimate. Few people at the ceremony agreed with that decision, but no-one dared say so, although the choir's singing was pointedly muted. Richard wore purple velvet for the occasion, his wife 'a rych serkelet of golde with many preciouse perles and stones sett therin.'

> The King and Queene came downe to the high Alter and there they
> hade great observance and service and in the meane while the King

and the Queene departed from their robes and stode naked from the medle upwarde and anone the bishops anointed boethe the King and the Queene, and after that this was done the King and the Queene changed their robes into clothe of gold and than the Cardenall of Caunterburye and all the byshopes crowned boeth the King and the Queen with great solempnite.

Henry VIII was only 17 at his coronation on June 24 1509. He walked to the Abbey from Westminster Palace along a carpet of royal blue. The crowd were so enthusiastic that they fell on the carpet and cut it up for souvenirs while Henry was still in the Abbey.

Anne Boleyn, the second of Henry's six wives, was crowned queen on June 1 1533. The ceremony was performed by **Archbishop Cranmer** (author of the prayerbook). It lasted eight hours and at one point required Anne to lie prostrate in front of the altar – not easy, when she was six months pregnant. Anne was beheaded three years later after failing to produce a son.

Elizabeth I (Anne's daughter) was crowned on January 15 1559, the last time the ceremony was held in Latin. Preceded by three drawn swords representing her three kingdoms, Elizabeth knelt before the altar and kissed the paten (the dish used at Eucharist). Then she withdrew to Edward the Confessor's chapel (behind the altar) to avoid a Roman Catholic part of the service that she did not agree with.

Charles II's coronation on April 23 1661 was very grand, designed to show the watching ambassadors that England was no longer a republic. The Abbey was decorated in red throughout, and Charles himself wore crimson and gold. A great shout went up when the crown was placed on his head, the nobles queuing up to touch it, 'promising by that Ceremony to be ever ready to support it, with all their Power'. The capes first worn by the clergy at his coronation are still worn at coronations today.

William III's coronation in 1689 was spoiled by having his purse stolen (see box, page 22). How's your money?

George III foolishly held his coronation at lunchtime on September 22 1761.

The Archbishop of Canterbury mounted the pulpit to deliver the sermon; and, as many thousands were out of the possibility of hearing a single syllable, they took the opportunity to eat their meal, when the general clattering of knives, forks and plates, and glasses that ensued, produced a most ridiculous effect.

George IV's big day (July 19 1821) was marred by his estranged wife's attempt to gatecrash the ceremony. Barred from the west cloister, Caroline drove angrily around the Abbey, crying 'Let me pass. I am your queen. I am Queen of Britain', while the crowd alternately cheered and booed. At Westminster Hall she was seen 'standing behind the door on her own ten toes, with the crossed bayonets of the sentry under her chin'. From there she proceeded to the Chapter House, hoping to enter the Abbey by the little door in Poets' Corner, before finally admitting defeat.

Did you know?

? The Coronation Chair has been used in every coronation since 1308. It was commissioned by **Edward I** to house the Stone of Scone, captured from the Scots in 1296. The Stone was kept under the seat for 700 years before finally being returned to Scotland in 1996. The chair itself is displayed behind Henry V's chantry (further up the Abbey) between coronations. Some naughty schoolboys carved their names on it in the 18th century.

? King of England until his death in 1066, **Edward the Confessor** was buried below ground at first but was raised to a more imposing tomb 'in the side of the choir' on becoming a saint in 1163. **Thomas à Becket** (himself a saint, after his murder at Canterbury) was present as the coffin was reinterred. Edward was moved again in 1269, as part of Henry III's rebuilding plans, to a specially built chapel behind the altar.

Edward the Confessor's Chapel

This is the final burial place of **St Edward (the Confessor)**. He was brought here in 1269, when

> the xiii daye of October, the kynge lette translate with great solempnytie the holy body of seynt Edwarde kynge and confessour, that before laye in the side of the quere, into the chapell at the back of the hygh aulter of Westmester abbey, and there layde it in a ryche shrine.

Unfortunately, the shrine was partly destroyed in 1540 during the dissolution of the monasteries, when shrines everywhere were attacked in a drive against idolatry. The only part to survive was the base, which was hurriedly dismantled and hidden away until the storm had passed. It was reassembled in

1557, not quite on the same spot as before, and a new upper part was added to house the saint's coffin.

Edward's body was last seen in 1685, when a falling plank knocked a hole in the coffin and revealed the saint's head 'sound and firm, the upper and lower jaws full of teeth, a list of gold round the temples'.

Did you know?

? Edward's shrine was a magnet for pilgrims in the Middle Ages convinced of its miraculous powers. The base contains recesses for the sick, who knelt there praying for a cure. Among them was **Henry IV**, who was taken ill here in March 1413, before his death in the Jerusalem Chamber (see page 17).

? Pursued by a howling mob, an unpopular gaoler threw himself on the saint's mercy on June 15 1381 during the Peasants' Revolt. 'Great numbers of the commons came into Westminster Abbey at the hour of Tierce (9am), and there they found Richard Imworth, Marshal of the Marshalsea and warden of the prisoners, a tormentor without pity; he was at the shrine of St Edward, embracing a marble pillar, to crave aid and succour from the saint to preserve him from his enemies. But the commons wrenched his arms away from the pillar of the shrine, and dragged him away to Cheapside, and there beheaded him.'

? **Richard III** came here during his coronation in 1483, 'upon ray clothe bare foted into Saint Edwardes Shrine and all the noble lordes goinge with him every lorde in his degre... first Trompettes and clarions and then harouldes of armes with the Kinges cote armour upon theim and after them the Crose with a riall (royal) procescion.'

? The teenaged **Victoria** came too, during hers on June 28 1838: 'I then again descended from the Throne, and repaired with all the Peers bearing the Regalia, my Ladies and Train-bearers, to St Edward's Chapel, as it is called; but which, as **Lord Melbourne** [Prime Minister] said, was more *unlike* a Chapel than anything he had ever seen; for, what was *called* an *Altar* was covered with sandwiches, bottles of wine &c. The Archbishop came in and *ought* to have delivered the Orb to me, but I had already got it. There we waited for some minutes; Lord Melbourne took a glass of wine, for he seemed completely tired.'

Henry V's Chantry

Built in the shape of a giant 'H', the Chantry houses the tomb of Henry V, the victor of Agincourt. He was so admired during the Middle Ages that his tomb became a shrine. The steps to it have been worn down by millions of visitors over the past seven centuries.

One of the earliest visitors was Henry's inadequate son, **Henry VI**, who came here often during the Wars of the Roses to try and draw strength from his father's memory. He once spent an hour in the Chantry chapel above the tomb, looking gloomily down the nave and hoping for a way out of his troubles. But it was not to be. Henry was quietly murdered in 1471 and the Wars of the Roses got on much better without him.

Did you know?

? Henry V's beautiful French wife, Catherine de Valois, was buried next to her husband, but not until 1878. Victim of various rebuilding schemes, she was lying near the Chantry in a simple wooden coffin when **Samuel Pepys** showed his family round the Abbey on February 23 1669: 'Here we did see, by perticular favour, the body of Queen Katherine of Valois, and had her upper part of her body in my hands. And I did kiss her mouth, reflecting upon it that I did kiss a Queen, and that this was my birthday, 36 year old, that I did first kiss a Queen.'

? Catherine's body was only shown to privileged visitors. She was still on view in 1742, 'the Bones firmly united, and thinly cloth'd with Flesh, like scrapings of tann'd Leather.'

? Henry VI wanted to be buried near his father as well. He got the abbey mason to mark the spot with an iron pick. In the event, he was buried elsewhere, but a long scratch on the floor between the tombs of Henry V and Henry III probably marks the spot he chose.

? Did **William Shakespeare** ever stand here while writing his play *Henry V*? It's an interesting thought.

Henry VII Chapel

Henry VII was the king who beat Richard III at the battle of Bosworth, bringing the Wars of the Roses to a close. In 1503 he decided to rebuild this end of the abbey as a suitable burial place for royalty. The result was a sensation in its day.

Henry is buried just behind the altar, next to his wife (the playing card queen – see page 17). His funeral on May 11 1509 was lavish. His sword, shield, helmet and spurs were offered up and the choir sang *'Libera me'* as he was lowered into his grave. Henry's chief ministers broke their staves of office and threw them onto the coffin. Then:

> All the herauds did cast their cote armours and did hange them
> upon the rayles of the herse: crying lamentably in ffrench 'Le Noble
> roi Henri le Septieme est mort', and assoone as they had so done,
> everie heraud put on his cote-armor againe and cryed with a loud
> voyce: 'Vive le noble Henri le Huitesme' **Henry VIII**.

Did you know?

? Among the many other monarchs buried here (see plan, page 20) is **George II**, the last English king to lead his troops into battle. **Horace Walpole** attended his funeral on November 13 1760. 'When we came to the chapel of Henry VII all solemnity and decorum ceased – no order was observed, people sat or stood where they could or would, the yeomen of the guard were crying out for help, oppressed by the immense weight of the coffin... The Duke of Cumberland, who was sinking with heat, felt himself weighed down, and turning round, found it was the Duke of Newcastle standing upon his train to avoid the chill of the marble.'

? England's only republican leader was buried here too – for a while. Following his death in 1658, **Oliver Cromwell** was interred in what is now the Battle of Britain chapel, just beyond the grave of Henry VII. After the restoration of the monarchy however, he was exhumed on January 30 1661 – the 12th anniversary of Charles I's execution: 'This day were the Carkasses of that arch-rebell Cromewell, Bradshaw the Judge who condemn'd his Majestie & Ireton... draged out of their superbe Tombs (in Westminster amongst the Kings), to Tyburne, & hanged on the Gallows there from 9 in the morning til 6 at night, & then buried under that fatal & ignominious Monument, in a deepe pitt.'

? Henry VII's Chapel used to have fine stained-glass windows until they were smashed by Cromwell's Puritans in the 1640s. The fan-vaulted ceiling is rivalled only by King's College Chapel in Cambridge.

? The walls are hung with the banners of the Knights of the Bath, an old order of chivalry whose members used to undergo a ritual cleansing as part of their initiation (see Tower of London, see page 54).

Poets' Corner

Like most poets, **Edmund Spenser** was desperately poor. He wrote the *Faerie Queene* (1590, 1596) and was revered by his contemporaries as the finest poet since Chaucer. But he died penniless in January 1599, perhaps of starvation. There was no money for his wife and children, let alone a decent funeral.

Fortunately, the Earl of Essex paid for him to be buried near **Geoffrey Chaucer**, in a part of the Abbey that has since come to be known as Poets' Corner. Literary London turned out in force for the occasion, 'his Hearse being attended by Poets, and mournfull Elegies and Poems with the Pens that wrote them thrown into his Tomb.'

William Shakespeare admired Spenser's work, so he may well have been one of those who stood here and threw their pens into the grave.

Did you know?

? Spenser was a kinsman of **Lady Diana Spencer, Princess of Wales**, whose own funeral service was held in the Abbey in 1997 before her burial in Northamptonshire.

? Although Poets' Corner is mostly for writers, the composer **George Frederick Handel** was buried here too on April 20 1759. His funeral was supposed to be private but 3,000 people turned up uninvited.

? Thousands came also for the actor **David Garrick**'s burial on February 1 1779 – among them **Dr Johnson** (in tears), **Edmund Burke, Sir Joshua Reynolds, Edward Gibbon** and **Charles James Fox**.

? **Charles Dickens** was buried secretly on June 14 1870 to avoid similar crowds. But so many wanted to pay their respects that the grave had to be left open anyway until they had all filed past.

The Chapter House

After the coronations at the High Altar, this is probably the second most historic spot in England. According to one account, it is where **Simon de**

Montfort's Parliament met, the first to elect ordinary people as well as lords – the beginning of the House of Commons.

Henry III was forced to summon Parliament on January 20 1265.

> In which Parliament, on St Valentine's Day, it was made public in the Chapter House at Westminster that the Lord King had bound himself, on oath, by his charter that neither he nor the Lord Edward in time to come would do injury to, nor cause to be injured, the Earls of Leicester (Simon de Montfort) and Gloucester, nor the citizens of London or any of those who adhered to them, on account of anything done in the former time of disorder in the kingdom.
>
> And he ordered expressly that the charters of liberties (Magna Carta) … should be kept inviolate.

De Montfort had led a revolt against the powers of the king. He did not enjoy his triumph for long because he was killed later in 1265 and his body dismembered by the king's supporters. But the seeds of parliamentary democracy had been sown…

Did you know?

? The earliest known reference to an English Parliament is 1081, but they are not regularly mentioned before 1236.

? Although it also met elsewhere, the House of Commons continued to use the Chapter House until the 1540s. This greatly annoyed the monks of the Abbey, who came here daily to have a chapter of the Bible read to them.

? In the early 1300s, the Pyx chamber next to the Chapter House was used as a strong room for the royal treasury. But robbers broke in on April 24 1303 and stole jewellery and plate. Some of them were hanged the following March. It seems likely that the ringleader was flayed as well because an examination of the door 500 years later revealed pieces of human skin under the hinges. He had probably been nailed up there as a warning to others.

? The museum next door contains **Henry V**'s shield and saddle, the funeral effigies of several other monarchs, and a contemporary waxwork of **Lord Nelson** in his own uniform. The waxwork is a very good likeness, according to his mistress Lady Hamilton. She observed, 'the direction and form of the nose, mouth and chin and the general carriage of the body was exactly his'.

CABINET WAR ROOMS
Winston Churchill
12
Corner of King Charles Street and Horse Guards Road

Less dramatic than it appears in films, this was the nerve centre of the British war effort from 1939 to 1945 – an underground network of bomb-proof rooms filled with maps, telephones, typewriters and radio transmitters, all the equipment needed to fight World War II.

The rooms operated 24 hours a day from September 3 1939 to August 16 1945. In all that time, the lights in the central map room were never once switched off. People lived, ate and slept underground, working shifts around the clock so that there was always someone on duty. They saw so little daylight that they had to be given ultra-violet light for their health.

Winston Churchill held many meetings here in the darkest days of the war. He preferred to work elsewhere but the bombing of 10 Downing Street (see page 10) persuaded him it would be safer underground. His office and bedroom can still be seen, as well as the radio room from where his speeches were broadcast to the free world.

The sandbagged entrance is a modern addition. In 1940 the rooms were top secret, entered discreetly from the building above.

Did you know?

? On the night of October 21 1940, bombs were raining down on London as Churchill sat in the radio room making a broadcast to occupied France. 'We are waiting for the long-promised invasion,' he told the French defiantly. 'So are the fishes.'

? **Q** Which of the buildings on this walk was bombed during the Blitz: Horse Guards Parade, 10 Downing Street, the Houses of Parliament, Westminster Hall, Westminster Abbey or Buckingham Palace?
A All of them. You are probably standing on an unexploded bomb right now.

? There are lavatories and a restaurant in St James' Park.

ST JAMES' PARK
James Boswell
13

In November 1762, an ambitious young Scotsman arrived in London, determined to conquer the town. His name was **James Boswell**, the future biographer of **Dr Johnson**. His plan was to get a commission in the Guards and then take London society by storm. But first he needed a place to live. Boswell tramped the streets for days, until

> at last I fixed in Downing Street, Westminster. I took a lodging up two pair of stairs with the use of a handsome parlour all the forenoon... The street was a genteel street, within a few steps of the Parade; near the House of Commons, and very healthful.

The lodging has since been demolished. But it never meant much to Boswell anyway. He was far more interested in the neighbouring St James' Park, where all sorts of extraordinary things went on after dark:

> March 25 1763. As I was coming home this night, I felt carnal inclinations raging through my frame. I determined to gratify them. I went to St James' Park, and, like Sir John Brute, picked up a whore. For the first time did I engage in armour, which I found but a dull satisfaction. She who submitted to my lusty embraces was a young Shropshire girl, only seventeen, very well-looked.

> March 31. At night I strolled into the Park and took the first whore I met, whom I without many words copulated with free from danger, being safely sheathed. She was ugly and lean and her breath smelt of spirits. I never asked her name. When it was done, she slunk off.

> June 4. I went to the Park, picked up a low brimstone, called myself a barber and agreed with her for sixpence, went to the bottom of the Park arm in arm, and dipped my machine in the Canal and performed most manfully.

Did you know?

? The park was a busy place in the 18th century. Itinerant condom salesmen did a roaring trade. The condoms were made of animal gut, intended to protect men from venereal disease rather than prevent pregnancy.

? **Giacomo Casanova** frequented the park in the same year as Boswell. He went there 'to watch the Great Beauties parading', but was disconcerted to see people defecating in the bushes instead: 'Going towards Buckingham

House, I see in the shrubbery to my left a piece of indecency which surprises me. Four or five people at different distances were attending to their needs and showing their behinds to the passers-by. "It is disgusting", I said to Martinelli. "Those pigs should be facing us instead.'"

BUCKINGHAM PALACE
George III, W A Mozart, Queen Victoria, Kaiser Wilhelm

14

Named after a previous owner, Buckingham House was bought by **George III** in 1763 as a wedding present for his wife. It was to be her private home, the Queen's House, a retreat from the official entertaining and stuffy protocol of St James' Palace.

The newly-weds were very happy here. They filled the house with art, furniture and books, employing the best craftsmen of the day. They enjoyed music, the queen taking singing lessons from **Johann Christian Bach**, the king accompanying her on his flute. In 1764, they invited eight-year-old **Wolfgang Amadeus Mozart** to play the organ for them, an event recorded by his father in a letter home:

> On April 27th we were with the King and Queen in the Queen's Palace in St James's Park... Their easy manner and friendly ways made us forget that they were the King and Queen of England. At all courts up to the present we have been received with extraordinary courtesy. But the welcome which we have been given here exceeds all others.
>
> A week later we were walking in St James's Park. The King came along driving with the Queen and, although we all had different clothes on, they recognized us nevertheless and not only greeted us, but the King opened the window, leaned out and saluted us and especially our Master Wolfgang, nodding to us and waving his hand.

Buckingham Palace has been the monarch's official London residence since 1837, when **Queen Victoria** succeeded to the throne. A new front was added shortly afterwards, featuring a central balcony for the royal family to show themselves to the public. On February 28 1854, the queen appeared on the balcony to see the Scots Guards off to the Crimean War. She remembered

> the gradual, steady but slow approach of the Band, almost drowned by the tremendous cheering of the dense crowd following. The soldiers gave three hearty cheers which went straight to my heart.
>
> Carriages with ladies, sorrowing wives, mothers and sisters were there, and some women in the crowd were crying. The men were quite sober, in excellent order and none absent... May God protect these fine men, may they be preserved and victorious! I shall never forget the touching, beautiful sight I witnessed this morning.

Since Victoria's time, it has become traditional for the royal family to appear on the balcony on special occasions – weddings, the monarch's birthday, the end of World War II – providing a focal point for moments of national celebration.

The palace has seen many comings and goings over the years, perhaps none more poignant than the funeral of **Edward VII** on May 20 1910:

> There were eight crowned heads, King George V, the German Emperor, the Kings of Norway, Greece and Spain, of Bulgaria, Denmark and Portugal, with in addition to our own royal Princes, about thirty others, including the Arch Duke Franz Ferdinand of Austria. There was a babel of tongues and a clashing of hooves all round me. At last at a given signal they were all mounted and the royal cortège passed slowly before me out into the Forecourt.

Four years later, Archduke Ferdinand was assassinated at Sarajevo, precipitating World War I. Among those who lost their thrones as a result was the German Emperor, Kaiser Wilhelm.

During World War II, the palace was bombed several times, most famously at 11am on September 13 1940, when a German aircraft flew up the Mall in broad daylight and dropped a stick of high explosive across the forecourt. The king and queen were in a small room overlooking the front quadrangle at the time. **Queen Elizabeth** (mother of Elizabeth II) was outraged:

> We heard the unmistakable whirr-whirr of a German plane. We said 'ah, a German', and before anything else could be said, there was the noise of aircraft diving at great speed, and then the scream of a bomb. It all happened so quickly, that we had only time to look foolishly at each other, when the scream hurtled past us, and exploded with a tremendous crash in the quadrangle...

> Everybody remained wonderfully calm, and we went down to the shelter. I went along to see if the housemaids were alright, and found them busy in their various shelters. Then came a cry for 'bandages', and the first aid party, who had been training for over a year, rose magnificently to the occasion, and treated 3 poor casualties calmly and correctly.

Did you know?

? It was a brilliant raid. As soon as it was over, a policeman stepped across the rubble and told the queen so, as she stood surveying the wreckage: 'A magnificent piece of bombing, ma'am, if you'll pardon my saying so.' Credit where it's due!

? After the United States had entered the war, **Eleanor Roosevelt** (wife of the US President) came to stay in October 1942: 'The restrictions on heat and water and food were observed as carefully in the royal household as in any other home in England. There was a plainly marked black line in my bathtub above which I was not supposed to run the water. We were served on gold and silver plates, but our bread was the same kind of war bread that every other family had to eat...'

WHITE'S CLUB
William Pitt

15

Top end of St James' Street between Piccadilly and Jermyn Street

William Pitt was only 24 when George III made him Prime Minister in 1783, against the wishes of Parliament. It was a time of great political turmoil, with much bitterness between rival factions.

On February 28 1784, Pitt's coach was approaching White's Club when it was attacked by a mob carrying broken chair poles.

> Several desperate blows were aimed at Mr Pitt, and I recollect endeavouring to cover him, as well as I could, in his getting out of the Carriage.
>
> Fortunately however, by the exertions of those who remained with us, and by ye timely assistance of a Party of Chairmen, and many Gentlemen from Whites, who saw his danger, we were extricated from a most unpleasant situation, and with considerable difficulty, got into some adjacent houses... and from thence to White's.

The old entrance to White's is now the bow window. Pitt quickly recovered from his ordeal, although his coach was almost demolished. The incident was blamed on his political opponents and won him great sympathy, ensuring his survival as Prime Minister.

White's Club

Did you know?

? Founded in 1693 as a chocolate house, White's soon became a gentlemen's club, on its present site since 1755. Every Prime Minister from 1721 to 1846 was a member.

? The bow window was installed in 1811 and immediately monopolised by **Beau Brummell**, the most fashionable dandy of the time. 'In the zenith of his popularity he might be seen at the bay window of White's

Club, surrounded by the lions of the day, laying down the law, and occasionally indulging in those witty remarks for which he was famous.'

16 ST JAMES' SQUARE
George IV, Waterloo

16

On June 21 1815, Mrs Edward Boehm held a glittering ball in her magnificent house at 16 St James' Square. The guest of honour was the Prince Regent (later **George IV**) and the party was very lavish. Mrs Boehm spared no effort to ensure that the evening was a success.

A crowd gathered outside to watch the fun. They were rewarded with the sight of Major Henry Percy, 'a dirty bloodstained officer', emerging from a carriage with a French standard in each hand. The party guests were just lining up for the first quadrille when Percy burst in, fell to one knee and laid the captured flags at the prince's feet. 'Victory, sir!' he told the startled prince. 'Victory!'

Napoleon had been beaten at Waterloo. The prince was so delighted that he promoted Percy on the spot. But he ended the evening in tears as details of the casualties emerged, including several of his own friends. The party should have turned into a victory celebration but distress at the number of casualties ruined it for everyone.

Did you know?

? News of an earlier military triumph reached the square on October 16 1759, when **William Pitt** the Elder was Prime Minister. He was living at 10 St James' Square when he received 'the joyful news that Quebec is taken, after a signal and compleat victory over the French army'. Canada became British as a result and church bells all over London rang in celebration.

? St James' Square was also the headquarters for the planning of Operation Overlord, the Allied invasion of Normandy in 1944.

Norfolk House (No 31, southeast corner) witnessed many meetings between **Dwight Eisenhower** and his cantankerous subordinate, **Bernard Montgomery**. On January 20 1944, Eisenhower arrived by car for an important planning session only to discover that the parking spot reserved for the

Supreme Commander had already been taken – as a deliberate provocation – by General Montgomery. Eisenhower wasn't bothered, but the incident was typical of Montgomery. The situation was quickly smoothed over by **Kay Summersby**, Eisenhower's British driver, leaving her boss free to concentrate on the real enemy across the Channel.

? In 1848, Bonaparte's nephew, Napoleon III, lived briefly around the corner at 1c King Street before returning to France to become head of state.

SCHOMBERG HOUSE
Lady Hamilton
80–82 Pall Mall

17

In the spring of 1781, a very pretty teenage girl worked for a few months at Schomberg House, the 18th-century equivalent of a strip club. The girl's name was Emma Lyon. Later she would become **Lady Hamilton**, the mistress of **Lord Nelson**. For the moment though she was horribly hard up – and Schomberg House was better than walking the streets.

It wasn't called a strip club, of course. It was the Temple of Health and of Hymen, a quasi-medical establishment run by a quack doctor who claimed to help infertile couples conceive. All they had to do was hire his 'Grand Celestial Bed, with pink sheets and Mattresses filled only with the Hair of English Stallions'. With music playing as well, and a mirror-lined ceiling, what more could anyone want?

To get them in the mood, Emma acted the role of Vestina, Rosy Goddess of Youth and Health. She stood naked on a pedestal, striking erotic poses and talking about love, while elderly gentlemen sat and stared. But Emma didn't enjoy the work very much. She left as soon as she could and went to live with a baronet in Sussex.

Did you know?

? Musicians at intimate parties were often blindfolded in those days – so they needed to know the score.

? In later years, Lady Hamilton was so pretty that even the empress Catherine of Russia heard about her and asked to see a picture.

? While Emma stood on her pedestal, the west wing of Schomberg House was occupied by the artist **Thomas Gainsborough**, who exhibited some of his

most famous work here. Gainsborough was a keen amateur musician, although not very good. His friend **Johann Christian Bach** (son of the more famous J S Bach) thought he should stick to what he did best: 'Once Bach called upon him in Pall Mall, and, going straight to his painting-room, he found him fagging hard at the bassoon, an instrument that requires the wind of a forge bellows to fill. Gainsborough's cheeks were puffed, and his face was round and red as the harvest moon. Bach stood astounded. "Put it away, man, put it away; do you want to burst yourself, like the frog in the fable?"'

? The house next door (No 79) has been rebuilt on the site of a previous house owned by **Nell Gwyn**, **Charles II**'s favourite mistress. Nell moved here in 1671 and was frequently visited by the king, the father of her children. She died in 1687, proud to the last of being a 'Protestant whore.'

THE ATHENAEUM CLUB
Charles Dickens and W M Thackeray   18
White building, corner of Pall Mall south and Waterloo Place west

Charles Dickens and **William Makepeace Thackeray** were the two giants of Victorian literature, but for years they refused to speak to each other. A friend of Dickens had made a public attack on Thackeray's work, and Thackeray held Dickens responsible.

The quarrel dragged on until December 1863 when the two novelists bumped into each other at the Athenaeum. According to Dickens, he had just gone in and was hanging up his hat when he saw a haggard Thackeray at the foot of the stairs. 'Have you been ill?' he asked, and they patched up their differences on the spot.

According to a bystander, however, Dickens passed Thackeray without a flicker of recognition. It was Thackeray who approached Dickens at the foot of the stairs.

> Dickens turned to him, and I saw Thackeray speak and presently hold out his hand to Dickens. They shook hands, a few words were exchanged, and immediately Thackeray returned to me saying 'I'm glad I have done this.'

The reconciliation was well timed – Thackeray died a few days later.

Did you know?
? The Athenaeum's membership has always been intellectual – bishops, Nobel laureates, university professors. Past members have included **Sir Walter Scott, Lord Macaulay, John Stuart Mill, Michael Faraday, Anthony Trollope, Benjamin Disraeli** and **Charles Darwin.**

? **William Gladstone** lived across the road at 11 Carlton House Terrace, overlooking the steps to the Mall.

DUKE OF YORK'S STEPS
William Gladstone

19

Carlton House Terrace, steps leading down to the Mall

Four times Prime Minister, **William Gladstone** was the Grand Old Man of British politics in the late 19th century, a great parliamentarian and a towering figure of moral rectitude. But he also had a seamy side, because he loved the company of prostitutes. He liked to take them home, sit knee to knee, and preach the virtues of a better life. There is no evidence that he ever slept with one but entries in his diary suggest that he almost certainly flagellated himself after their visits.

Gladstone lived across the road from the Athenaeum, in the house overlooking the steps to the Mall. At about 11.30pm on the night of May 6 1882, he was walking back to Downing Street when he was accosted by a prostitute on the steps. She was dressed in black satin. Gladstone stopped and had a talk with her under the gaslight.

Unfortunately for the Prime Minister, he was recognised by at least two people, one of whom, Colonel Tottenham, was an opposition Member of Parliament. Tottenham was only too delighted to make trouble for the old goat, who took such a high moral tone in public while behaving quite differently in private.

The colonel had been dining at the Athenaeum. He wasted no time telling people what he had seen. Within days it was the talk of fashionable London. Gladstone hotly denied any wrongdoing – 'It may be true that the gentleman saw me in such conversation, but the object was not what he assumed, or, as I am afraid, hoped' – but his words fell on deaf ears. For several months afterwards his enemies had him followed to see if there was any more dirt that they could dig up and use in an election campaign.

Did you know?

? The other eyewitness was a Mr Parkinson. He was so disappointed that he sat down at once and wrote to Gladstone: 'Had I seen the Heavens open & an angel descend & said such a thing (as I saw), I should have asked the Earth to open & swallow that angel as a liar.'

? This happened the same day as the Phoenix Park murders, when the British Viceroy in Ireland (Gladstone's nephew) was stabbed to death by Fenians. Gladstone heard the news as soon as he got back to Downing Street.

ROYAL OPERA ARCADE
Harriette Wilson

20

Haymarket end of Pall Mall

Soon after dawn on a January day in 1825, an excited crowd gathered outside the Royal Opera Arcade waiting for the bookshop at No 24 to open. They stood ten deep on the pavement and were so unruly that there was almost a

riot. The bookseller had to barricade his windows for his own protection.

The crowd were waiting for the first instalment of *The Memoirs of Harriette Wilson, written by herself*. Harriette was a prostitute who had slept with half of fashionable London in her prime. But she had lost her looks now and fallen on hard times. So she had written her memoirs to provide a nest egg for her old age.

And what memoirs they were! 'I shall not say why and how I became, at the age of fifteen, the mistress of the Earl of Craven,' ran the opening sentence. 'Whether it was love, or the severity of my father, the depravity of my own heart, or the winning arts of the noble lord...'

There was much worse to follow. Lord Melbourne's son abandoning her penniless, Lord Ponsonby forgetting to mention her to his wife, the Marquess of Worcester tearfully begging her to marry him, the Duke of Argyll putting on Harriette's nightcap and pretending to be her chaperone when the Duke of Wellington called unexpectedly. They had all made fools of themselves with Harriette. Now here she was, blowing the whistle on them at the Opera Arcade.

The first instalment sold out at once and was reprinted at least 35 times before the end of the year. Later instalments sold out as well, despite frantic attempts by the aristocracy to stop them. Harriette was the hit of the season in London. Everybody had heard of her. There were even jokes made about her in the House of Commons. And the Duke of Wellington's alleged response to Harriette – 'Publish and be damned' – has since entered the language, a phrase familiar to English speakers all over the world.

Did you know?

? To cash in on Harriette's notoriety, her publisher also sold prints of a naked woman purporting to be *The Redemption of Coventry by the Countess Godiva*. Respectable people were outraged: 'This most disgusting and indecent painting has been, and now is, exhibited by the reptile who purchased it, at his bagnio in the Opera Colonnade, and we need not tell our readers that the sole object in effecting this purchase has been to entice young men of fashion to see it, and by tampering their appetites with a lustful style, to induce them to purchase, at an exorbitant price, the engravings taken from it.'

? At the end of each instalment of her memoirs, Harriette published a list of those who were to appear in the next issue. They could buy her silence if they wished, to keep their names out of it. Quite a few did, although not the **Duke of Wellington**. Far from the 'Publish and be damned' of popular legend, he actually threatened to sue instead, pointing out that Harriette was trying to blackmail him.

HAYMARKET
Verdi, Oscar Wilde, Dostoevesky

21

It was the world premiere of **Giuseppe Verdi**'s latest opera. *I masnadieri* had been specially written for Her Majesty's Theatre and was performed here for the first time on July 22 1847. Verdi himself was conducting and **Jenny Lind** was singing. **Queen Victoria** and **Prince Albert** were in the audience. So were the **Duke of Wellington**, **Prince Louis Napoleon** and half the aristocracy of London.

It soon became clear to the audience that *I masnadieri* was not Verdi's greatest work, but nobody minded in the least. It was enough that the great man was here, in London, and everyone could set eyes on him. He was followed with opera glasses from the beginning of the performance to the end, and the evening was a triumph.

> From the Overture to the Finale there was nothing but applause, evvivas, recalls and encores. The Maestro himself conducted sitting on a chair higher than the others, with baton in hand. As soon as he appeared in the orchestra pit, applause broke out and continued for a quarter of an hour... The Maestro was cheered, called onto the stage, both alone and with the singers, and pelted with flowers. All you could hear was '*Evviva* Verdi! Beautiful!'

Afterwards, the management begged Verdi to stay on and become musical director of the theatre. He declined and left for Paris instead. Verdi loved London but, like all Italians, was appalled by the weather. 'If only London had the climate of Naples,' he observed, 'there would be no need to sigh for Paradise.'

Did you know?

? An extract from her diary records Queen Victoria's response to Verdi's opera: 'Went to the Opera, where we saw the production of Verdi's *I masnadieri* in 4 acts.... Lind sang and acted most exquisitely as Amalia & looked very well & attractive in her several dresses. She was immensely applauded.'

Across the street from Her Majesty's, the pillared Theatre Royal was the scene of a glittering first night on April 19 1893. **Sir Herbert Beerbohm Tree** was playing the lead in **Oscar Wilde**'s latest comedy, *A Woman of No Importance*. The theatre was packed for the occasion because a new play by Mr Wilde was always a big event, and this one was no exception.

The evening was a success and the actors were heartily applauded at the end. So was the author, although a few people had reservations, as Tree's half-brother, **Max Beerbohm**, quietly observed:

When little Oscar came on to make his bow there was a slight mingling of hoots and hisses, though he looked very sweet in a new white waistcoat and a large bunch of little lilies in his coat.

Theatre Royal

Behind the scenes, however, it was a very different story. There was a young man waiting for Wilde at the stage door that night. His name was William Allen and he was a homosexual blackmailer. He had a letter of Wilde's, addressed to Lord Alfred Douglas as 'My Own Boy' and making it quite clear that the two of them had been lovers. Would Oscar like to buy it for £10?

'Ten pounds!' Wilde was insulted. 'You have no appreciation of literature! If you had asked me for £50, I might have given it to you.'

Wilde told him to keep the letter and sent him away with half a sovereign. He had called the young man's bluff, as he had called many others. But his days were numbered, nevertheless. In 1895, he was found guilty of sodomy and sentenced to two years' imprisonment with hard labour. His career never recovered.

Did you know?

? The Theatre Royal's stage door is at the rear, 18 Suffolk street. Approach from Pall Mall.

? **Fyodor Dostoevsky** made a flying visit to London in July 1862 and took a stroll down the Haymarket. He was impressed by the girls – 'there are no women in the world as beautiful as the English' – but horrified by the prostitution. 'In the Haymarket I noticed mothers who brought their little daughters to make them ply the same trade. Little girls, aged about 12, seize you by the arm and beg you to come with them.'

TRAFALGAR SQUARE
Victory in Europe

22

Dominated by the statue of Lord Nelson in the middle, Trafalgar Square is the traditional place for a party when the country has something to celebrate. The square enjoyed its best ever party on May 8 1945, the day the war in Europe finally came to an end.

I went into London to walk through Whitehall, Trafalgar Square and Piccadilly. The sun came out, and London was gay, gay and densely thronged… It was a crowd light-hearted, wearing its red, white and blue rosettes as on a Cup Final day, and wearing, too, a host of comic little hats, silver cones, tricoloured cones, and in one instance, small royal crowns…

I heard *Marching through Georgia* in Whitehall, and the *Volga Boatmen's Song* in the Haymarket... In the heavens a number of Flying Fortresses were moving on, pleasure bent. From Trafalgar Square five or six in formation seemed to be flying up Northumberland Avenue. Over the Admiralty one dropped two cerise flares, and later I saw a Lancaster let fall a Very light over St James' Park. Girls had climbed on to various clumps of stone and turned themselves into living statues; the lions' heads in Trafalgar Square were being sat upon...

Tonight the city was thronged. The king and Mr Churchill have been on to the palace balcony and have been greeted with the sort of delight shipwrecked mariners bestow on a sail. Buildings have been floodlit so that Admiralty Arch seemed to be rising out of the ground, and Horatio Nelson, standing aloft in a greenish ray of light, was as romantic as even he could have wished...

And then the heavens were pierced by swords of light as so often they have been pierced by those searchlight beams which sought the enemy. Now they wove in a kind of geometric dance of rejoicing, and we watched the beauty of them and tried to realise, and as for me, found it very hard to realise, that we shall not be bombed again.

Did you know?

? The diarist **Harold Nicolson** was there too. 'I walked back through the happy but quite sober crowds to Trafalgar Square. The National Gallery was alive with every stone outlined in flood-lighting, and down there was Big Ben with a grin upon his illumined face. The statue of Nelson was picked out by a searchlight, and there was the smell of distant bonfires in the air... Looking down Fleet Street, one saw the best sight of all – the dome of St Paul's rather dim-lit, and then above it a concentration of searchlights upon the huge golden cross.'

? The light was wonderful to Londoners. There had been a blackout for almost six years, not a chink of illumination showing anywhere after dark. But now the war was over. The lights were back on, no more bombs were going to fall, and the blackout curtains had been torn down for ever.

CHARING CROSS
Charles I statue

23

Whitehall

Looking down Whitehall towards Parliament and the place where he was beheaded, this equestrian statue of Charles I marks the spot where the Parliamentarians who signed his death warrant were themselves executed after the restoration of the monarchy in 1660.

The first to die was Thomas Harrison. **Samuel Pepys** came to watch his execution on October 13 1660.

Statue of Charles I

> I went out to Charing-cross to see Major-Generall Harrison hanged, drawn, and quartered – which was done there – he looking as cheerfully as any man could do in that condition. He was presently cut down and his head and his heart shown to the people, at which there were great shouts of joy… Thus was it my chance to see the King beheaded at White-hall and to see the first blood shed in revenge for the blood of the King at Charing-cross.

After the executions were over, the statue of Charles I was erected in their place. It was powerfully symbolic, as **Daniel Defoe** (author of *Robinson Crusoe*) observed in 1724:

> We see the great equestrian statue of King Charles the First in brass, a costly, but a curious piece… he faces the place where his enemies triumphed over him, and triumphs, that is, tramples in the place where his murtherers were hanged.

Did you know?

? Although not erected here until later, the statue actually dates from 1633. Parliament sold it for scrap after Charles' execution, but the scrap-dealer buried it instead in the belief that England's flirtation with republicanism would not last long. The statue was dug up again after the restoration of the monarchy and returned as good as new.

? The statue stands also on the site of the original Charing cross, a stone monument to Edward I's wife, Queen Eleanor, who died in the Midlands in 1290. Her body was brought to Westminster Abbey for burial, and Edward erected a cross in her memory at every place on the way where the body lay overnight.

? The cross stood here until 1647. It was one of the great assembly points of medieval London, the very centre of the city and the spot from which distances to the capital have always been measured.

? Because it's an old assembly point, the spot is also one of the four places in London where the death of a monarch is traditionally announced by the Garter King of Arms. Escorted by a detachment from the Household Cavalry, he stands by the statue and declares: 'The king is dead. Long live the king!' in the presence of trumpeters and the Earl Marshal.

WHAT NOW?

The National Gallery (north side of Trafalgar Square) houses a stupendous art collection: **Titian, Rembrandt, Giotto, da Vinci, Caravaggio, Rubens, Vermeer, Van Dyck, Velázquez, Van Gogh, Renoir** etc.

The National Portrait Gallery (round the side of the National Gallery, to the right as you face it) is full of original portraits from the history books, all the famous people from Britain's past. It's the place to go if you want to put a face to the people in this guide.

Benjamin Franklin's old house (see page 123) is just off Trafalgar Square at 36 Craven Street. Go up the Strand and turn right before Charing Cross station.

Just before it, you will pass Northumberland Street. The Sherlock Holmes pub (towards the bottom of the street at No 10) has a faithful reproduction of Holmes and Watson's sitting room and other Holmes memorabilia.

Nearest public lavatories Parliament Street, Westminster Bridge, St James' Park, Green Park Underground, Piccadilly Circus Underground, Charing Cross railway station

⊖ Piccadilly Circus, Charing Cross

WHERE TO EAT

There are fast food places everywhere, including Whitehall and St James' Park. Simpson's (100 Strand) requires a collar and tie but is worth the effort. The National Gallery has a good restaurant. Beyond it lies Soho (page 127), with every kind of restaurant under the sun.

Try also Jermyn Street, just south of Piccadilly and parallel to it. **Sir Isaac Newton** used to live at No 87, although the house has since been rebuilt.

The Tower of London

The Tower was begun by **William the Conqueror** in 1078. It stands just inside the old Roman wall around London and was designed primarily as a fortress, capable of withstanding a siege. But it also served as a royal palace and the seat of government. Later it served as arsenal, treasury, mint and state prison as well.

The original Tower was the four-turreted structure in the centre. Subsequent monarchs added two rows of defensive walls and a moat. It was a place of dungeons, torture chambers, bloody executions, and horrible murders in the night. It is also where the Crown Jewels are kept, and a superb display of medieval weapons and suits of armour. There's nowhere else quite like it in the world.

WALK AT A GLANCE

Features London's ancient citadel, with 900 years of very colourful history in a single building.
Time Allow several hours.
Length ¹/₂ mile.
⊖ Tower Hill

1 **Traitors' Gate**
  - Sir Thomas More comes cheerfully ashore
  - Anne Boleyn falls to her knees in panic
  - Sir Thomas Wyatt is threatened with immediate death
  - Princess Elizabeth refuses to get out of the boat.

2 **Bloody Tower**
  - the two little princes are murdered in their beds
  - Sir Walter Ralegh grows tobacco.

3 **Wakefield Tower**
  - Henry VI is quietly assassinated during the Wars of the Roses.

4 White Tower
- William the Conqueror builds it
- St Thomas à Becket occupies a suite of rooms
- the Peasants Revolt through it
- the Knights of the Bath keep a vigil in the chapel
- Edmund Campion and Guy Fawkes are tortured on the rack
- Tsar Peter the Great comes to inspect the axe that killed Charles I.

5 Martin Tower
- Thomas Blood steals the Crown Jewels.

6 Bowyer Tower
- the royal Duke of Clarence is murdered face down in a barrel of wine.

7 Waterloo Block
- the Crown Jewels include the Koh-I-Noor diamond, the Cullinan diamond, and the Black Prince's ruby, worn by Henry V at the battle of Agincourt.

8 Tower Green
- Lord Hastings is seized by Richard III and beheaded on a log
- Anne Boleyn and Catherine Howard are executed for adultery
- Lady Jane Grey sees her husband's corpse before following him to the scaffold
- Sir Walter Ralegh comes to watch the execution of his rival, the Earl of Essex.

9 Devereux Tower
- Essex spends a sleepless night before his execution wondering if Elizabeth I will reprieve him.

10 Beauchamp Tower
- waiting for his execution, Lady Jane Grey's husband carves her name on the wall of his dungeon.

11 Bell Tower
- Sir Thomas More waits in darkness for execution
- Princess Elizabeth expects to be murdered.

12 Queen's House
- Guy Fawkes is interrogated
- William Penn contemplates emigration to America
- Lord Nithsdale cheats death by dressing as a woman
- Rudolph Hess admires British troops.

13 Queen's Stair
- Henry VIII kisses Anne Boleyn
- Sir Thomas More's daughter hugs him for the last time
- Thomas Blood refuses to let go of the crown
- Peter the Great sails for home.

14 Middle Tower
- an elephant lives by the gate
- a polar bear fishes in the Thames.

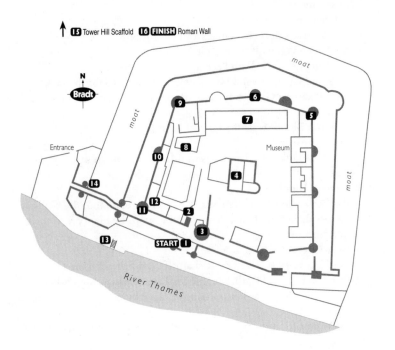

15 Tower Hill

- the Archbishop of Canterbury is beheaded by peasants
- Sir Thomas More dies graciously
- Sir Thomas Wyatt is cut into four quarters
- the Duke of Monmouth is still alive after five blows of the axe.

16 Roman Wall

- the best preserved piece of the wall that once encircled Roman London.

TRAITORS' GATE
Sir Thomas More, Anne Boleyn, Sir Thomas Wyatt, Princess Elizabeth
1

This was the main entrance to the Tower in medieval times, when people usually arrived by water. Known originally as the Watergate, it owes its present name to the large number of political prisoners who passed through it on their way to imprisonment in the Tower. Some stayed only a few weeks, others for ever. More than a hundred suffered the unkindest cut of all and were executed on the block.

One of the most famous prisoners to arrive here was **Sir Thomas More**, the Roman Catholic saint. Unwilling to swear an oath acknowledging Henry

VIII's supremacy over the Pope, he was brought from Westminster on April 17 1534. Sir Thomas was wearing his gold livery chain, a reminder of his past service to the king, and was met at the landing stage by the Lieutenant of the Tower and the porter to the wicket gate.

It was customary for prisoners to give their 'upper garment' to the porter as a tip for his services. Sir Thomas was supposed to hand over his gown but decided to make a joke of it instead. He took off his cap and offered it apologetically to the porter. 'I am very sorry it is no better for you.'

'No, sir,' said the porter firmly. 'I must have your gowne.' Sir Thomas surrendered it gracefully and was led away to his cell.

Did you know?

? St Thomas the Martyr has been a Roman Catholic saint since 1935, but he was something of a fanatic in his own lifetime. As Lord Chancellor, he thought nothing of sending heretics to the Tower to be tortured before execution, for no other crime than questioning the authority of the Pope.

Anne Boleyn, the second of Henry VIII's six wives, was a sworn enemy of More, who did not approve of her marriage to the king. On May 2 1536, however, she too fell foul of the king and was arrested in Greenwich on charges of incest, adultery and high treason. She was taken at once to the Tower, accused of betraying the king with several lovers, including her own brother. But her real crime was her failure to provide Henry with the son and heir that he so badly needed.

The penalty for incest was burning at the stake. Stunned by the suddenness of her arrest, and the injustice of the charges against her, Anne hardly knew which way to turn when she arrived at the Tower. She was met at the Court Gate by the Constable, Sir William Kingston. He was a decent man, but Anne promptly lost all control at the sight of him:

> 'Master Kingston, shall I go in to a dungeon?'
>
> 'No, Madam, you shall go into your lodging that you lay in at your coronation.'
>
> 'It is too good for me. Jesu, have mercy on me!' and she kneeled down weeping a great pace, and in the same sorrow fell into a great laughing, and she hath done so many times since.

In 1553, Henry's eldest daughter **Mary** succeeded to the throne. A devout Roman Catholic, she at once dedicated her reign to restoring the old religion,

Traitors' Gate

against the wishes of most of her subjects. When she became engaged to the King of Spain, it was the last straw for **Sir Thomas Wyatt** of Kent. He led a march on London aimed at preventing the marriage and perhaps putting Mary's half-sister Elizabeth on the throne.

But the rebellion found little support. Forced to surrender, Wyatt was brought to the Tower on February 8 1554.

> At v. of the clock this Wyat… wer brought… by water to the Tower
> as prysoner.'

Sir Thomas was wearing boots, spurs, a chainmail shirt, a velvet cassock, and a hat trimmed with fine lace. He was met at the wicket gate by the Lieutenant of the Tower, who threatened to kill him on the spot:

> Then came in sir Thomas Wyat, who sir John of Bridges toke by
> the coller in most rygorouse maner, and saide theis or moche-like
> wordes, 'Ohe! thou villayn and unhappie traytour! Howe couldest
> thou finde in thine hart to worke such detestable treason to the
> quenes maiestie?'… 'Yf yt was not (saith he) that the lawe must
> justly passe apon thee, I wolde strike thee throughe with my
> dagger.'

> And in so saying, havinge one hand apon the coller of the said maister
> Wyat, and the other on his dagger, shaked his bossome; to whom
> Wyat made no answer, but holdinge his armes under his side, and
> looking grevously with a grym looke upon the saide livetenant, saide,
> 'Yt is no maistery nowe.' And so they passyd on.

The penalty for treason was beheading with dismemberment. It was duly carried out. Sir Thomas had every reason to look grim as they took him away.

If Wyatt's rebellion had succeeded, the obvious beneficiary would have been Princess Elizabeth (later **Elizabeth I**). She too was brought to the Tower on suspicion of having secretly plotted with the rebels:

> The xviij th of Marche, being 1554, the lady Elizabethes grace, the
> quenes syster, was conveyed to the Tower from the court at
> Westminster about x th of the clocke in the forenoone by water.

Elizabeth was terrified. At the age of just 20, she had been very careful to have nothing to do with Wyatt's rebellion but who would believe her? Certainly not Queen Mary, who didn't trust her half-sister. Elizabeth thought she was being taken to the Tower to be killed like her mother (Anne Boleyn) before her. Like her mother, too, she cracked up when she arrived at the Tower. Elizabeth took one look at the grim fortress looming over her in the rain and refused to get out of the boat.

> At landing she fyrst stayd and denyd to land ther, neyther well could she onles she goo over her show [shoe]. The lords were goone out of the bote before, and asked why she came not. One of the lords went bak agayne to her, and brought word that she would not come. Then said one of the lordes that shalbe nameles that she shuld not chuse. Because yt dyd then rayne, the same lord offered to her his clock, which she, puttyng yt back with her hand, refused. So she comyng out, havyng one foote upon the stayre, sayd, 'Here landeth the truest subject, being a prysonner, that ever landed at these stayres… I come yn no traytour, but as true a woman to the quenes majesty as eny is nowe lyving: and theron will I take my deathe.'

Did you know?

? Elizabeth was convinced she was going to die. She even expressed the hope that she would be beheaded with a sharp French sword (like her mother) rather than a blunt English axe. But there was no firm evidence against her so she was released after a few weeks, although she had to remain under house arrest for several more months.

? Traitors' Gate is part of St Thomas' Tower, built by Edward I for his own use soon after becoming king in 1272. Edward was a warrior king, 'the hammer of the Scots'. He lived in St Thomas' Tower whenever he was in London. More often than not though he was in Scotland, campaigning against William Wallace (the Scottish leader played by Mel Gibson in the movie *Braveheart*).

BLOODY TOWER
The two little princes, Sir Walter Ralegh

2

Known originally as the Garden Tower, this is reputedly where the **two little princes** were murdered in the autumn of 1483. No-one knows for sure what happened to them but, according to a confession by one of their murderers, they were smothered with a pillow while they slept. Their bodies were then taken across to the White Tower and buried in a wooden chest under the stairs leading to the Chapel of St John.

The princes were the sons of Edward IV. He died in April 1483, when they were only 10 and 12 – too young to rule the country. Their uncle put them in the Tower instead and had himself illegally crowned in July as **Richard III**.

The boys lived for some time after the coronation: 'The children of King Edward were seen shoting [shooting arrows? shouting?] and playing in the garden of the Tower at sundry times.' Before long though, 'he and his brother were withdrawn into the inner apartments of the Tower proper, and day by day began to be seen more rarely behind the bars and windows, until at length they ceased to appear altogether.'

Wakefield Tower (left) and Bloody Tower

How were they killed? 'Some said they were murdered between two feather beds, some said they were drowned in malmsey, and some said they were pierced with a venomous poison.' According to one account, Richard asked the Constable of the Tower to kill the princes. But the Constable refused, so Richard asked Sir James Tyrell instead:

> Tyrell devised that they should be murdered in their beds, to the execution whereof he appointed Miles Forest, one of the four that kept them, a felowe fleshed in murther before time. To him he joined one John Dighton, his own horsekeeper, a big, brode, square, strong knave. Then, all the others being removed from them, this Miles Forest and John Dighton about midnight (the children lying in their beds) came into the chamber and suddenly lapped them up among the clothes – so bewrapped them and entangled them, keeping down by force the featherbed and pillows hard unto their mouths, that within a while, smothered and stifled, their breath failing, they gave up to God their innocent souls into the joys of heaven, leaving to the tormentors their bodies dead in the bed.

> After that the wretches… laid their bodies naked out upon the bed and fetched Sir James to see them. Which, upon the sight of them, caused those murderers to bury them at the stair foot, meetly deep in the ground, under a great heap of stones.

Did you know?

? That account was published in 1513. More than 150 years later, on Friday, July 17 1674, some workmen were digging at the bottom of the stairs leading to the chapel in the White Tower when they discovered the bones of two children in a wooden chest about 10 feet underground. The larger skeleton lay on its back, the smaller one face down on top. They were aged about 10 and 12. 'This day I, standing by the opening, saw working men dig out of a stairway in the White Tower the bones of those two Princes who were foully murdered by Richard III. They were small bones of lads in their teens, and there were pieces of rag and velvet about them.' Velvet suggested royalty. So did 'very certain indications' found with the bodies. Charles II commissioned Sir Christopher Wren to design an urn for the remains and had them reburied in the Henry VII chapel at Westminster Abbey. They lie there to this day.

? Did Richard have his nephews killed? Plenty of people thought so at the time but there has never been any direct evidence linking him to their disappearance. He himself was killed at Bosworth two years later and the history books were then rewritten to blacken his memory — giving him a hunchback, for instance, that no-one had noticed during his lifetime. Richard was a brave soldier and a good administrator with many fine qualities. On balance though, the circumstantial evidence surely suggests that he must have had a hand in the princes' death.

Another prisoner held in the Bloody Tower was **Sir Walter Ralegh**. He had risen to prominence under Elizabeth I but had made enemies along the way and did not prosper under her successor. Within a few months of James I's accession in 1603, Ralegh had been sent to the Tower on trumped-up charges of plotting to overthrow the new king.

Ralegh was allotted two rooms in the Bloody Tower. Unless the king relented, he was to stay there for the rest of his life. For a man of 50, the sudden fall from grace was so calamitous that he seriously contemplated suicide for a while.

But then he rallied and made the best of it. He was allowed conjugal visits at first. Lady Ralegh arrived in style, insisting on driving her carriage through the gate. Their younger son Carew was conceived and born in the Tower. Ralegh was allowed the use of the Lieutenant's garden (originally at the top of the wall to the left, through the gate) and converted an old chicken shed there into a makeshift laboratory. He grew all sorts of rare plants and tried to make a cure for headaches out of tobacco.

Indeed, he spent so much time in the garden that he became one of the sights of the Tower. A new Lieutenant eventually tightened up the rules in case Ralegh was chatting to foreign spies over the fence. Conjugal visits were banned, and from then on Ralegh had to spend much more time in his room.

But his health suffered in the Bloody Tower. His doctor called for him to be 'removed from the cold lodging where he lieth unto a warmer, that is to say, a little room which he hath built in the garden adjoining to his still-house.' The Lieutenant took the view that the Tower was a prison, not a hotel, and left Ralegh where he was.

But some good came of it. Ralegh used his enforced idleness to write several books, including *The History of the World*, a monumental work that kept him busy for years. In all, he stayed more than 12 years in the Bloody Tower and was not released until 1616.

Did you know?

? Now built over, the garden beside the Bloody Tower belonged to the Lieutenant of the Tower. The royal family had a garden too, in the southeast corner near the Salt Tower. It is not known which one the little princes played in. Perhaps both.

? Ralegh hadn't been a prisoner very long when Guy Fawkes and the other conspirators in the Gunpowder Plot were also imprisoned in the Tower. The plot to blow up the king had nothing to do with him, but Ralegh worried that James wouldn't see it that way, especially as Ralegh's wife was related to one of the conspirators. He managed to avoid being implicated, but his chances of an early release were at an end.

? Among the Bloody Tower's other prisoners was **Archbishop Cranmer** (author of the prayer book), who spent some time here in 1553 before being burned at the stake for heresy. 'The xiiij th of September, the busshope of Canterbury was brought to the Tower as prysoner, and lodged in the Tower over the gate anenst the water-gate'.

? And **Judge Jeffreys**, who asked to be put in the Tower for his own protection. After the Duke of Monmouth failed to overthrow James II in 1685, Jeffreys sentenced so many of the West Country rebels to slavery or transportation that their descendants in the Caribbean still speak with a West Country accent today. James lasted another three years before fleeing abroad in 1688. Jeffreys tried to flee too, but was spotted by an angry mob and chose the security of the Tower instead.

? The Bloody Tower's portcullis weighs two tons and still works.

WAKEFIELD TOWER
Henry VI

3

In July 1465, during the Wars of the Roses, a forlorn and pathetic prisoner was brought to the Tower on horseback. His spurs had been struck off, his feet were tied under the horse with leather thongs, a straw hat had been placed on his head and he had been mocked by the crowd as he rode through the streets. He was **Henry VI**, who had been deposed as king four years earlier and replaced by his cousin Edward IV.

Henry was mentally inadequate, not at all suited to the demands of kingship. He had been wandering the north of England disguised as a monk before his capture. But now he was a prisoner in the Tower, a pawn in other people's games. His enemies would keep him alive for as long as it suited them, and then get rid of him without compunction.

Henry was badly treated in the Tower. He was allowed his breviary and a few pets, but he also had to endure 'hunger, thirst, mockings, derisions, abuse and many other hardships'. The end came in 1471, after Henry's only son was killed at the battle of Tewkesbury. With the son out of the way, there was no longer any reason for keeping the father alive.

Edward IV's victorious troops marched on London. Henry waited for them. According to tradition, he was praying in the oratory, upstairs in the Wakefield Tower, when they found him.

> And the same night that King Edward came to London, King Harry, being in ward in prison in the Tower of London, was put to death the 21st day of May on a Tuesday night between eleven and twelve of the clock... and on the morrow he was chested and brought to [St] Paul's and his face was open that every man might see him. And in his lying he bled on the pavement there; and afterwards at the Black Friars.'

Did you know?

? According to William Shakespeare, Henry was personally done to death by the future Richard III. There's no hard evidence for that, but Shakespeare certainly wasn't the only one to believe it.

? It is not known exactly how Henry was killed, but an examination of his bones in 1910 yielded a few clues: 'The skull bones were much broken... To one piece of the skull was attached some hair of a brown colour, which in one place was darker and apparently matted with blood.'

? Henry founded Eton College, England's most famous public school, and King's College, Cambridge. Every year, on the anniversary of his death, the Provost of Eton lays a bunch of lilies at the site of his murder and the Provost of King's a bunch of roses.

WHITE TOWER
William the Conqueror, Thomas à Becket, Peter the Great

4

This is the original Tower of London, commissioned by **William the Conqueror** in 1078 to dominate the city and show the people who was boss. It was given a coat of whitewash in 1240 and has been known as the White Tower ever since.

In medieval times there were dungeons and torture chambers in the basement. The monarch lived on the top floor, frequently conferring with his barons in the council chamber. The first floor (the entrance floor) was occupied by the Constable of the Tower. In the 1150s, the Constable was **Thomas à Becket**. Unusually for a saint, he had begun his working life as an accountant in the City of London. But his talents were spotted by the king and he rose rapidly in royal service.

He rose so rapidly that when Henry II was away in France, Becket at the Tower was the most powerful figure in the land.

His dress was gorgeous, his retinue of knights as splendid as the king's. His hospitalities were boundless. His expenditure was enormous. The wealthiest peer in England did not maintain a more costly household, or appear in public with a more princely surrounding.

Becket was later made Archbishop of Canterbury and promptly became a thorn in the king's side. Quite a few people felt that he got what he deserved when he was murdered at Canterbury in 1170.

Did you know?

? Modern visitors enter the White Tower by the same door as the Normans did, up a wooden flight of stairs. Take away those stairs, barricade the door, and the Tower was impregnable.

? The walls are 15 feet thick at the bottom, 11 feet thick at the top. Garderobes (lavatories) were built into them at intervals, with shoots to the outside. A few shoots can still be seen on the first and second floors, on the north side facing away from the river. The smell was so bad that Henry III commissioned a new garderobe for his private use in 1245.

? In the Middle Ages, it was customary for new monarchs to stay the night in the White Tower before their coronation at Westminster next day. On the eve of his coronation in 1399, Henry IV created 46 Knights of the Bath in the Tower. After a ceremonial bath, they laid their armour in front of the altar in the Chapel of St John on the top floor and kept an all-night vigil over their weapons before joining the procession to Westminster next morning.

? The Tower has a fabulous collection of armour and weapons from the Middle Ages, on show to the public since the 17th century. **Peter the Great** came to see it in 1698. The Russian tsar was a forthright monarchist, so they didn't let him see the axe that killed Charles I, 'as it was feared that he would throw it in the Thames'.

? The White Tower was also used as a state prison from time to time. The first recorded escape was made by Rannulf Flambard, Bishop of Durham,

METHODS OF TORTURE AT THE TOWER

Manacles One of the 'gentler tortours'. Prisoners were handcuffed to the wall, with no support under their feet. They usually fainted from the pain, but were not permanently crippled.

The Rack The Tower had the only one in England. It was a wooden frame like a bed, with rollers at each end. The prisoner's wrists and ankles were tied to the rollers. His interrogators then stretched him, slowly levering the rack until 'bones and joints were almost plucked asunder'. Wise prisoners confessed at once. Stupid ones were permanently disabled before they gave in. The rack was so unpopular with the general public that it was only used as a method of last resort.

The Scavenger's Daughter Iron hoops which crushed the body until blood spurted out of nostrils, mouth, anus and sometimes even hands and feet.

Pressing to death The prisoner was sentenced to be 'put in some low dark room. He shall lie without any litter or anything under him. One arm shall be drawn to one quarter of the room with a cord, and the other to another. His feet shall be used in the same manner. As many weights shall be laid on him as he can bear and more… He shall not eat the same day upon which he drinks, nor drink the same day upon which he eats, and he shall so continue till he die.'

The dungeon of Little Ease A four-foot cube so small that prisoners couldn't stand or lie inside. They just had to crouch there in the dark for several days at a time.

The dungeon amongst the rats Below water level. When the tide rose, so did rats from the river. They ate prisoners alive while they slept.

Water torture Drip by drip on the prisoner's head until he went mad.

Thumbscrew

The Bilboes Squeezed the ankles.

The Pilliwinks Squeezed the fingers.

The Brakes A device for breaking teeth.

The 'gratynge of an arrowe through the fingers'

These were just a few. The Tower had plenty of ways of making people talk. Don't try any of them at home.

towards the end of 1100. A rope was smuggled to him in a cask of wine. Rannulf threw a party for his gaolers and shinned down the rope while they were enjoying the wine. The rope turned out to be too short, so he had to jump the last few feet to the ground, but managed to pick himself up and escape safely to France.

? Less fortunate was the Welsh prince Gruffydd, who tried the same trick on the night of

March 1 1244: 'Having (in the night) made of the hangings, sheets, towels and table cloths a long line, he put himself down from the top of the Tower. But in the sliding, the weight of his body (being a very big and a fat man) brake the rope, and he fell and brake his neck withal; whose miserable carkass being found in the morning by the Tower wall, was a most pitiful sight to the beholders. For his head and neck were driven into his breast between both the shoulders.'

Torture at the White Tower

There was certainly a torture chamber in the basement, but the Tower's reputation for torture is a little exaggerated. It was against the law, for one thing. It required a warrant signed either by the monarch or a member of the Privy Council under the royal prerogative. Warrants were only signed in exceptional circumstances.

Nevertheless, there were times in the 16th century when the rack 'seldom stood idle in the Tower', especially when Jesuits were being persecuted for their supposed allegiance to Spain. **Father John Gerard** was tortured several times here in April 1597 but survived to tell the tale, later translated from the Latin.

Gerard was interrogated in Queen's House. When he refused to reveal the whereabouts of other Jesuits, he was taken to the White Tower for torture, perhaps through an underground passage beneath the cobbles. The torture chamber lay deep in the bowels of the White Tower.

> We went in a sort of solemn procession, the attendants preceding us with lighted candles, because the place was underground and very dark, especially about the entrance. It was a place of immense extent, and in it were ranged divers sorts of racks, and other instruments of torture. Some of these they displayed before me, and told me I should have to taste them every one...
>
> Then they led me to a great upright beam or pillar of wood, which

was one of the supports of this vast crypt. At the summit of this
column were fixed certain iron staples for supporting weights. Here
they placed on my wrists gauntlets of iron, and ordered me to mount
upon two or three wicker steps; then raising my arms, they inserted
an iron bar through the rings of the gauntlets and then through the
staples in the pillar, putting a pin through the bar so that it could not
slip.

Gerard was suspended by his wrists and left to hang. He was so tall that the
tips of his toes still touched the ground, so his torturers dug the earth away
from underneath. The pain began almost immediately.

The worst pain was in my breast and belly, my arms and hands. It
seemed to me that all the blood in my body rushed up my arms into
my hands; and I was under the impression at the time that the blood
actually burst forth from my fingers and at the back of my hands.
This was, however, a mistake; the sensation was caused by the
swelling of the flesh over the iron that bound it.

Gerard fainted eight or nine times before he was taken down. He still refused
to talk, so he was suspended again next day. He fainted so badly this time that
he looked as if he was going to die. He was hurriedly taken down and hot
water was forced down his throat until he revived. But still he refused to talk,
so his torturers decided to try something more drastic:

They took him lately to the rack, and the torturers and examiners
were there ready; but he suddenly, when he entered the place, knelt
down and with a loud voice prayed to our Lord that, as He had given
grace and strength to some of His saints to bear with Christian
patience being torn to pieces by horses for His love, so He would be
pleased to give him grace and courage, rather to be dragged into a
thousand pieces than to say anything that might injure any person or
the Divine glory. And so they left him without tormenting him,
seeing him so resolved.

In fact, several of Gerard's gaolers were closet Catholics and sympathetic
towards him. No-one enjoyed watching him suffer. The Lieutenant of the
Tower resigned in disgust soon afterwards, after only a few months in the
job. Gerard himself escaped six months later, climbing down a rope from
the Cradle Tower and making his getaway across Tower Wharf to a waiting
boat.

Did you know?

? Gerard was not the only Jesuit to suffer here. In 1581, **Edmund Campion**
was tortured three times on the rack at the Tower. 'He used to fall down at
the rackehowse dore upon both knees to commend himself to God's mercie
and to crave His grace of patience in his paines. As also being upon the racke
he cried continually with much myldeness upon God and the holy name of

Jesus.' The experience left Campion unable to use his hands or feet. 'He likened himselfe to an elephant, which being downe could not rise.'

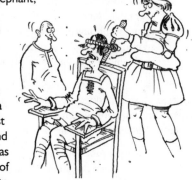

? But it was not only Jesuits who suffered. In 1536, Mark Smeaton, a young court musician, was brought to the Tower, accused of being Anne Boleyn's lover. Smeaton denied it indignantly, but Henry VIII needed a pretext for bringing charges against Anne, so a rope was knotted around Smeaton's forehead and a stick was twisted into the loop. A few turns of the stick and Smeaton was ready to confess to anything. He was executed on Tower Hill, along with Anne's other alleged boyfriends.

? Where did all this happen? In the basement of the White Tower, now a gift shop for tourists. Think of Smeaton, and poor Father Gerard, as you stand there buying postcards and Beefeater dolls!

The Tower under attack

The Tower has been attacked several times, most notably during the Peasants' Revolt of June 1381. A mob rampaged through the streets, surrounding the Tower and demanding to speak to the king about their grievances. Still only 14, **Richard II** struggled to handle the crisis on his own:

> The king was in a turret of the great Tower of London and saw the manor of the Savoy and the Hospital of Clerkenwell... all in flames. He called all the lords about him into a chamber, and asked their counsel as to what should be done in such a crisis. But none of them could or would give him any counsel.

The following day (June 14), the boy-king went out to meet the rebels at Mile End. While he was there, a breakaway group of peasants invaded the Tower in his absence. It was defended by 600 archers and 600 men-at-arms, but none of them lifted a finger to stop the peasants:

> '**Wat Tyler**, **Jack Straw** and **John Ball** and more than 400 entered into the Tower and brake up chamber after chamber, and at last found the archbishop of Canterbury... These gluttons took him and strake off his head... these four heads were set on four long spears and they made them to be borne before them through the streets of London and at last set them a-high on London Bridge.

While in the Tower, the peasants barged into the king's private quarters with their filthy sticks. They stroked the beards of several knights, lay on the king's bed, and made some suggestions to his mother that she did not consider at all suitable. But it ended in disaster, because Wat Tyler was killed next day and

the revolt fell apart. The ringleaders were
executed and order was rapidly restored to the
country.

Did you know?

? On June 13, the first day of the
crisis, thousands of peasants
gathered at St Katharine's, just
east of the Tower. The king
spoke to them from a 'little
turret' on that side – no-
one knows which, but the
Develin Tower or the Brass Mount
seem the most likely.

? The Peasants' Revolt had its origins in the Black Death. So many people died
of plague that there was an acute shortage of labour. Wages should have risen
accordingly, but were artificially held down by old rules of serfdom that were
no longer relevant. So the peasants revolted.

? Really they were rebelling against the rigid class system, which they saw in
biblical terms. 'When Adam delved and Eve span, who was then the
gentleman?'

? The peasants weren't all bad. One of their cries as they rioted through the
streets was 'Kill the lawyers!' They did too, all the ones they could find!

? The Archbishop of Canterbury was an old enemy of John Ball, one of the
peasant leaders. He had several times imprisoned him for preaching against
the ruling class. As the mob advanced on the Tower, the Archbishop tiptoed
down to Traitors' Gate to try to escape by boat. But a peasant woman
spotted him and raised the alarm. The Archbishop scuttled back into the
Tower – only to be beheaded a few hours later.

The Tower was briefly besieged in 1460, during the Wars of the Roses. It was
held by the Lancastrian party (red rose), while the Yorkists (white rose)
occupied the rest of London. A few cannon-balls whistled to and fro, but the
Lancastrians didn't have enough food for a long siege, so they negotiated a
quick surrender and most were given safe passage out of London.

The Tower found itself under threat again in February 1554, during Sir
Thomas Wyatt's rebellion. A force of two thousand rebels advanced from
Deptford towards Southwark, just across the river from the Tower:

> Which their comyng, so soone as it was perceyved, ther was shot off
> out of the White tower a vj. or viij. shott; but myssed them,
> somtymes shoting over, and somtymes shoting short.

As well as the cannons in the White Tower, there was 'one culvering on the
Devyls tower, and iij. fawkenetes over the Water-gate, all being bent towardes
Southwarke.' The drawbridge was cut down and the gates closed. The Mayor
of London and the sheriffs donned armour and ordered everyone to shut their

shops and windows and await developments.

In the event, the Tower looked so formidable that Wyatt's rebels thought better of it and crossed the river further along. They were quickly defeated in a running battle between Charing Cross and St James' Park. The noise of shrieking women was so loud that it could be distinctly heard from the battlements of the White Tower.

MARTIN TOWER
Thomas Blood, Sir Isaac Newton

5

During the reign of Charles II, the Crown Jewels – the crown, orb and sceptre used at coronations – were stored in the basement of the Martin Tower, under the care of Talbot Edwards, an old soldier of 76. On a spring morning in 1671, they were stolen in broad daylight by an audacious gang of thieves who shot their way out of the Tower and would have got clean away if they hadn't run out of ammunition just as their pursuers caught up with them.

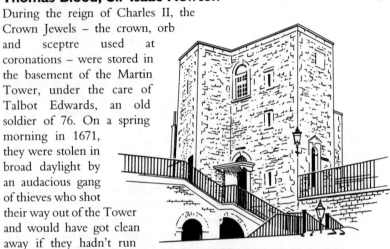

The gang's leader was **Thomas Blood**, an incorrigible adventurer who had fought on both sides in the Civil War. His Irish estates had been confiscated on the restoration of Charles II, so he had decided to steal the Crown Jewels to get even.

> About three Weeks before this Blood made his Attempt upon the Crown, he came to the Tower in the Habit of a Parson, with a long Cloak, Cassock and Canonical Girdle, and brought a Woman with him whom he called Wife... This pretended Wife desired to see the Crown; and having seen it feigned to have a Qualm come upon her Stomach, and desired Mr Edwards (who was Keeper of the Regalia) to send for some Spirits, who immediately caused his Wife to fetch some; whereof when she had drunk, she courteously invited her up Stairs to repose her self upon a Bed: Which Invitation she accepted, and soon recovered. At their Departure they seemed very thankful for this Civility.

A few days later, 'Parson' Blood returned to the Martin Tower with four pairs of white gloves as a thank-you present for Mrs Edwards. Several more visits followed, until he had won the Edwards' trust. Then he proposed a marriage between their two families.

You have a pretty Gentlewoman to your Daughter, and I have a young
Nephew who hath two or three Hundred a Year Land, and is at my
Disposal. If your Daughter be free, and you approve of it, I will bring
him hither to see her, and we will endeavour to make it a Match.

Edwards approved. A meeting was arranged for 7am on May 9.

The old Man was got up ready to receive his Guest, and the Daughter
had put her self into her best Dress to entertain her gallant; when
behold Parson Blood, with three more came to the Jewel House, all
Armed with Rapier Blades in their Canes, and every one a Dagger,
and a pair of Pocket Pistols. Two of his Companions entred in with
him, and the Third stayed at the Door, it seems, for a Watch.

Blood asked if they could see the Crown Jewels while waiting for his 'wife' to
arrive.

As soon as they were entred the Room where the Crown was kept,
and the Door (as usually) was shut behind them, they threw a Cloak
over the Old Man's Head, and clapt a Gag into his Mouth… at the
same time they fastened an Iron Hook to his Nose, that no Sound
might pass from him that Way neither…

Then one of them named Parrot put the Globe into his Breeches.
Blood held the Crown under his Cloak. The Third was designed to
file the Sceptre in two (because too long to carry) and when filed it
was to be put into a Bag brought for that Purpose.

But before this could be done, young Mr Edwards (Son of the Old
Gentleman)… chanced to arrive at the very Instant that this was
acting… they forthwith hasted away with the Crown and Globe, but
left the Sceptre, not having time to file it. The Old Man returning to
himself got upon his Legs, pulled off the Gag… and cryed out
'Treason! Murther!'

The gang fled, shooting as they went. They got out of the Tower and turned
left along the wharf, where their horses were waiting. But Blood and Parrot

were caught before they could escape. They were thrown into the White Tower to await interrogation by the king himself. Unbelievably, Charles was so amused by Blood's impudence that instead of sending him to the gallows he gave him a royal pardon and arranged for his Irish income to be restored to him.

Did you know?

? A few weeks later, Blood was dining out on the experience: 'At Mr Treasurers where dined... one Bloud that impudent bold fellow, who had not long before attempted to steale the Imperial Crowne it selfe out of the Tower... How he came to be pardoned, & even received to favour, not onely after this, but severall other exploits almost as daring... I could never come to understand: some believed he became a spie... & did his Majestie services that way... The Man had not onely a daring but a vilanous un-mercifull looke, a false Countenance, but very well spoken, & dangerously insinuating.'

? The Crown Jewels have moved since Blood's time. They live now in the Waterloo Block – under heavy guard. The Martin Tower has been converted into... a jewellery shop.

? In 1696, **Sir Isaac Newton** became Master of the Mint and was given a small house between the two curtain walls to the north of the Martin Tower. But he disliked living in the Tower and moved to Piccadilly instead. Newton was often at the Tower, overseeing an ambitious programme of recoinage. The Russian Tsar **Peter the Great** visited the Mint in 1698 and particularly asked to meet him, so that he could learn about gravity from the man himself.

? Below the wall east of the Martin Tower, there is a miniature rifle range in the East Casemates (part of the defensive wall). Eleven German spies were shot there during World War I. To date, the last person to be executed at the Tower was another German, Sergeant Josef Jacobs. He parachuted into England during World War II, but twisted his ankle on landing. He was put in a chair and shot for spying on August 4 1941.

BOWYER TOWER
The Duke of Clarence

6

Behind the Waterloo Block, not open to the public

Partly rebuilt in the 19th century, the Bowyer Tower was originally occupied by the king's bow maker, who kept the Tower garrison supplied with bows and arrows. The Tower was the scene of a bizarre murder in February 1478, when the royal Duke of Clarence was seized and drowned headfirst in a barrel of wine.

Clarence was the middle brother between Edward IV and the future Richard III. He hated them both, for different reasons. He hated Edward because he was king. Clarence claimed that his elder brother was illegitimate and he was therefore the rightful king. He claimed that Edward's sons (the two little princes) were illegitimate too and should not be allowed to succeed their father.

He hated Richard because Richard wanted to marry the sister of Clarence's wife, thus reducing her inheritance by half. Clarence even went so far as to kidnap the girl and put her to work as a kitchenmaid. But Richard tracked her down and married her anyway, an act of defiance which Clarence took very badly.

He intrigued shamelessly against both of his brothers, brazenly joining their enemies during the Wars of the Roses while being all smiles to their faces. He switched back again when the brothers looked like winning and couldn't be trusted an inch in his determination to replace Edward as king. So Edward got rid of him:

> The duke was cast into the Tower, and therewith adjudged for a
> traitor, and privilie drowned in a butt of malmesie.

Did you know?

? A butt of malmsey? Contemporary accounts all agree that Clarence was 'plunged into a jar of sweet wine', but it does seem odd. Perhaps one was handy at the time.

? Uneasy lies the head that wears a crown. The Plantagenet brothers were not a close-knit family, but little worse than anyone else at the time. If Richard had not got rid of the little princes, for instance, their mother and her family would have got rid of him. Then, as now, politics was all about pre-emptive strikes. The Plantagenets were just taking care of business – like the Mafia.

WATERLOO BLOCK
Crown Jewels

7

The Crown Jewels are worn by the monarch and other members of the royal family on ceremonial occasions such as coronations or the annual opening of Parliament. The jewels used to be kept in the Pyx chamber at Westminster Abbey. After the robbery of 1303, however, it was decided to move them to the Tower (see page 28). They have been here ever since.

Some of the jewellery is very old, but most dates from after the restoration of the monarchy in 1660. Oliver Cromwell's Parliamentarians sold the original Crown Jewels after the execution of Charles I, arguing that there was no longer any need for them without a monarchy. But canny dealers kept a few of the pieces and sold them back to the Crown after Charles II's return.

In fact, the jewels were often pawned during the Middle Ages to finance various wars. The collection was greatly enhanced during the days of the

British Empire with spectacular diamonds from India and South Africa. Today, it is one of the most fabulous collections in the world.

Did you know?

? The oldest crown in the collection is St Edward's Crown, used only for coronations. In its present form it was first worn by Charles II in 1661. But the base of the crown is much older and may well have been used at Edward the Confessor's coronation in 1043.

? The richest piece is the Imperial State Crown. It is encrusted with more than 3,000 jewels, including:

St Edward's sapphire Removed from Edward the Confessor's tomb in 1163 and set now in the Maltese cross at the top of the crown.

Queen Elizabeth's pearls Four perfect tears, three of which belonged to Elizabeth I, hanging now below the orb above the crown.

The Black Prince's ruby Given to Edward III's son by the King of Castile in 1367. Worn by **Henry V** at the battle of Agincourt – he nearly lost it when the French cavalry knocked his crown off. Perhaps worn also by **Richard III** at the battle of Bosworth and retrieved either from his corpse or from under a hawthorn bush where a looter had hidden it.

The **Second Star of Africa** (just under the ruby) One of nine stones cut from the **Cullinan Diamond**.

? See also the **Star of Africa** in the sceptre. This too was taken from the Cullinan and, at 530 carats, is the biggest cut diamond in the world.

? And don't miss the **Koh-I-Noor** in the Queen Mother's crown. The 'Mountain of Light' was probably mined in India in 1655. It passed through many hands and caused enormous trouble before being looted by the British in 1849. It has brought disaster to so many male owners that it is now considered very bad luck for a man to own it. That's why they allowed the Queen Mother to have it!

TOWER GREEN
Lord Hastings, Anne Boleyn, Catherine Howard, Lady Jane Grey, the Earl of Essex

8

The execution site stands outside the chapel of St Peter-ad-Vincula

There were two places of execution at the Tower. One was Tower Hill, outside the walls. The other was here, on the green beside the White Tower.

Most people were executed in public on Tower Hill, where their last agonies were watched by thousands. Tower Green was much more private, reserved chiefly for women and royalty. Only seven people lost their lives here, and five of those were women. It was a great privilege to be beheaded on Tower Green, even if the victims didn't think so!

The first person to die on the green was **Lord Hastings** on June 13 1483. But his death was more an assassination than a formal execution.

Hastings was part of the council that ruled England after the death of Edward IV. The new king was Edward V, the elder of the two little princes in the Tower – a boy of only 12. Hastings was loyal to the two princes. If he had known that their uncle Richard was planning to declare them illegitimate and make himself king, he would never have agreed to it. So Richard had him killed to get him out of the way.

On the day of his death, Hastings rode unsuspectingly to the Tower, arriving in time for a 9am meeting to discuss the arrangements for Edward V's coronation. Making his way to the White Tower, he joined his friend Richard and other nobles in the council chamber.

Richard was in a good mood at first. 'My lord,' he told the Bishop of Ely. 'You have very good strawberries at your garden in Holborn. I require you, let us have a mess of them.'

Richard left the room while the strawberries were being fetched. He returned between 10 and 11 o'clock in a very different frame of mind. He suddenly accused Lord Hastings of treachery. Banging his fist on the table, he gave the signal for a squad of armed men to come rushing into the room.

'I arrest thee, traitor!' Richard told Hastings.

'What me, my lord?'

'Yea thee, traitor!'

Hastings was seized. Everyone else scattered. Lord Stanley was wounded by a blow that would have killed him if he hadn't dived under the table. Richard told Hastings to prepare for death and confess to a priest at once. 'For by Saint Paul, I will not to dinner till I see thy head off.'

In mounting shock, Hastings gabbled a quick confession before being bundled outside.

> So was he brought foorth into the greene beside the chappell within
> the Tower, and his head laid downe upon a long log of timber, and
> there striken off.

Two weeks later, Richard was king.

Did you know?
? You can see it all in *The Tragedy of King Richard the Third* by **William Shakespeare**. He didn't invent a thing!

The first queen to die here was **Anne Boleyn**. Henry VIII needed her out of the way so he could remarry and have a son.

Anne was executed at about 8am on Friday, May 19 1536. The Tower was cleared of foreigners for the occasion and the gates were shut, but there was still a large audience to watch her die. She was executed by a swordsman especially brought over from France – a great privilege, because Continental two-handed swords were much more efficient than English axes. The executioner hid his weapon underneath the straw on the scaffold and waited for Anne to appear from the bottom end of the green.

She walked the 50 yards uphill, accompanied by four ladies-in-waiting. She was wearing a grey, fur-lined damask gown, a crimson petticoat, and an ermine mantle and hood. She looked as if she was happy to die – a welcome release after all the trouble she had been through.

Anne mounted the scaffold and made her last speech.

> Good Christian people. I have not come here to preach a sermon. I
> have come to die... As for mine offences, I here accuse no man. God
> knoweth them. I remit them to God, beseeching Him to have mercy
> on my soul.

The mantle was removed. Anne's hair was tucked into a cap. One of her
attendants blindfolded her. 'To Jesu Christ, I commend my soul.' Anne knelt
down, but kept turning her head towards the executioner, even though she
couldn't see what was coming. The executioner fooled her by calling for
someone to bring his sword. Anne looked that way and the executioner
whipped her head off before she knew what was happening.

After the blood had subsided, a lady-in-waiting picked the head up and
covered it in a white cloth. The other three wrapped the body in a sheet and
carried it into the Chapel of St Peter-ad-Vincula next to the scaffold. Anne's
clothes were removed and given to the Tower staff, as was customary. Her body
and head were dumped in a box originally designed to carry bow staves. She was
buried in the chancel of the chapel, just in front of the altar. She's there now.

Did you know?

? These days, royal ladies-in-waiting never carry anything heavier than a
handbag or a bunch of flowers.

? Foreigners all over Europe were amazed that Anne didn't have to be tied up
for her execution. They had forgotten about Britain's stiff upper lip in times
of crisis!

? A slight exception to this trend was the Countess of
Salisbury, beheaded here on May 27 1541. She was an
old lady, daughter of the Duke of Clarence who
was drowned in malmsey (see page 62).
She had done nothing wrong, but her
son opposed Henry VIII's divorce, so
Henry had her killed as a warning to the
son. Because she was innocent, Lady
Salisbury refused to lay her head on the
traitors' block. She kept moving it
about instead as the axeman
took aim. He was just a
boy, a novice at the job. He
gouged great chunks out of
Lady Salisbury's head and
shoulders before she finally
stopped fidgeting and lay still at last.

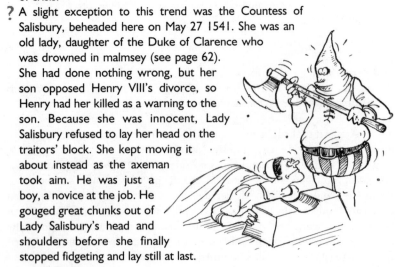

Catherine Howard was Henry VIII's fifth wife, a silly girl of 20 married to a
fat old man. She had had lovers before her marriage to the king and continued
to have them afterwards. Bad mistake.

The lovers were tortured and beheaded. One who wasn't a gentleman was castrated and disembowelled as well. Catherine herself was executed at 7am on Monday, February 13 1542. She put up a fight when they brought her to the Tower and had to be forced into the boat. But she soon became resigned to her fate and asked to have the block brought to her beforehand, 'that she might know how to place herself' when the time came.

Catherine was so terrified on the scaffold that she couldn't think of anything interesting to say before she was beheaded. She was followed by her lady-in-waiting, Viscountess Rochford, who confessed her sins and prayed for the king before laying her head on a block still wet with Catherine's blood. Both were then buried in the chapel. Catherine lies in front of the altar, next to Anne Boleyn – her cousin.

Did you know?

? Catherine had known all about boys since her mid-teens. 'At the flattering and fair persuasions of Mannox, being but a young girl, I suffered him at sundry times to handle and touch the secret parts of my body.'

? 'Francis Dereham by many persuasions procured me to his vicious purpose and obtained first to lie upon my bed with his doublet and hose and after within the bed and finally he lay with me naked and used me in such sort as a man doth his wife.'

? There was also Thomas Culpepper, who continued to see Catherine after her marriage. Her lady-in-waiting, Viscountess Rochford, arranged late night trysts for them. Catherine and Culpepper both stoutly insisted that nothing improper had occurred in her bedroom between 11 o'clock at night and 3 o'clock the next morning, but nobody believed them for a moment.

Lady Jane Grey was only 16 when she died. A great niece of Henry VIII, she was a threat to her cousin Queen Mary for as long as she remained alive. So Mary had her killed on Monday, February 12 1554.

Jane's 17-year-old husband **Lord Guildford Dudley** was executed the same day. He wasn't royal, so he was taken outside the walls of the Tower and beheaded on Tower Hill, shortly after 10am. Then:

> His carcas throwne into a carre, and his hed in a cloth, he was
> brought into the chappell within the Tower, wher the ladye Jane,
> whose lodging was in Partrige's house, dyd see his ded carcase taken
> out of the cart, aswell as she dyd see him before on lyve going to his
> deathe – a sight to hir no lesse than death.

> By this tyme was ther a scaffolde made upon the grene over agaynst
> the White tower, for the saide lady Jane to die apon… The saide
> lady, being nothing at all abashed, neither with feare of her owne
> deathe, which then approached, neither with the sight of the ded
> carcase of hir husbande, when he was brought in to the chappell,
> came fourthe, the levetenaunt leading hir, in the same gown wherin
> she was arrayned, hir countenance nothing abashed, neither hir eyes

> enything moysted with tears, although her ij gentylwomen, mistress
> Elizabeth Tylney and mistress Eleyn, wonderfully wept, with a boke
> in hir hande, wheron she praied all the way till she cam to the saide
> scaffolde...

Jane admitted her sins to the crowd but insisted that she had never wanted to
be queen. Kneeling down, she asked everyone to pray for her and said the
psalm *Miserere mei Deus* in English.

> Then she stode up and gave her maiden mistris Tilney her gloves and
> handkercher, and her book to maister Bruges, the lyvetenantes
> brother; forthwith she untyed her gown. The hangman went to her to
> help her of therewith; then she desyred him to let her alone, turning
> towardes her two gentlewomen, who helped her off therwith...
> geving to her a fayre handkercher to knytte about her eyes.

> Then the hangman kneeled downe, and asked her forgevenesse,
> whome she forgave most willingly. Then he willed her to stand upon
> the strawe: which doing, she sawe the block. Then she sayd, 'I pray
> you dispatch me quickly.' Then she kneeled down, saying, 'Wil you
> take it of before I lay me downe?' and the hangman answered her,
> 'No, madame.'

> She tyed the kercher about her eys; then feeling for the blocke, saide,
> 'What shall I do? Where is it?' One of the standers-by guyding her
> therunto, she layde her heade down upon the block, and stretched
> forth her body and said: 'Lorde, into thy hands I commende my
> spirite!' And so she ended.

Did you know?

? Jane was a nice girl, quiet and scholarly – 'that fayre Ladye, whom nature had
not onely so bewtified, but God also had endewed with singular gyftes and
graces'. She was familiar with Latin, Greek, Hebrew, Italian and French, but
had little interest in politics. It was an attempt by her father to put her on the
throne, with himself the power behind the scenes, that caused her downfall.
Jane was proclaimed queen after the death of her cousin Edward VI, but ruled
for only nine days before happily surrendering to Mary, the rightful successor.
Mary kept Jane prisoner for a while, then put her to death a few days after
Sir Thomas Wyatt's abortive coup.

? Jane was a skinny little thing, so small that she had to wear three-inch soles
on her clogs for people to see her in a crowd. She found her nine days as
queen so stressful that her skin flaked and her hair began to fall out.

? She refused to meet her husband the night before their execution in case
either of them broke down. But she did agree to watch from the window
next morning as he was led away to his death.

? Partridge's house, from where Jane watched, is now the Yeoman Gaoler's
House, No 5 Tower Green (in between Queen's House and the Beauchamp
Tower).

BEEFEATERS

It's only a nickname. They're really either Yeomen of the Guard, who used to guard the Tower gates, or Yeomen Warders, who guarded the prisoners. They were first appointed by Henry VII after the death of Richard III at the battle of Bosworth.

> On the 22nd day of August 1485 Henry, Earl of Richmond, was by public acclamation saluted on the battle field of Bosworth King over England... In the first year of his reign, the Yeoman of the Guard was first ordered of which the Yeomen Waiters or Warders of the Tower hath the seniority.

Today's Yeomen are all ex-servicemen, mostly army. Their best uniform of scarlet and gold hasn't changed since Elizabeth I introduced it nearly 450 years ago. They don't wear it every day because it's too expensive to look after.

? Along with the rest of his family, Lord Guildford Dudley had been incarcerated next door in the Beauchamp Tower. In one of the dungeons, the name IANE is still clearly visible on the wall (see page 72). Did he carve it there, thinking about his wife as he sat waiting for execution?

? An hour before her death, Jane was examined to see if she was pregnant. She wore a black gown to the scaffold. She thought the executioner was trying to help her take it off, but actually he just wanted it as part of his fee.

? The prayer book she carried to her death is now in the British Library at St Pancras (see page 185). She wrote various farewell messages in the margins, including this to Sir John Bridges, the Lieutenant of the Tower who escorted her to the scaffold: 'Forasmutche as you have desired so simple a woman to wrighte in so worthye a booke mayster lieutenaunte therefore I shall as a frende desyre you and as a christian require you to call uppon god to encline youre harte to his lawes.'

? No-one followed Jane's execution more closely than Princess Elizabeth, herself imprisoned a month later. 'You had best come in, Madam, for here you sit unwholesomely,' Sir John Bridges told her, as she sat glumly in the boat at Traitors' Gate. 'Better sit here than in a worse place,' Elizabeth replied. She wasn't to know then that she had a great and glorious reign in front of her.

The only man to be formally executed on Tower Green was Robert Devereux, **Earl of Essex**. He was a favourite courtier of Elizabeth I, the virgin queen almost old enough to be his grandmother. Essex knew her well enough to walk into her bedroom in the morning before she had got her face on, or her wig.

But he overreached himself in 1601 by staging a rebellion against the old lady's increasingly erratic rule. Elizabeth was most reluctant to sign his death warrant, yet felt she had no option. Essex was duly axed just after 7am on Wednesday, February 25.

It was announced at the time that he was executed in the privacy of the Tower as a special favour to an old courtier. In fact, there might have been a riot if he had been executed on Tower Hill. Essex was popular with ordinary people. He articulated the growing belief that the monarch should not be the only person to have a say in how the country was governed.

He wore a black satin suit for his execution and a black velvet cloak. A hundred people watched him die, including his old enemy **Sir Walter Ralegh**. Essex called for his servant to help him off with his cloak and ruff, forgetting that he didn't have a servant any more. Kneeling down on the straw, he said the Lord's Prayer, then removed his black doublet to reveal a scarlet waistcoat underneath.

The first stroke hacked into his shoulder. The second missed as well. The third severed his head and Essex was dead at last. But the mob got hold of the executioner later that day and beat him senseless in revenge.

Did you know?

? Sir Walter Ralegh was Captain of the Guard at the time of Essex's death. As rivals for the queen's favour, they had been enemies for years. The other onlookers at the execution disapproved of Ralegh's presence, feeling that he had only come to gloat. So he removed himself from the actual beheading and watched it discreetly from a distant window.

? Essex was buried in the Chapel of St Peter-ad-Vincula, just beyond the execution site. The present chapel dates from 1520, replacing the previous one destroyed by fire. Two saints are buried there (St **Thomas More**, St **John Fisher**), and two queens (**Anne Boleyn**, **Catherine Howard**). So are **Lady Jane Grey**, **Lord Guildford Dudley**, the **Duke of Monmouth** and many others.

? Admission to the Tower is usually free on Sundays to people attending services in the chapel, but there are no services in August.

DEVEREUX TOWER
The Earl of Essex
Behind the chapel, not open to the public

Originally the Devyl's Tower, this was later renamed the Devereux Tower after its most famous inmate, Robert Devereux, Earl of Essex. It was from here that he walked the few yards to his execution on Tower Green on February 25 1601.

In happier days, Essex had been close enough to Elizabeth I to stay in her apartments until the small hours, although probably not as a lover. It was said that she had given him a ring, promising that if ever they quarrelled, he only had to return it and all would be forgiven.

THE CEREMONY OF THE KEYS

A nightly ritual for more than 700 years, the ceremony takes place at ten o'clock every evening, when the Tower is closed up for the night. Escorted by four guardsmen with lanterns, the Chief Warder locks all the gates, then returns to the Bloody Tower with the Keys. He is challenged by the sentry on duty, who points a rifle and bayonet at him.

Sentry: 'Halt, who comes there?'

Warder: 'The Keys.'

Sentry: 'Whose Keys?'

Warder: 'The Queen's Keys.'

Sentry: 'Pass, Queen Elizabeth's Keys. All's well.'

The troops proceed through the archway to the inner court, where the rest of the guards are drawn up on the steps leading towards the execution site. They salute, the bugler sounds 'Last Post', and at ten o'clock precisely the Warder falls out to deliver the Keys to the Tower Governor for the night.

Did you know?

? The Ceremony of the Keys has taken place in some form or another every night for the past 700 years. The only time it was nearly abandoned was April 16 1941, when a German bomb blew the escort off their feet. But the men picked themselves up, resumed their places and carried on as normal...in the middle of an air raid!

? Easily the most atmospheric of all the Royal Guard duties in London, the ceremony is open to 70 members of the public every night, but only by ticket in advance. Ask a Beefeater for details.

The story goes that Essex did return the ring, a few days before his execution. Opening a window in the Devereux Tower, he summoned a pageboy to give the ring to Lady Scrope, who would return it to the queen and thus save Essex's life. But the boy gave it instead to Lady Scrope's sister, wife of one of Essex's enemies. The ring never reached the queen and Essex was not reprieved.

It's almost certainly untrue. Ring or no ring, Elizabeth could have reprieved Essex any time she wanted. What *is* true though is that she wore a ring Essex had given her until the day she died. The museum at Westminster Abbey has a gold ring with a sardonyx cameo of the queen which is said to be the one that Essex sent her.

Did you know?

? Essex didn't sleep a wink the night before his execution. 'Pray for me,' he told the guards outside his cell. 'Tomorrow you shall see in me a strong God in a weak man. I have nothing left but that which I must pay to the Queen tomorrow in the morning.' And pay he did.

BEAUCHAMP TOWER
Lord Guildford Dudley

10

Pronounced 'Beecham' and often used as a prison in the 16th and 17th centuries. Its most famous prisoners were the Dudley family (the Duke of Northumberland and his five sons), held here in 1553 after the duke's abortive attempt to install his daughter-in-law,
Lady Jane Grey on the throne.

The Dudleys had time to kill before their execution. They busied themselves carving elaborate family inscriptions on the walls, all still there today. Most poignant of all is the single word IANE, almost certainly carved by 17-year-old **Lord Guildford Dudley**, Lady Jane's husband, as he sat waiting to die.

BELL TOWER
Sir Thomas More, Princess Elizabeth

11

The tower is not open to the public. It is best viewed from outside the walls.

After his arrival at Traitors' Gate on April 17 1534, **Sir Thomas More** was escorted to a cell in the Bell Tower, which had recently been converted to accommodate important prisoners. The tower was divided into two – the Upper Bell and the Lower Bell – and could only be reached through a door in Queen's House, where the Lieutenant Governor lived.

More was placed in the Lower Bell. It wasn't nice, but for the first few months he was allowed the freedom of the Tower and could walk in the grounds or go to mass, as he wished. Later though, after his continued refusal to recant, he was confined to his cell and all his privileges were withdrawn.

He could have gone free if he had recanted. His wife tried to talk him into it.

> I marvel that you that have been alwaies hitherto taken for so wise a
> man will nowe so play the foole to lye here in this close, filthy prison,
> and be content thus to be shut upp amongst mise and rattes.

But More was determined to be a martyr. 'Is not this house as nighe heaven as my owne?' Even when they took away his writing materials, forcing him to scribble secretly with bits of charcoal, he refused to capitulate. Through a tiny window he watched three Carthusian monks being taken to execution, 'as chearefully goinge to their deaths as bridegromes to their Mariage'. In his last weeks he had the windows closed and sat in darkness for most of the time. He was executed on Tower Hill on July 6 1535.

Did you know?

On March 18 1554, in the pouring rain, **Princess Elizabeth** arrived at the Bell Tower, convinced that her half-sister Queen Mary was going to have her beheaded, as her cousin Lady Jane Grey had been only a few weeks before.

Elizabeth hated her imprisonment. She was treated royally by her gaolers, dining at night with the Lieutenant Governor. But she was certain she was going to follow her mother and her cousin to the block. She dreaded the sound of approaching footsteps, the sudden knock on the door. She wondered how long it would be before they came for her.

She was probably imprisoned upstairs. For the first month, her only exercise was along the leads, a rooftop walkway between the Bell and Beauchamp Towers (not visible from the inner ward). From there she could look out over the battlements towards St Paul's Cathedral a mile away and Westminster Abbey beyond. She could also see the scaffold on Tower Hill.

Elizabeth was watched round the clock, in case Queen Mary's enemies tried to contact her. One of the Beefeaters' sons liked to bring her flowers, but was threatened with a beating in case he was passing her secret messages. 'Mistress,' he called through the bars. 'I may bring you no more flowers.' Her food was examined too, and her attendants were searched.

But there was no evidence against Elizabeth and she was far too popular to kill. Mary released her from the Tower after a couple of months. Elizabeth hated the place so much that for the rest of her life she always avoided it if she could.

QUEEN'S HOUSE
Anne Boleyn, Princess Elizabeth, Guy Fawkes, William Penn, Rudolph Hess

12

Queen's House is the L-shaped black and white building at the bottom of the green

Soon after midnight on November 5 1605, a group of Beefeaters carrying lanterns entered an old coal cellar beneath the House of Lords at Westminster. They discovered 36 barrels of gunpowder hidden under a pile of firewood – enough to blow the whole place to pieces when **James I** arrived later that day to open Parliament.

They also discovered a tall, bearded man, dressed in boots and spurs, wearing a hat and cloak, and carrying a supply of slow matches. He gave a false name, but it didn't take long to discover that he was **Guy Fawkes**, a fervent Roman Catholic. He was part of a conspiracy to blow up king and Parliament in revenge for the persecution of Catholics then taking place.

Guy Fawkes was arrested and brought to Queen's House for questioning. He refused to talk, so the king signed a warrant for his torture, stipulating that 'the gentler tortours are to be first usid unto him,' before anything nastier was tried.

Queen's House

Guy Fawkes confessed within a couple of days. He was probably stretched on the rack in the White Tower. But he was certainly interrogated in Queen's House, because a plaque commemorating the event was erected in the house's council chamber (top floor, right) in 1608 and is still there on the wall. Fawkes was executed at Westminster (see page 16) on January 31 1606.

? 'Remember, remember, the fifth of November'. The Gunpowder Plot is still commemorated every November 5 with fireworks and bonfire parties all over the country.

Queen's House was built in the 1530s as a residence for the Lieutenant Governor of the Tower. It also housed important prisoners from time to time. **Anne Boleyn** may have set out for her execution from here. Her daughter **Elizabeth I** certainly dined in the house while a prisoner in the Bell Tower.

One of the luckiest prisoners to be kept here was a Scottish rebel, the **Earl of Nithsdale**. He was awaiting execution in 1716 for supporting the Jacobite rebellion – an attempt to replace the new German king with the old Scottish one. On February 23, however, a few hours before he was to die, he made a dramatic escape, disguised as a woman, and was never seen again.

The escape was organised by his wife. Accompanied by two women in riding hoods, she arrived at Queen's House to say goodbye to her husband. One of the women

> had the precaution to hold her handkerchief to her face, as was very natural for a woman to do when she was going to bid her last farewell to a friend on the eve of his execution.

> I had, indeed, desired her to do it, that my Lord might go out in the same manner. Her eyebrows were rather inclined to be sandy, and my Lord's were dark and very thick: however, I had prepared some paint of the colour of hers to disguise his with. I also bought an artificial head-dress of the same coloured hair as hers; and I painted his face with white and his cheeks with rouge, to hide his long beard, which he had not had time to shave.

Donning the woman's hood, Lord Nithsdale kept a handkerchief to his face and wept copiously as he walked past the guards. Lady Nithsdale stayed in his cell.

> When I was in the room, I talked to him as if he had been really present, and answered my own questions in my Lord's voice as nearly as I could imitate it. I walked up and down, as if we were conversing together, till I thought they had time enough thoroughly to clear themselves of the guards.

Then she rejoined her husband in

> the house of a poor woman directly opposite to the guard-house. She had but one small room, up one pair of stairs, and a very small bed in it. We threw ourselves upon the bed, that we might not be heard walking up and down.

They lay low for two days, while the redcoats hunted everywhere for them. Then Lord Nithsdale escaped to Italy, disguised as a servant of the Venetian ambassador, and was reunited with his wife in Rome.

Did you know?

? An earlier and less dramatic prisoner here was the Quaker **William Penn**. Imprisoned in 1668 for an intemperate religious pamphlet, he stoutly declared 'My prison shall be my grave before I will budge a jot'. After his release, Penn went to the colonies to found Sylvania. The word Penn was added to the title deeds in honour of Penn's father, a distinguished admiral.

? The most bizarre prisoner of all was **Rudolph Hess**, Deputy Fuhrer of Nazi Germany. He spent four days in Queen's House in May 1941 while his captors wondered what on earth to do with him. In the middle of World War II, Hess had flown himself to Scotland and then parachuted to earth, with the apparent aim of making peace with the British. His captors didn't know what to make of him at all. Hess was kept in a room on the first floor, at the northern end of the house. It gave him a good view of the changing of the guard on the green. 'From my window, I could see the Guards parade each

THE TOWER RAVENS

Keen scavengers, ravens have always thrived at the Tower, feeding on the refuse thrown over the wall or into the moat. There is a tradition that without them the Tower will fall and the kingdom too. So they are actively encouraged to stay. There are six on the official strength, fed and cared for by the Ravenmaster. He also clips their wings, to make sure they can't escape.

In 1675, the Royal Observatory was established in the northeast turret of the White Tower, under Sir John Flamsteed, the Astronomer Royal. But there were so many ravens in those days that they often obscured the view. It's sometimes said that Charles II became so irritated with the birds one day, as he was trying to peer through a telescope, that he decided to move the observatory to Greenwich to get away from them. Nice idea, but actually the observatory was moved to get away from London's smog.

day, displaying enormous stamina and a drill that would have done them proud in Prussia. They even had a military band, though I could have done without the bagpipes – as could many of the English, or so they confessed to me.'

QUEEN'S STAIR
Henry VIII, Anne Boleyn, Sir Thomas More, Captain Blood, Peter the Great

13

Outside the Tower at Tower Wharf

The Queen's Stair was used by royalty and other distinguished visitors to the Tower arriving by boat. They were welcomed on the wharf by the Lieutenant Governor and escorted across the moat to the little postern gate in the Byward Tower, royalty's private entrance. It was here that **Henry VIII** stood waiting to greet his new wife **Anne Boleyn** on May 29 1533, a couple of days before her coronation as his second queen.

Anne came from Greenwich by boat. It was a lavish procession because Henry wanted to put on a good show. His divorce from his first wife had not been popular, so he made a spectacle of Anne's coronation to provide everyone with an excuse for a party. Although six months pregnant, Anne was 'apparelled in rich cloth of gold', with luxurious dark hair stretching down almost to her waist. Her boat was escorted by 50 barges, all decked out for the occasion, with minstrels playing and everyone dressed in their best clothes. There were so many other boats following behind that the flotilla stretched for four miles along the river.

A thunder of artillery greeted Anne's arrival at Tower Wharf – so loud that it shattered every pane of glass in the Tower. Anne came ashore to applause from the nobility and officers of state, anxious not to offend the king's new squeeze. Henry himself stepped forward and kissed Anne publicly, 'with loving countenaunce at the postern by the waters' side'. Three years later, he had her head cut off.

While Anne was still queen, **Sir Thomas More** was tried at Westminster on July 1 1535 and sentenced to a traitor's death.

> You are to be… hanged till you be half dead, after that cut down yet alive, your bowels to be taken out of your body and burned before you, your privy parts cut off, your head cut off, your body to be divided in four parts, and your head and body to be set at such places as the King shall assign.

With his sentence ringing in his ears, More was taken back to the Tower to await execution. His daughter Margaret hurried ahead to try and get one last glimpse of him before he disappeared inside.

> She gave attendaunce aboute the Tower wharf, where she knewe he should passe by, before he could enter into the Tower… As soon as she sawe him… she hastinge towards him, without consideracion or care of her self, pressinge amonge the thronge and company of the garde that with halberd and bills wente round aboute him, hastely ranne to him, there openly, in the sight of them all, imbraced him, toke him about the neck, kissed him…

> The beholding whereof was to many of them that were present so lamentable that it made them for very sorowe to mourne and weape.

More than a century later, on the morning of May 9 1671, **Captain Thomas Blood** and his gang came hastening along the wharf with the Crown Jewels hidden under their clothes (see page 60).

Blood was disguised as a clergyman, with the crown under his cloak. Parrot had the Black Prince's ruby in his pocket and the orb down his trousers. With a hue and cry behind them, they were doing their best to look natural as they hurried east towards St Katharine's, where their horses were waiting.

> The Villains got over that Drawbridge, and through the outward Gate upon the Wharf, and made all possible haste toward their Horses, which attended at St Katharine's Gate… crying themselves, as they ran, "Stop the Rogues!". And they were by all thought innocent, he being in that grave Canonical Habit, till Captain Beckman got up to them.

> Blood discharged his Second Pistol at Captain Beckman's Head, but
> he stooping down avoided the Shot, and seized upon the Rogue, who
> had the Crown under his Cloak; yet had Blood the Impudence, altho'
> he saw himself a Prisoner, to struggle a long while for the Crown.

Blood was damned if he was going to let go of it. Beckman had to snatch it
from him in the end and the crown was damaged in the process.

> In the robustious struggle for the Crown... the great Pearl and a fair
> Diamond fell off, and were lost for a while, with some other smaller
> Stones. But the Pearl was found by Katharine Maddox (a poor
> Sweeping Woman to one of the warders) and the Diamond by a
> Barber's Apprentice... The fair Ballas Ruby belonging to the Sceptre,
> was found in Parrot's Pocket. So that not any considerable Thing was
> wanting. The Crown only was bruised and sent to repair.

The crown was remodelled and returned to the Tower. It looked as good as
new when Elizabeth II wore it at her coronation in 1953.

On May 2 1698, at the end of a four-month stay in England, **Peter the Great**
paid a final visit to the Tower to say goodbye before returning to Russia. He
had visited the Mint several times to learn about English coinage, spending so
much time in the local pubs that a tavern in Great Tower Street was renamed
the 'Czar of Muscovy' in his honour. But now he had come to distribute
presents and gifts of money while his yacht, the *Royal Transport*, waited for
him in the Thames.

From Tower Wharf, Peter sailed to Woolwich to say goodbye to the officials
at the arsenal, and from there to Gravesend, Chatham and Margate, where an
English naval squadron escorted him to Holland. Peter never returned to
England, but remained fond of the place. 'The English island is the best and
most beautiful in the world!'

THE MIDDLE TOWER

14

The pit outside the Middle Tower (the modern entrance for tourists)
used to house the royal menagerie. Henry III kept an elephant at the Tower in
1255. There were also lions at various times, leopards,
and a polar bear that was allowed to fish in the
Thames with its keeper.

In 1278, the old elephant house provided
emergency accommodation for an overflow of
Jews, imprisoned in the Tower on suspicion
of clipping the coinage. The Jewish
community were distinctly ambivalent about
the Tower. They fled there for safety from
pogroms, but they were also hanged from the
walls on occasion, and rounded up there
before their expulsion from England in 1290.

TOWER HILL SCAFFOLD
The Archbishop of Canterbury, Sir Thomas More, Lord Guildford Dudley, Sir Thomas Wyatt, the Duke of Monmouth

15

Trinity Square Gardens

The Tower Hill scaffold stood across the road from the Tower, in the middle of what is now Trinity Square Gardens. The exact spot is marked by a memorial, but it is not easy to find. Aim for the sunken garden recording the merchant navy dead from World War II. The scaffold stood immediately outside the garden at the southwest corner, and the spot is marked by a set of memorial tablets at ground level, bearing the names of some of those executed here.

Unlike the scaffold inside the Tower, the Tower Hill scaffold was a semi-permanent structure. The scaffold posts stood here for several centuries and were not finally removed until after the last execution in 1780. In the 400 years up to then, at least 125 people were executed on Tower Hill. A few were common criminals, but most were heretics or political prisoners. Upper-class prisoners were beheaded. The rest were hanged, and sometimes disembowelled as well.

An execution was always a big spectacle, attended by thousands of Londoners. Viewing stands were erected and the public paid good money for the best seats. In return, they got to see a man hanged until he had lost consciousness, then revived in time for his penis to be cut off and shoved  into his mouth. His stomach was cut open and his intestines thrown into a pot of boiling water. His heart was shown to him before he was beheaded. The head was then lightly boiled, so it would last longer when displayed on London Bridge. With speeches beforehand, and a chance to dip their handkerchiefs in the blood afterwards, it was a great day out for all the family!

The first person to die here was the **Archbishop of Canterbury** during the Peasants' Revolt of 1381. He had taken refuge in the White Tower when the peasants broke in. They went from room to room, looting everything they could find, until they found the Archbishop hiding in the Chapel of St John.

> They therefore laid hands on him; and dragging him out of the chapel, they drew him forth of the Tower gate, to the Tower Hill; where being compassed about with many thousands, and seeing swords about his head drawn in excessive manner, threatening death to him… kneeling down, he offered his head to him that should smite off his head.
>
> Being stricken in the neck, but not deadly, he putting his hand to his neck, said: 'Aha, it is the hand of God'. He had not removed his hand

from the place where the pain was, but that being suddenly stricken
again, his fingers ends being cut off, and part of the arteries, he fell
down; but yet he died not, till being mangled with eight several
strokes in the neck and head, he fulfilled most worthy martyrdom.

Three other courtiers suffered the same fate. The heads of all four were stuck
on poles and paraded through the streets to Westminster Abbey. They were
then exhibited on London Bridge, the traditional site for traitors' heads. The
peasants responsible were soon caught and executed in their turn, but too late
for the unfortunate Archbishop and his companions.

Sir Thomas More was executed on Tower Hill at 9am on July 6 1535. His
sentence of hanging and disembowelment had been commuted to a simple
beheading, an act of clemency for which he was duly grateful. He dressed in his
best clothes for the occasion, but was persuaded to change by the Lieutenant
Governor, who pointed out that the clothes would be taken by the executioner,
a worthless fellow. More wanted the man to have his best clothes anyway, but
eventually changed into a coarse robe and gave him a gold coin instead.

> And so was he by master Leiutenaunte brought out of the Tower,
> from thence led to the place of execution. Where, goinge vppe the
> scaffold, which was so weake that it was ready to fall, he said merilye
> to master Leiutenaunte: 'I pray you, master Leiutenaunte, see me saif
> vppe, for my cominge downe let me shifte for my self.'

A huge crowd had assembled to watch More die. He was bearded and haggard,
and carried a red cross. Someone had offered him a cup of wine on his way up
the hill but he had refused it, pointing out that Jesus had only been offered
vinegar and gall. He was received on the scaffold by the executioner in a scarlet
robe, a mask and a horn-shaped hat. The man knelt down to ask More's
forgiveness and was given a kiss in return.

> Then desired he all the people thereaboute to pray for him, to beare
> witnes with him that he should suffer death in the faith of the holy
> chatholik churche. Whiche done, he kneled downe, and after his
> prayers said, turned to the executioner, with a cheerefull
> countenaunce spake to him: 'Plucke vpp thy spirites, man, be not
> afrayde to do thine office; my necke is very shorte; take heede
> therefore thow strike not awrye, for savinge of thine honestye.'

More was decapitated with one blow. His head was boiled and placed on
London Bridge, but his daughter retrieved it after a few days and kept it
hidden. It is buried now in a family vault in Canterbury.

Lord Guildford Dudley, 17-year-old husband of Lady Jane Grey, was
executed here in 1554 (see page 72).

> The monday, being the xij th of Februarie, about ten of the clocke,
> ther went out of the Tower to the scaffolde on Tower hill, the lorde

Guilforde Dudley, husbande to the lady Jane Grey, who at his going out tooke by the hande sir Anthony Browne and many other gentyllmen, praying them to praie for him.

Without the bullwarke the sheryve receyved him and brought him to the scaffolde, where, after a small declaration, having no gostlye father with him, he kneeled downe and said his praiers; then holding upp his eyes and handes to God many tymes; and at last, after he had desyred the people to pray for him, he laide his hedd upon the block, which was at one stroke of the axe taken from him.

Dudley was tall and handsome. He had asked for a Protestant clergyman to accompany him to the scaffold, but his request had been refused. His body was thrown into a cart and wheeled back to the Tower. Lady Jane watched from a window of the Yeoman Gaoler's house as it was taken for burial in the Chapel of St Peter, just beyond her own scaffold on the green.

Lady Jane and her husband would probably have survived if **Sir Thomas Wyatt** hadn't led a rebellion against Queen Mary. Two months after their execution, he too followed them to the block.

The xj th of Aprell, being wenysdaye, was sir Thomas Wyat behedded upon the Tower-hill... He was brought out with a boke in his hande; and at the garden pale the lorde chamberlayne tooke his leave of him, to whome master Wyat said: 'I praie you, sir, pray for me, and be a meane to the quene for my poore wife and chilldren'...

When he was uppe apon the scaffolde he desired eche man to praye for him... without more talke he tourned him, and put of his gown and untrussyd his pointes; then he plucked of his doblet and wastcote, unto his shirte, and knelyd downe upon the strawe, then laied his hed downe awhile, and rayse on his knees agayne, then after a fewe wourdes spoken, and his eyes lyft upp to heaven, he knytt the handekersheve himself about his eyes, and a lyttel holding upp his hands sobdenly laid downe his hed, which the hangeman at one stroke toke from him.

Then was he forthwith quarteryd apon the scaffolde, and the next day his quarters set at dyverse places, and his hed apon a stake apon the galloss beyond saynte James. Which his hed, as ys reported, remayned not there x. dayes unstolne awaye.

Did you know?

? **John Fisher**, Sir Thomas More's fellow Catholic saint, was executed two weeks before him, on June 22 1535. Fisher was so old and feeble that he had to be carried up Tower Hill in a chair. As soon as he had been axed, the crowd rushed forward to dip their handkerchiefs in his blood. This was traditional at important executions. A martyr's blood was held in awe – a holy relic and a remedy for all sorts of aches and pains.

? The **Duke of Monmouth** was beheaded here on July 15 1685. He was very good-looking, the illegitimate son of Charles II and a prostitute. He tried to overthrow his uncle, James II, and paid the price of failure. The execution itself was a disaster, needing repeated blows of the axe and then a knife to finish him off.

The axeman 'made five Chopps before he had his head off, which so incens'd the people, that had he not ben guarded & got away they would have torne him in pieces'. It was thought that no pictures existed of the duke, so according to one account his head was hurriedly sewn back on after his death and his portrait painted before his burial. The picture is in the National Portrait Gallery, just off Trafalgar Square, but opinion is divided as to whether it really is Monmouth or not.

? Beheadings continued until the 18th century. The last person to lose his head here was **Lord Lovat** on April 9 1747. The axe and block are still on show in the Tower. Lovat was a Scottish rebel, a supporter of the Jacobite rebellion. So many people came to watch him die that one of the stands collapsed, killing up to 20 spectators. Lovat didn't mind a bit.

? There were no more beheadings after Lovat, but hangings continued on Tower Hill until 1780. The very last people to be hanged were two prostitutes and a soldier who had taken part in the anti-Catholic Gordon riots. They destroyed a tavern belonging to a foreign Catholic and were hanged for it on July 11.

TOWER HILL UNDERGROUND
Roman wall

16

Near the entrance to the Underground station stands one of the last remaining segments of the Roman wall that once encircled London. The wall was built around AD200 and originally stood 20 feet high. Today it is 35 feet high – the first 14 Roman, the rest a medieval addition.

With the introduction of modern artillery in the 17th century, defensive walls became obsolete and were eventually demolished. Most of London's wall had disappeared by the end of the 18th century and very little now remains. The statue at the base is thought to be of the Emperor Trajan (AD98–117).

WHAT NOW?

Several companies along Tower Wharf offer boat trips upriver to Westminster Pier, or downriver to the National Maritime Museum at Greenwich (with a longitude of 0). Tower Bridge offers a tour of the Tower Bridge experience, or you can walk across the river and visit HMS *Belfast*, a World War II battle-cruiser converted into a floating museum.

The Tower Hill pageant is just up the hill from the entrance to the Tower. Beyond it, the best of **Jack the Ripper**'s murder sites is at Mitre Square (see page 203), 400 yards due north along Cooper's Row.

The diarist **Samuel Pepys** is buried in the crypt of St Olave's church, Seething Lane, across the road from Pepys Street where he used to live (just north of Tower Hill). The church also has a bust of his long-suffering wife in the nave, carefully sited so that he could see it from his pew.

Nearest public lavatories By the Underground station, or across the road from the entrance to the Tower

⊖ Tower Hill

WHERE TO EAT

There are fast food places by the entrance to the Tower and a café/restaurant in the Tower itself. The café on Tower Wharf has nice views of the river. Just beyond Tower Bridge, the Tower Thistle hotel does more serious food.

St Paul's Cathedral and the Temple

WALK AT A GLANCE

Features Sir Christopher Wren's masterpiece, and other historic buildings that survived the Blitz.
Time Allow one hour for looking round St Paul's, and at least another hour for wandering the narrow alleyways towards the end of the walk.
Length I mile, or just over two if you take the optional detour.
⊖ St Paul's

1 St Paul's Cathedral
- Admiral Nelson and the Duke of Wellington are buried
- Sir Winston Churchill receives a state funeral
- Lady Diana Spencer marries Prince Charles
- George Frederick Handel and Felix Mendelssohn play the organ.

2 Newgate Street
- Marconi gives the first public demonstration of radio.

Optional detour, adding just over one mile to the walk:

3 Smithfield
- Wat Tyler is killed outside St Bartholomew church
- Benjamin Franklin learns to print.

4 Charterhouse
- Elizabeth I prepares for her coronation
- John Wesley runs round the green
- W M Thackeray rehearses *Vanity Fair*.

5 St John's Gate
- Dr Johnson launches his literary career.

6 Clerkenwell Green
- Lenin plots the downfall of capitalism
- Oliver Twist learns how to pick a pocket or two.

Return to main walk:

7 Old Bailey/Newgate Gaol
- Charles Dickens and William Makepeace Thackeray see a man hanged
- Oliver Twist visits Fagin in the condemned cell.

8 **Gough Square**
   - Dr Johnson works on his dictionary.
9 **The Cheshire Cheese**
   - Voltaire, Mark Twain and Theodore Roosevelt all ate here.
10 **St Dunstan's church**
   - Samuel Pepys tries to pick up a girl during the sermon.
11 **Middle Temple Hall**
   - the first known performance of William Shakespeare's *Twelfth Night*.
12 **Middle Temple Garden**
   - medieval barons choose sides for the Wars of the Roses.

ST PAUL'S CATHEDRAL 1

A brilliant sailor and a well-loved national hero, **Admiral Nelson** commanded the British fleet at Trafalgar in 1805. The battle was a sensational victory for the British, destroying for ever Napoleon's chances of mounting an invasion. But Nelson himself was killed at the moment of triumph, and the nation was stunned with grief.

He was buried in St Paul's on January 9 1806. His body lay overnight at the Admiralty (see page 11) and was then drawn through the streets on a huge funeral car decked out in black to look like the admiral's flagship. Fifes and muffled drums played the 'Dead March' from *Saul* as the cortège set out. An immense crowd lined the route, but they were as silent as the grave as Nelson's coffin passed. The only sound was a noise like the murmur of waves along the seashore as thousands of people removed their hats in respect.

At St Paul's, the coffin was lifted from the funeral car by 12 sailors from HMS *Victory*, Nelson's flagship. In all, 300 men from the *Victory* attended the funeral. It had been postponed for several weeks because they insisted on being there.

Dressed in blue jackets and white trousers, each with a black armband and a gold Trafalgar medal around his neck, the 12 sailors carried the coffin slowly up the steps and into the cathedral. The choir sang 'I am the Resurrection and the Life' as they proceeded along the nave to the choir. There they were met by six admirals in full dress uniform, with black waistcoats, who took charge of the coffin for the service.

It was a very moving ceremony. The scene was lit by a huge lantern, specially suspended from the cathedral dome, which illuminated the coffin as the winter afternoon began to fade. The *Victory*'s battle ensigns were held proudly aloft – large ragged flags, riddled with shot. The choir sang Handel's funeral anthem 'The ways of Zion do mourn', muting the words 'His body is buried in peace', then bursting into full cry for the line 'But his name liveth evermore'.

At the end, the sailors were supposed to fold the battle flags reverently and lay them on the coffin. But they tore off a large strip first and divided it into smaller pieces among themselves. Then Nelson disappeared dramatically from view, lowered slowly through a trapdoor into the crypt below. There wasn't a dry eye in the house as he vanished. He was buried on the floor of the crypt

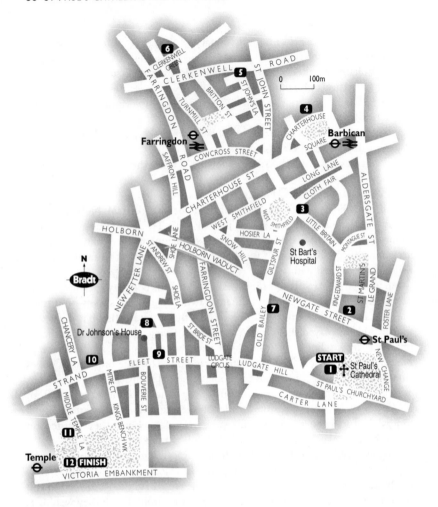

immediately beneath the cathedral's central crossing. A memorial to him was later erected in the south transept. The trapdoor through which he disappeared is still there.

Did you know?

? Nelson's funeral was attended by everyone who was anyone in London: his wife and family, the future **George IV**, the future **William IV**, half the aristocracy, 31 admirals, 100 Royal Navy captains – everyone, that is, except the woman he loved, his mistress **Lady Hamilton**. She wasn't invited.

? As he lay dying in *Victory*'s cockpit, Nelson summoned Captain Hardy to him. 'Take care of my dear Lady Hamilton, Hardy. Take care of poor Lady Hamilton. Kiss me, Hardy.' The captain did his best but the Government refused to help Lady Hamilton, who later died in poverty.

? Hardy was present at Nelson's funeral. So too was **Admiral Villeneuve**, the French commander at Trafalgar. Now a prisoner, he wanted to pay his respects to a man admired by sailors everywhere, regardless of nationality.

? Nelson's bloodstained uniform from Trafalgar is on display at the National Maritime Museum, Greenwich.

The **Duke of Wellington** finished what Nelson had started by defeating Napoleon at Waterloo in 1815. He later became Prime Minister, dying in 1852 at the ripe old age of 83.

He was buried at St Paul's on November 18. More than a million people turned out to watch, on a bitterly cold day. Wellington had never been loved as Nelson was loved, but he was greatly admired and respected. The country felt lost without him.

His body lay in state at Horse Guards (see page 8) the night before the funeral. Next morning it was loaded onto a funeral car even more bizarre than Nelson's – 'for forms of ugliness, horrible combinations of colour, hideous motion and general failure, there never was such a work achieved as the Car' – or so **Charles Dickens** thought.

The procession set off for Buckingham Palace first, where **Queen Victoria** was watching from the balcony. From there it turned towards Wellington's house at Hyde Park Corner before doubling back towards St Paul's. There were 3,000 infantry in the procession, eight squadrons of cavalry, three batteries of guns, and a host of foreign dignitaries – among them Count Alexandre Walewski, illegitimate son of **Napoleon**.

The bands played various dirges. The soldiers carried their weapons in reverse. Wellington's riderless horse was led by his groom, with a pair of Wellington boots reversed in the stirrups. The horse was too much for Queen Victoria, who burst into tears at the sight of it.

At the west door of the cathedral, the unloading mechanism proved so unwieldy that it took an hour to get the coffin down from the top of the car, 15 feet above the ground. When at last it was carried into the cathedral, 13,000 people rose to their feet. Among the official mourners were private soldiers from every regiment in the British army. The coffin was lit by six tall candlesticks for the service, and the address was given by **Benjamin Disraeli**.

At the end, the 'Dead March' was played as the coffin was ceremonially lowered into the crypt. Then came 'Sleepers Awake' and the distant boom of a gun salute from the Tower of London. Wellington was laid to rest in a chamber leading to the centre of the crypt, only a few yards from Lord Nelson. They had met only once in life, but in death it was felt that they should lie close to each other, two of the greatest heroes in British history.

Did you know?

? Traditionally such heroes were supposed to be buried in Westminster Abbey, the British Valhalla. But there was no room left by the time of Nelson's death, so St Paul's was chosen instead. The aim was to turn it into a pantheon of heroes, like the one in Paris.

WHAT TO SEE (clockwise from main entrance):

North aisle of the nave Wellington monument. Not his tomb, which is in the crypt, but a magnificent sculpted memorial completed in 1912.

North transept (Left of the central dome area) *The Light of the World*, one of three versions of **William Holman Hunt**'s painting of Jesus holding a lantern and knocking on a door, waiting for admittance.

Choir The organ, with five keyboards, 138 organ stops and 7,189 pipes. Built in 1695, it has since been refurbished but retains its original case. **George Frederick Handel** liked it so much that he brought his royal pupils to hear him play on August 24 1724:

> On Monday last the Royal Highnesses, the Princess Anne and
> Princess Caroline, came to St Paul's Cathedral, and heard the
> famous Mr Handel (their Musick Master) perform upon the Organ.

Handel often played for himself as well.

> When Handel had no particular engagements, he frequently went
> in the afternoon to St Paul's church... The truth is, that Handel
> was very fond of St Paul's organ... which was then almost a new
> instrument... The tone of the instrument delighted Handel; and a
> little intreaty was at any time sufficient to prevail on him to touch
> it, but after he had ascended to the organ-loft, it was with
> reluctance that he left it; and he has been known, after evening
> service, to play to an audience as great as ever filled the choir.

In summer, 'often stript into his shirt', he played on until eight or nine o'clock at night.

Felix Mendelssohn loved the organ too. On a visit to London in 1833, he played at St Paul's every Sunday, drawing capacity crowds. He was playing

---

? As with Nelson, the mourners all removed their hats as Wellington's coffin passed. To one eyewitness, it looked like 'the sudden rising from the ground & settling again of a huge flock of birds'.

Sir Winston Churchill's funeral on January 30 1965 was the first full state funeral for a commoner since the Duke of Wellington's a century earlier. His body lay in Westminster Hall for several days beforehand, where 300,000 people came to pay their respects. On the day of the funeral, the coffin was placed on a gun carriage and hauled to St Paul's by sailors from the Royal Navy. Big Ben was silenced for the occasion and did not strike again until after the funeral was over.

Six reigning monarchs and 15 heads of state attended the service at St Paul's. The coffin stood beneath the great dome, lit by the same six candlesticks that had illuminated the Duke of Wellington's in 1852. At the end of the ceremony, in Birmingham Cathedral once when the congregation refused to leave after the service, remaining rapt in their seats as Mendelssohn continued pouring out his magic. In the end, the bellows operator gave up, letting the wind out of the organ so they could all go home.

Apse (Far end of the cathedral, behind the high altar) American Memorial Chapel, dedicated 'To the American dead of World War II from the people of Britain.' A roll of honour contains the names of 28,000 Americans killed in or around the British Isles and is available for inspection.

South Choir Aisle Shrouded effigy of **John Donne**, Dean of St Paul's in the 1620s. It stood in the medieval cathedral and was one of very few statues to survive the Great Fire of 1666 – albeit with scorch marks still visible on its base. Donne was a fine poet as well as a priest. 'For whom the bell tolls' was a line of his poetry 300 years before it became the title of a novel by Ernest Hemingway and of a Hollywood movie.

South Transept Nelson monument and **Captain Robert Scott** memorial (to the man who famously died returning from the South Pole in 1912). Entrance also to the crypt, containing the tombs of **Sir Christopher Wren**, **Lord Nelson**, the **Duke of Wellington**, **Admiral Beatty** and **Earl Jellicoe**, and monuments to **Florence Nightingale**, **George Washington**, **Lawrence of Arabia** and others. Here too are lavatories, shop, café and restaurant.

South transept junction with nave Entrance to the Whispering Gallery, 259 steps up inside the dome. Whispers against the wall can be heard on the other side of the dome, 32 metres away. Entrance also to the Stone Gallery, 378 steps up, and the Golden Gallery, 530 steps. These are both external, running around the outside of the dome. Great views of London… for people with healthy hearts who don't mind heights!

a trumpeter in the Whispering Gallery sounded the Last Post and reveille. Churchill's body was then taken by barge along the Thames to Waterloo station for burial next to his parents in Oxfordshire. All the cranes at the dockside lowered their booms in unison as he passed, while jet fighters roared overhead in salute.

Did you know?

? The tradition of the Royal Navy hauling the body on a gun carriage began at the Duke of Wellington's funeral, when his funeral car got stuck in the mud and some nearby sailors were hurriedly roped in to help.

? The President of the United States did not attend Churchill's funeral because Churchill had failed to attend President Roosevelt's in 1945. But ex-President **Eisenhower** was there.

On a happier note, St Paul's is also where **Lady Diana Spencer** married **Prince Charles** in the summer of 1981. The whole nation celebrated, and the ceremony was seen on television by a global audience of 750 million.

Diana felt like 'a lamb to the slaughter' as she proceeded up the aisle.

> I remember being so in love with my husband that I couldn't take my eyes off him. I just absolutely thought I was the luckiest girl in the world.

After the ceremony, she walked back down the aisle on Prince Charles' arm, searching for his former mistress in the sea of faces. **Camilla Parker Bowles** wore a veiled pillbox hat, but Diana identified her without difficulty and remembered the moment for the rest of her life.

The marriage went wrong in the end but, for that day at least, everything was fine. The sun was shining, the bride was radiant, the people were delighted. They came out on the streets in tens of thousands and had a wonderful party. The whole country was happy.

History of St Paul's

There has been a house of worship on this hill overlooking the City of London since Roman times. The first Christian cathedral was built here in AD604. Dedicated to St Paul, it burned down in AD675. Its replacement was destroyed by Vikings in AD962. Two more cathedrals also burned down, the second most spectacularly in the Great Fire of London which destroyed most of the old city in 1666.

The present cathedral was built between 1675 and 1710 – a miraculously short time given that medieval cathedrals usually took a century to complete. The architect throughout was **Sir Christopher Wren**. Immediately after the Great Fire of London he had produced an ambitious plan for rebuilding the whole city in classical style. His plan was ignored, but he was commissioned instead to design a palatial new cathedral to complement the new city that was arising from the ashes of the old – the richest new city in the world.

It was no easy task. The design problems were immense, and Wren was hampered by an interfering committee that continually obstructed his work. He ended up erecting screens around the work in progress so that no-one could see what he was up to until it was complete. But the job was finished at last, and Wren was there for the topping out ceremony when his son (born the year the foundation stone was laid) added the final brick to the lantern on top of the cathedral dome. In old age, he often returned to the

cathedral to sit quietly and contemplate his masterwork. He is buried in the crypt with these Latin words on his tomb: *'Lector, si monumentum requiris, Circumspice'* ('Reader, if you want a monument, look around').

Did you know?

? One example of Wren and the committee at loggerheads: the committee wanted a stone balustrade around the outside of the dome but Wren declared it 'contrary to the principles of Architecture' and refused to cooperate. **Sir Isaac Newton** was deputed to talk him round. Wren gave in, probably correctly, since the balustrade does not offend the eye.

St Paul's and the Blitz

The cathedral was bombed several times during World War II, but miraculously survived each time. On September 12 1940, an 800lb bomb landed in front of the main steps, but failed to explode. A team of workers tunnelled 26 feet through gas-mains, electrical cables and mud to reach it. The bomb was hauled slowly to the surface and driven to Hackney Marshes, where it promptly blew a crater one hundred feet wide and broke windows half a mile away.

Far more serious was the raid of December 29 1940, when the Luftwaffe targeted the City of London (the 'square mile', London's ancient financial centre), using St Paul's as an aiming point. The cathedral was hit by 28 incendiary bombs, most of which were quickly dealt with by volunteers on the roof. But one bomb lodged in the dome, beyond anybody's reach, and set fire to the lead. Luckily it fell out when the lead melted and burned out harmlessly on the parapet.

The raid was well timed. December 29 was a Sunday. All the City offices were empty and locked. The tide was out on the Thames, so when the water-mains were bombed the fire brigade were unable to replenish their hoses from the river. About 1,500 fires started that night, raging out of control in two great firestorms that swept the length and breadth of the City. When the country woke up next morning, London's financial district had been gutted from end to end.

But St Paul's was still standing. It was famously photographed against the smoke, its dome still intact while everything else lay in ruins. The dome's survival became a symbol for the British, a sign that, however bad things might be, the country was still in business and would fight on to the bitter end.

Ritchie Calder was in the City that night.

I saw such a sight as none has seen since Samuel Pepys took boat at Tower Hill and from the river saw London ablaze in 1666 (see page 194)… The roof-tops of Fleet Street seemed a stockade of flames. The Middle Temple library was hopelessly alight. Johnson's London, those narrow back courts which are the hinterland of Fleet Street, was a flaming acre. Part of the *Daily Telegraph* building was burning furiously. The spire of St Bride's, parish church of journalism, was a macabre Christmas tree festooned in fire, and its inner pillars burning like candles.

Other Wren churches were torches. St Paul's was etched against a lurid sky; the fires seemed to be lapping round its dome. Fires in Cheapside, fires by St Martin's-le-Grand. Stationers' Hall Court, Ave Maria Lane and Paternoster Row a furnace fed by their own books; fires across the river, charring Little Dorrit's London; great fires that fused into greater until it seemed that puny man could never master them. Standing on that roof one felt like a Smithfield martyr must have felt as the faggots were lit around him.

Did you know?

? The Luftwaffe used three main kinds of bomb on London: high explosive, which blew up straight away; incendiary, which started fires that were difficult to put out; and delayed action, which lay in the ground for everyone to see, and were bad for the nerves since no-one knew when they would blow. This was a new kind of warfare, never before seen on such a scale. The German air force sowed the wind in the skies above St Paul's. In due course, the cities of Berlin, Dresden, Cologne and elsewhere reaped the whirlwind.

BRITISH TELECOM
Guglielmo Marconi
Newgate Street

2

In the summer of 1896, BT's smart building on the corner of King Edward Street was known simply as the Post Office. It was here that a bouncy 22-year-old arrived one morning, carrying two bags of electrical equipment and a letter of introduction to William Preece, the Engineer-in-Chief of Britain's postal services:

> Dear Mr Preece,
>
> I am taking the liberty of sending to you with this note a young Italian of the name of Marconi who has come over to this country with the idea of getting taken up a new system of telegraphy without wires, at which he has been working… From what he tells me he appears to have got considerably beyond what I believe other people have done in this line.

Guglielmo Marconi did not invent radio, but he was among the first to see its potential. He had designed an apparatus for transmitting 'electrical impulses and signals through the air, earth or water by means of electric oscillations of high frequency'. He had failed to sell it in Italy, so had turned to his mother's country instead because Britain was a maritime nation looking for ways to improve its communications at sea.

Preece was immediately impressed and gave Marconi the run of his laboratory. A few weeks later, on July 27, the young man was ready to give the first ever public demonstration of radio. Setting up his equipment on the Post Office roof, he proposed to send a signal to the Savings Bank Department on Queen Victoria Street, the other side of St Paul's. Post Office worker George Kemp spotted him from the pavement below.

'What are you doing there?' he shouted up to Marconi.

'Come on up and I'll show you,' Marconi replied.

Kemp joined him on the roof and watched in fascination as Marconi fiddled with his strange apparatus of black box, rods, terminals and brass balls. The experiment was a success. The signal travelled a quarter of a mile, through solid brick walls, and was received at the other end. Marconi was in business and George Kemp worked for him for the next 36 years.

Did you know?

? Marconi won the Nobel Prize for physics in 1909. Most of his early equipment is on display at the Science Museum, South Kensington.

? On the day of his funeral, radio transmitters all over the world fell silent for two minutes in tribute.

If you've decided to do the longer walk to Smithfield, Charterhouse, etc, go up King Edward Street and turn left along Little Britain towards St Bartholomew-the-Great church at West Smithfield.

If you're doing the shorter walk, go west along Newgate Street until you come to the Old Bailey on your left.

You may also want to visit the Museum of London at the junction of Aldersgate Street and London Wall (up King Edward Street). It's full of Roman wall paintings, reconstructed street scenes, both 18th-century clothes and the 1960s mini-skirt, and working models of the Great Fire of 1666 and the Blitz – something for everyone.

ST BARTHOLOMEW-THE-GREAT CHURCH

3

Wat Tyler, Benjamin Franklin

West Smithfield, corner of Little Britain

Wat Tyler led the Peasants' Revolt of 1381. At the height of the rebellion, 20,000 of them gathered at Smithfield ('smooth field'), which was then a large open space bordered on one side by the Norman priory of St Bartholomew. The peasants had just taken London by storm. They had assembled now to discuss with their leaders what the next move should be.

They were debating whether to loot the city when the king appeared, accompanied by a retinue of 60 horsemen. **Richard II** was a boy of only 14, but he did not shrink from a challenge.

When he reached the Abbey of St Bartholomew which stands there, he stopped and looked at the great crowd and said that he would not go on without hearing what they wanted. If they were discontented, he would placate them.

Entrance to Abbey of St Bartholomew

Wat Tyler rode forward from the west to negotiate with the king by the abbey. Tyler was a roofer from Kent, emboldened by the peasants' success. He spoke insolently to the king, and also to the Lord Mayor of London who was with him. In reply, the Lord Mayor produced his sword and struck Tyler on the head. He fell to the ground and was surrounded by the king's retainers, one of whom finished him off with a stab wound to the stomach while the peasants looked on helplessly.

They were about to launch into a massacre when Richard hurriedly retrieved the situation. Ordering his retainers to stay where they were, he rode forward alone and calmed the mob. 'I am your king,' he told them. 'You have no other leader but me.' The situation remained tense for some time, but the crowd eventually dispersed. The Peasants' Revolt was over. The peasants went home and their remaining leaders were later hunted down and hanged without mercy.

Did you know?

? No longer surrounded by open space, St Bartholomew is one of very few Norman churches in London. It is much smaller now than it was in 1381. The priory that the peasants knew reached as far as the gateway (the entrance to the nave is still there under the gatehouse at Little Britain, looking on to Smithfield), but was pulled down after Henry VIII dissolved the monasteries. Only the choir was left standing – today's church.

? After the dissolution of the monasteries, the church's Lady Chapel was used for non-religious purposes, including a printing works. **Benjamin Franklin** learned his trade there in 1725.

? Across the road from the church, the houses at 41 and 42 Cloth Fair are very rare examples of 17th-century homes that survived the Great Fire of 1666.

? One account of Wat Tyler's death claims that he did not die at once, but was taken to St Bartholomew's hospital (on its present site at Smithfield since 1123). 'Wat had been carried by a group of the commons to the hospital for the poor near St Bartholomew's, and put to bed in the chamber of the master of the hospital. The mayor went there and found him, and had him carried out to the middle of Smithfield, in the presence of his companions, and had him beheaded.'

? The hospital is also where the fictional Dr Watson met Sherlock Holmes for the first time, in *A Study in Scarlet*. '"Dr Watson, Mr Sherlock Holmes," said Stamford, introducing us. "How are you?" he said cordially, gripping my hand with a strength for which I should hardly have given him credit. "You have been in Afghanistan, I perceive."'

THE CHARTERHOUSE
Elizabeth I, John Wesley, W M Thackeray
Charterhouse Square

4

The Charterhouse is a bit of old London that somehow survived the worst of the bombing in this part of the City during World War II. Founded in 1371 as a religious house for Carthusian monks, it was later occupied by **Elizabeth I** as she prepared for her coronation in 1558. She arrived on November 23 and stayed for five days before moving on to the Tower of London. There her first action was to sack the Lieutenant of the Tower, who had been her gaoler during her imprisonment in 1554 (see page 73).

The Charterhouse later became a school. One of its most famous alumni in the early 19th century was **William Makepeace Thackeray**, a pupil there from 1822 until 1828. He boarded at the school at first, then went to live with a friend's parents in Charterhouse Square. Thackeray loathed the place and always remembered it with a mingled sense of horror and masochistic nostalgia common among the alumni of English boarding schools. The teaching was terrible, homosexuality was rife, and the only amusements were attending hangings at Newgate, leering at local prostitutes, or listening to the animals being slaughtered at Smithfield meat market.

But Thackeray recalled the school in his most famous novel, *Vanity Fair*. Thinly disguised as the Whitefriars, it's where Becky Sharp's son Rawdon was educated, with the help of her lover, Lord Steyne.

> The Whitefriars… had been a Cistercian convent in the old days, when the Smithfield, which is contiguous to it, was a tournament ground. Obstinate heretics used to be brought thither convenient for burning hard by. Harry VIII, the Defender of the Faith, seized upon the monastery and its possessions, and hanged and tortured some of the monks who could not accommodate themselves to the pace of his reform. Finally, a great merchant bought the house and land adjoining, in which… he established a famous foundation hospital for old men and children…

The boys are very comfortably lodged, fed, and educated, and subsequently inducted to good scholarships at the University and livings in the Church. [Young Rawdon] ... only got that degree of beating which was, no doubt, good for him; and as for blacking shoes, toasting bread, and fagging in general, were these offices not deemed to be necessary parts of every young English gentleman's education?

Did you know?

? Thackeray was writing in 1847. Charterhouse School outgrew the site in 1872 and moved to Godalming, in Surrey.

? Another Charterhouse alumnus was **John Wesley**, founder of the Methodist Church, who joined the school in 1714. On the advice of his father, he used to run three times round Charterhouse Green every morning to keep fit.

ST JOHN'S GATE
Dr Johnson

5

Top of St John's Lane

Born and bred in Staffordshire, **Samuel Johnson** intended at first to be a country schoolmaster. He set up a school at Edial and advertised for pupils in the *Gentleman's Magazine*. But the school was not a success, although the future actor **David Garrick** was one of his pupils. So Johnson gave up schoolmastering in March 1737 and set off for London, taking Garrick with him, to try and earn a living as a writer.

His first port of call in London was the office of the *Gentleman's Magazine* at St John's Gate. By his own account, Johnson 'beheld it with reverence' the first time he saw it. The editor's office was above the archway. Johnson introduced himself and asked for work. He was taken on at once, and for many years the magazine provided him with his main source of income.

His friend Garrick often came to see him here while trying to get a job in the theatre. Garrick may even have given his first public performance at St John's Gate, playing in *The Mad Doctor* to an audience composed of the *Gentleman's Magazine* staff. The magazine saw a great deal of Johnson and his friends during their early years in London.

St John's Gate

Did you know?

? Johnson was so poor that he preferred to keep out of sight when the editor had other guests for dinner. 'You might observe I sent a plate of victuals behind the screen. There skulked the Biographer, one Johnson, whose dress was so shabby that he durst not make his appearance.'

? Built in 1504, St John's Gate was the entrance to the priory of St John, the English headquarters of the crusading Knights Hospitallers. They were based here from 1140 until the 1540s, when Henry VIII dissolved the monasteries.

? The original priory was looted and burned by Wat Tyler's men during the Peasants' Revolt. This was the 'Hospital of Clerkenwell' that Richard II saw in flames as he watched from a turret of the Tower of London (see page 58).

? In the early 1700s, the gate was run as a coffee-house by Richard Hogarth. His son, the artist **William Hogarth**, grew up in the neighbouring streets and knew the gate well.

37A CLERKENWELL GREEN
V I Lenin
6

Now the Marx memorial library, 37a is where **Vladimir Ilich Lenin** worked during his London exile. He had chosen England for his operations because the proletarian class struggle was more advanced here than elsewhere. He first arrived in April 1902 and immediately began production of *Iskra* (The Spark), a Russian Marxist newspaper that had been banned at home.

The library had been a school in the 18th century, but now housed a printing press devoted to English socialist publications, including the works of Marx and Engels. Lenin was given a small room on the first floor, with a single window looking out onto a blank wall. His arrival meant that everyone else had to move up, but Lenin was grateful for the help from his English friends:

> The British Social-Democrats, headed by Quelch, readily made their printing-plant available. As a consequence, Quelch himself had to squeeze up. A corner was boarded off at the printing-works by a thin partition to serve him as editorial room. This corner contained a very small writing-table, a bookshelf above it, and a chair. When the

present writer visited Quelch in this editorial office there was no
room for another chair.

Lenin produced a copy of *Iskra* every fortnight during his ten months at
Clerkenwell. And when Harry Quelch's son visited Moscow in 1920, the first
question from Russia's new leader was: 'How is everybody at Clerkenwell
Green?'

Did you know?

? Still containing some of the original furniture, Lenin's room at the library is now
a listed historic monument. It is usually open to the public, except in August.

? Lenin lived at 30 Holford Square (now Kingsway College, leading off Holford
Place at Pentonville) during his London stay. It was there that he met **Leon
Trotsky** for the first time, as Trotsky later recalled: 'A cab that I engaged
because I saw others doing so took me to an address jotted down on a piece
of paper, my destination. This was Vladimir Ilich's home... As far as I
remember, Nadezhda Konstantinovna Krupskaya opened the door for me; I
had fetched her out of bed with my knocking, as one can imagine. It was early
in the morning... Vladimir Ilich was still in bed, and he greeted me with
justifiable surprise. Under such conditions our first meeting and our first
conversation took place.'

In the 1830s, Clerkenwell was full of thieves' kitchens, the most notorious of
which was run by a receiver of stolen goods named Ikey Solomon. **Charles
Dickens** used him as the model for Fagin in *Oliver Twist*. After his arrival in
London, Oliver was befriended by the Artful Dodger and taught how to pick
pockets by Fagin. Then the boys went looking for someone to rob:

> They were just emerging from a narrow court not far from the open
> square in Clerkenwell, which is yet called by some strange perversion
> of terms "The Green", when the Dodger made a sudden stop; and,
> laying his finger on his lip, drew his companions back again, with the
> greatest caution and circumspection.
>
> 'What's the matter?' demanded Oliver.
>
> 'Hush!' replied the Dodger. 'Do you see that old cove at the book-stall?'
>
> 'The old gentleman over the way?' said Oliver. 'Yes, I see him.'
>
> 'He'll do,' said the Dodger.

CENTRAL CRIMINAL COURT
(formerly Newgate Prison)
Charles Dickens, W M Thackeray
Old Bailey

7

Across the road from St Sepulchre church lies the wall of Newgate Prison, the
scene of many public hangings in the 19th century. The prison was

demolished in 1902, but the stones were re-used to build the Central Criminal Court (Old Bailey) on the same site. The ground-floor wall of the Old Bailey is the original prison wall, refaced in Portland stone. The main entrance used to be the debtors' door to the prison, through which men, women and children emerged to be hanged on the gallows directly outside. St Sepulchre is still there too, silent witness to their last moments as they dangled helplessly at the end of a rope.

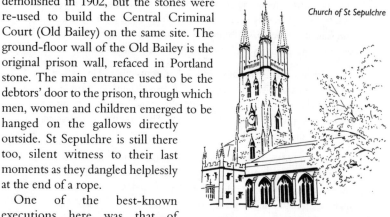

Church of St Sepulchre

One of the best-known executions here was that of Francois Courvoisier, who was publicly hanged on July 6 1840 for slitting his employer's throat. Courvoisier himself was unremarkable. But his death was witnessed by two young writers, **Charles Dickens** and **William Makepeace Thackeray**, both of whom were horrified by the public spectacle that was made of his execution.

Up to 40,000 people came to watch it happen. William Thackeray and his friends arrived very early in the morning to be sure of a good place.

> It is twenty minutes past four as we pass St Sepulchre's: by this time many hundred people are in the street, and many more are coming up Snow Hill. Before us lies Newgate Prison; but something a great deal more awful to look at, which seizes the eye at once, and makes the heart beat, is the gallows.
>
> There it stands black and ready, jutting out from a little door in the prison. As you see it, you feel a kind of dumb electric shock, which causes one to start a little, and give a sort of gasp for breath…
>
> The crowd has grown very dense by this time, it is about six o'clock, and there is a great heaving and pushing, and swaying to and fro… In one of the houses near us, a gallery has been formed on the roof. Seats were here let, and a number of persons of various degrees were occupying them… Some men were endeavouring to climb up a leaden pipe on one of the houses. The landlord came out, and endeavoured with might and main to pull them down…
>
> A thousand things of the sort related here came to amuse us. First the workmen knocking and hammering on the scaffold, mysterious clattering of blows was heard within it, and a ladder painted black was carried round, and into the interior of the edifice by a small side-door…
>
> It was past seven now… we turned back every now and then and looked at St Sepulchre's clock. Half an hour, twenty-five minutes… at last – ding, dong, dong, dong! – the bell is tolling the chimes of eight…

Just then, from under the black prison-door, a pale, quiet head peered out. It rose up directly, and a man in black appeared on the scaffold, and was silently followed by about four more dark figures. The first was a tall grave man: we all knew who the second man was...

His shirt was open. His arms were tied in front of him. He opened his hands in a helpless kind of way, and clasped them once or twice together. He turned his head here and there, and looked about him for an instant with a wild, imploring look. His mouth was contracted into a sort of pitiful smile.

He went and placed himself at once under the beam, with his face towards St Sepulchre's. The tall, grave man in black twisted him round swiftly in the other direction, and, drawing from his pocket a nightcap, pulled it tight over the patient's head and face. I am not ashamed to say that I could look no more, but shut my eyes as the last dreadful act was going on, which sent this wretched, guilty soul into the presence of God.

Charles Dickens did not enjoy it either.

From the moment of my arrival – down to the time when I saw the body with its dangling head, being carried on a wooden bier into the gaol – I did not see one token in all the immense crowd; at the windows, in the streets, on the house-tops, anywhere; of any one emotion suitable to the occasion. No sorrow, no salutary terror, no abhorrence, no seriousness; nothing but ribaldry, debauchery, levity, drunkenness, and flaunting vice in fifty other shapes.

Dickens knew all about Newgate. It's where Fagin sat in the condemned cell at the end of *Oliver Twist*, his novel of 1839. The book was fiction, but Dickens' knowledge of Newgate was hard fact:

Then came night – dark, dismal, silent night. Other watchers are glad to hear this church-clock strike, for they tell of life and coming day. To Fagin they brought despair. The boom of every iron bell came laden with the one, deep, hollow sound – Death. What availed the noise and bustle of cheerful morning, which penetrated even there, to him? It was another form of knell, with mockery added to the warning...

Those dreadful walls of Newgate, which have hidden so much misery and such unspeakable anguish ... From early in the evening until nearly midnight, little groups of two and three presented themselves at the lodge-gate, and inquired, with anxious faces, whether any reprieve had been received. These being answered in the negative, communicated the welcome intelligence to clusters in the street, who pointed out to one another the door from which he must come out, and showed where the scaffold would be built, and, walking with unwilling steps away, turned back to conjure up the scene...

It was some time before they left the prison. Oliver nearly swooned after this frightful scene, and was so weak that for an hour or more, he had not the strength to walk.

Day was dawning when they again emerged. A great multitude had already assembled; the windows were filled with people, smoking and playing cards to beguile the time; the crowd were pushing, quarrelling, joking. Everything told of life and animation, but one dark cluster of objects in the centre of all – the black stage, the cross-beam, the rope, and all the hideous apparatus of death.

Did you know?

? Executions were held outside Newgate from 1783, when Tyburn became uncontrollable, until 1868, when public hangings were abolished. The Magpie and Stump (18 Old Bailey, now refurbished) used to hire its upper rooms to spectators, perhaps including Dickens. The Viaduct Tavern (126 Newgate Street) still uses the prison's dungeons as cellars.

? A tunnel, since bricked up, ran under the road between St Sepulchre church and the condemned cell at Newgate. The night before a hanging, a priest would come through it ringing a handbell and chanting:

Watch and pray, the hour draws near

That you before the Almighty must appear.

All you that in the Condemned Hold lie

Prepare you, for tomorrow you shall die.

? The prison reformer **Elizabeth Fry** visited Newgate on March 4 1817 at the request of a woman due to be hanged next morning for robbery. 'Besides this poor young woman, there are also six men to be hanged, one of whom has a wife near her confinement, and seven young children. Since the awful report came down, he has become quite mad, from horror of mind. A strait waistcoat could not keep him within bounds: he had just bitten the turnkey; I saw the man come out with his hand bleeding, as I passed the cell.'

17 GOUGH SQUARE
Dr Johnson's house

8

Aim for the Cheshire Cheese, 145 Fleet Street. Johnson's house is signposted up Bolt Court or Wine Office Court

In 1746, **Samuel Johnson** was a struggling writer, so poor that he and his wife had to sell their most treasured possessions to pay the bills. He was thinking of giving it all up and returning to schoolmastering when a group of booksellers came to the rescue. They were planning to publish *A Dictionary of the English Language* defining more than 40,000 words and they wanted him to do the work.

Johnson started at once. His first move was to rent 17 Gough Square, which had a garret on the top floor big enough to house his six assistants. 'He had an upper room fitted up like a counting-house for the purpose, in which he gave to the copyists their several tasks.' The work went well, but conditions were primitive. A visitor invited to the garret 'found about five or six Greek folios, a deal writing-desk, and a chair and a half. Johnson giving to his guest the entire seat, tottered himself on one with only three legs and one arm...'

Johnson was so shabby and looked so odd with his nervous tics that people stopped to stare whenever he emerged from Bolt Court into Fleet Street. The dictionary was published in 1755 and established his reputation at once. But he remained dreadfully short of cash. On March 16 1756, he wrote an anguished letter from Gough Square to the novelist Samuel Richardson, author of *Clarissa*:

> I am obliged to entreat your assistance. I am now under an arrest for five pounds eighteen shillings... If you will be so good as to send me this sum, I will very gratefully repay you, and add it to all former obligations.

Johnson avoided a debtors' prison, but he left Gough Square soon afterwards and moved somewhere cheaper.

Did you know?

? All writers starve in garrets. Dr Johnson's is open to the public.

? Although a large man, he was terrified of being mugged. The chain he attached to the front door, to stop anyone breaking in, is still there.

? His friend **Oliver Goldsmith** later lived near by, at 6 Wine Office Court (now demolished). Goldsmith is best known as a playwright, but during his time at Wine Office Court (1760–2) was working on his novel *The Vicar of Wakefield*. He was behind with the rent, so Johnson offered to find him a publisher for the novel and got him 60 guineas for it.

YE OLDE CHESHIRE CHEESE
Voltaire, Mark Twain, Theodore Roosevelt
145 Fleet Street

9

Dr Johnson's favourite tavern in Fleet Street was the Mitre (long since demolished), but he is said to have frequented the Cheshire Cheese as well. It was certainly his nearest pub. A plaque in the restaurant marks the spot where he and **Oliver Goldsmith** are reputed to have been regulars, Johnson holding forth while everyone else sat and listened.

The Cheshire Cheese was rebuilt after the Great Fire of 1666 and has altered little since the early 18th century. It still has the same arrangement of small rooms, fireplaces and wooden benches that it did then, and has resisted all attempts at unsuitable modernisation. **Voltaire** drank here during his London exile. The poet **Alexander Pope** and the playwright **William Congreve** are thought to have done so as well.

In later years, **Dickens**, **Thackeray**, **Tennyson** and **Conan Doyle** came to the Cheese, as did American tourists **Longfellow**, **Mark Twain** and **Theodore Roosevelt**. The poet **W B Yeats** stopped by after visiting Dr Johnson's house, and the humorist **G K Chesterton** was a regular, sometimes dressing up as Dr Johnson. With such a famous clientele, the Cheshire Cheese has now become a tourist attraction in its own right, a rare example of a London tavern little changed in 300 years.

> He took him down Ludgate Hill to Fleet Street, and so, up a covered way, into a tavern. Here, they were shown into a little room, where Charles Darnay was soon recruiting his strength with a good plain dinner and good wine.
>
> Charles Dickens, *A Tale of Two Cities*

ST DUNSTAN-IN-THE-WEST CHURCH
Samuel Pepys

10

Fleet Street, between Chancery and Fetter Lanes

After enjoying Sunday lunch on August 18 1667 – 'we had a good haunch of venison, powdered and boiled, and a good dinner and merry' – **Samuel Pepys** left his wife at home and set off through the City for an afternoon stroll. 'I walked toward White-hall; but being weary, turned into St Dunstan's church, where I heard an able sermon of the Minister of the place.'

Pepys quickly recovered his strength when he took a look around.

> And stood by a pretty, modest maid, whom I did labour to take by the hand and the body; but she would not, but got further and further from me, and at last I could perceive her to take pins out of her pocket to prick me if I should touch her again; which seeing, I did forbear, and was glad I did espy her design.
>
> And then I fell to gaze upon another pretty maid in a pew close to me, and she on me; and I did go about to take her by the hand, which she

suffered a little and then withdrew.
So the sermon ended and the church
broke up, and my amours ended also;
and so took coach and home.

Did you know?

? Diagonally across the road from the church, Prince Henry's Room at 17 Fleet Street has a small museum over the gateway devoted to Pepys.

? The political philosopher **Edmund Burke** lodged at 16 Fleet Street in 1750, during his days as a law student at the Temple.

? A few yards to the west of No 16, Middle Temple Lane leads to the next stop on the walk.

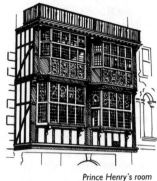

Prince Henry's room

MIDDLE TEMPLE HALL
The first known performance of William Shakespeare's *Twelfth Night*
Middle Temple Lane at Fountain Court

11

> If music be the food of love, play on.

It is widely believed that **Elizabeth I** came to the Middle Temple Hall on February 2 1602 to see the first performance of **William Shakespeare**'s latest play, *Twelfth Night*. The play was certainly performed in the Hall that evening, but the queen did not attend. Records show that she was elsewhere.

She is also believed to have formally opened the new Hall in 1576, but again the evidence is lacking. The Hall was (and is) a dining-hall for the student lawyers of the Middle Temple, but served also as a gathering place for the gentry, particularly in the Christmas season when feasts were held and comedies put on for their entertainment. The night of February 2 1602 was just such an occasion, as a lawyer later remembered in his diary: 'At our feast wee had a play called Twelue night or what you will much like the commedy

Middle Temple Hall and garden

of errors.' This was the first known performance of the play, and very possibly its world première.

Was Shakespeare there then? He may well have been, but again there's no written record of it.

Did you know?

? On a dais at the far end of the Hall, the high table is 29 feet long, constructed from a single oak tree reputedly presented to the Middle Temple by Elizabeth I. One of the smaller serving tables was made out of a hatch cover from the Golden Hind, the ship in which Sir Francis Drake circumnavigated the globe.

? The building was hit during World War II, but the original hammerbeam roof survived and is one of the finest examples of its kind. A scene from the movie *Shakespeare in Love* was filmed here.

? The Hall is best photographed from the Embankment by the river, the final stop on the walk.

MIDDLE TEMPLE GARDEN
The Wars of the Roses
Embankment

12

> And here I prophesy: this brawl today,
> Grown to this faction in the Temple garden,
> Shall send between the red rose and the white
> A thousand souls to death and deadly night.

Henry VI Part 1

If **William Shakespeare** is to be believed, the Temple gardens saw a dramatic confrontation in the summer of 1430, when rival nobles chose their emblems for the civil war that later became known as the Wars of the Roses. According to Shakespeare, the Duke of York plucked a white rose, the Earl of Somerset a red, and others followed suit, committing themselves to a conflict that raged for the next 55 years before the red rose finally defeated the white.

In fact, Shakespeare probably invented the scene, although the two sides certainly adopted roses as emblems. They may well have walked in the gardens too, which have been here since at least the 11th century and were known for their roses long before Shakespeare's time.

Did you know?

? In the 1430s, as now, the Temple was full of lawyers' offices (known as chambers). The area takes its name from the Knights Templar, whose English base was here after their expulsion from Jerusalem.

? The lawyers' names are listed on the doorways to their chambers. Those with QC after their name are Queen's Counsel, allegedly the best in the business, who charge more for their services than ordinary lawyers...a bit like tarts in a brothel.

WHAT NOW?

Somerset House and its fine art collection (see page 119) is 400 yards west along the Embankment.

Nearest public lavatory On the island in the Strand, just outside the Royal Courts of Justice

✪ Temple (**Baroness Orczy** was waiting for a train here in 1901 when she came up with the idea for *The Scarlet Pimpernel.*)

WHERE TO EAT

At St Paul's Café and small restaurant in the crypt.

At the Temple Somerset House has a restaurant and café. Otherwise, walk up to the Strand and along to Covent Garden.

Covent Garden and Somerset House

WALK AT A GLANCE

Features The bustling heart of 18th-century London, much of it still recognisable as such.
Time Allow 1 hour for the walk, more for shopping at Covent Garden and viewing the art at Somerset House.
Length ³/₄ mile.
⊖ Covent Garden

1 **Opera House**
 • Gustav Mahler conducts.

2 **Theatre Royal**
 • George III quarrels with his son.

3 **Russell Street**
 • James Boswell meets Dr Johnson.

4 **Covent Garden market**
 • Casanova picks up girls.

5 **St Paul's church**
 • opening scene of *My Fair Lady*.

6 **Henrietta Street**
 • Jane Austen goes to the theatre.

7 **Maiden Lane**
 • Edward VII dines with Lillie Langtry.

8 **Southampton Street**
 • Dr Johnson chides David Garrick.

9 **Tavistock Street**
 • Thomas De Quincey evades his creditors.

10 **Wellington Street**
 • Charles Dickens works on *A Tale of Two Cities*.

11 **Somerset House**
 • William Herschel discovers a new planet
 • Lord Nelson claims for his arm.

12 **Buckingham Street**
 • Samuel Pepys hears a eunuch sing.

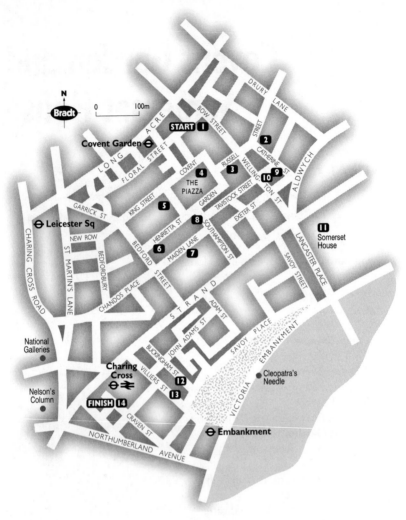

13 Villiers Street
- Rudyard Kipling sees a man cut his throat.

14 Craven Street
- former Prime Minister William Pitt visits Benjamin Franklin for urgent talks about the American crisis
- Heinrich Heine takes a dislike to the English
- Herman Melville reads De Quincey.

ROYAL OPERA HOUSE
Gustav Mahler
Covent Garden

The summer of 1892 was unforgettable for London's music lovers. **Gustav Mahler** was in town, conducting 18 separate performances in 45 days. He had brought a team of German singers with him and they were going to do everything of Wagner's, from *Tristan und Isolde* and *Tannhäuser* to *Der Ring des Nibelungen*, which London had only ever heard once before.

The first performance was *Siegfried*, at the Opera House on June 8. Mahler rehearsed strenuously beforehand. He was 32,

> rather short, of thin, spare build, with a dark complexion and small piercing eyes that stared at you with a not unkindly expression through large gold spectacles. I found him extraordinarily modest for a musician of his rare gifts and established reputation. He would never consent to talk about himself or his compositions… His efforts to speak English, even with those who spoke German fluently, were untiring as well as amusing.

The performance was a wild success. It began at 8pm and continued until half-past midnight. **George Bernard Shaw** considered himself lucky to have got the very last ticket for the stalls.

> The performance was vigorous, complete, earnest – in short, all that was needed to make *Siegfried* enormously interesting to operatic starvelings like the Covent Garden's frequenters… The impression created by the performance was extraordinary, the gallery cheering wildly at the end of each act… We all breathed that vast orchestral atmosphere of fire, air, earth, and water, with unbounded relief and invigoration.

Did you know?

? The Royal Opera House is Britain's best, and one of the finest in Europe. The main building dates from 1858, rebuilt after a fire two years earlier. Behind the scenes, a huge complex of workshops and state-of-the-art rehearsal rooms was reconstructed in 1999, making the opera-house as modern as any in the world.

? One of the last to attend a performance in the old opera-house before it burned down was the man himself, **Richard Wagner**. He came several times in the spring of 1855: 'The secretary of the Philharmonic Society… took the trouble to entertain me. I had to go once or twice to the Italian Opera at Covent Garden with his daughter. There I heard *Fidelio*, given in rather grotesque fashion by unclean Germans and voiceless Italians, and with recitatives. I subsequently avoided paying frequent visits to this theatre.'

? There has been a theatre on the site since 1732, when Covent Garden was one of only two licensed playhouses in London. Today, the facilities are shared between the Royal Opera Company and the Royal Ballet Company, with guest artistes from all over the world.

Royal Opera House

THEATRE ROYAL
George III
Catherine Street

2

The year was 1812 and the theatre had just been rebuilt after a fire. To celebrate its reopening, the king himself was honouring it with a visit. **George III** was very old now, frail and mentally ill, but he was still the country's sovereign. The theatre was agog for his arrival, desperate for the royal visit to pass off without a hitch.

The crowd stirred as the king's carriage drew up outside. Everyone bowed low as he was helped out. They bowed again as the royal party was escorted indoors and made its way through the foyer towards the lower rotunda and the royal box beyond. In the pit, the orchestra sat waiting, ready to strike up the national anthem as soon as the king appeared. The audience sat waiting as well, two thousand people preparing to sing 'God Save the King' as the royal party took their seats and settled down for the play to begin.

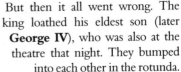

But then it all went wrong. The king loathed his eldest son (later **George IV**), who was also at the theatre that night. They bumped into each other in the rotunda. George immediately flew at his son and thumped him round the ear, while everyone else turned away in embarrassment. It was quite some time before order was restored and the king was at last persuaded to take his seat in the royal box.

Soon afterwards, the lower rotunda was placed off limits to royalty. Go in there now and you will see a sign proclaiming the KING'S SIDE over the left-hand door, and the PRINCE'S SIDE over the right. Never again were the two allowed to meet at Drury Lane. The theatre is unique also in having *two* royal boxes today, one each side of the stage, in case any future generations of royals decide to have a go at each other in public.

Did you know?

? Although it is always known as the Drury Lane theatre, the Theatre Royal's main entrance is actually on Catherine Street, facing Covent Garden.

? First built in 1663, it is easily the most historic of all London's theatres. The playhouses had been closed down in Puritan times, but they reopened under **Charles II** and enjoyed a great revival in the years that followed. It was in a previous building on this site that Charles first set eyes on **Nell Gwyn**, the orange-seller-turned-actress who later became his favourite mistress.

? It was here too that **David Garrick** revolutionised the profession of acting, introducing all sorts of ideas in the 18th century that are still in use today.

? Before Garrick's time, theatregoers could pay to go backstage and watch the girls undressing between numbers. This facility has since been withdrawn.

? Among the artistes who have appeared here are **Henry Irving**, **Beerbohm Tree**, **Richard Strauss**, **Nijinsky**, **Caruso**, **Lillie Langtry**, **Marie Rambert**, **Anna Pavlova**, **Noel Coward**, **Claude Rains**, **Paul Robeson**, **Stewart Granger**, **Gene Kelly**, **Ginger Rogers**, **Julie Andrews**, **Rex Harrison**, **Stanley Holloway** (in the first production of *My Fair Lady*), **Rudolph Nureyev**, **Yul Brynner**, **Bill Haley and the Comets**, **Petula Clark**, **Joan Collins** and **Catherine Zeta Jones**.

8 RUSSELL STREET
James Boswell and Dr Johnson

3

On Monday, May 16 1763, a great bear of a man stepped into this bookshop near the market which was run by a friend of his. The man was 53, large, awkward and slovenly, with a wig permanently singed in front by the candle he used for reading. His name was **Samuel Johnson**. He was a giant in more ways than one, the outstanding intellectual figure of his age. And he was about to meet the man who would one day write his biography.

James Boswell was a small but determined Scot, newly arrived in London and anxious to make his name. He had been hanging around the bookshop for weeks, hoping to meet the famous Samuel Johnson. Now was his chance.

> At last, on Monday the 16th of May, when I was sitting in Mr Davies's back-parlour, after having drunk tea with him and Mrs Davies, Johnson unexpectedly came into the shop; and Mr Davies having perceived him through the glass-door in the room in which we were sitting, advancing towards us, he announced his awful approach to me, somewhat in the manner of an actor in the part of Horatio, when he addresses Hamlet on the appearance of his father's ghost, 'Look, my Lord, it comes.'

> I found that I had a very perfect idea of Johnson's figure, from the portrait of him painted by Sir Joshua Reynolds soon after he had published his Dictionary, in the attitude of sitting in his easy chair in deep meditation…

> Mr Davies mentioned my name, and respectfully introduced me to him. I was much agitated; and recollecting his prejudice against the Scotch, of which I had heard much, I said to Davies, 'Don't tell where I come from.' – 'From Scotland,' cried Davies, roguishly.

'Mr Johnson, (said I) I do indeed come from Scotland, but I cannot help it.' I am willing to flatter myself that I meant this as light pleasantry to soothe and conciliate him... but this speech was somewhat unlucky; for with that quickness of wit for which he was so remarkable, he seized the expression 'come from Scotland'... and retorted, 'That, Sir, I find, is what a very great many of your countrymen cannot help.'

This stroke stunned me a good deal; and when we had sat down, I felt myself not a little embarrassed, and apprehensive of what might come next.

Fortunately, the two men hit it off, and *The Life of Samuel Johnson* is still in print.

Did you know?
? In 1791, James Boswell wrote of this address: 'No 8 – The very place where I was fortunate enough to be introduced to the illustrious subject of this work, deserves to be particularly marked. I never pass by it without feeling reverence and regret.'

COVENT GARDEN MARKET
Hogarth, Casanova

4

Famed for its piazza around the market, Covent Garden was a popular meeting place for 18th-century Londoners – including **William Hogarth**, who lived near by and drew some of his most perceptive pictures here. The piazza swarmed with prostitutes, one of whom was picked up by **Giacomo Casanova** in 1763.

I went to Covent Garden, and on meeting an attractive young woman, I accosted her in French, and asked her if she would sup with me.

'How much will you give me?'

'Three guineas.'

'Come along.'

'After the play, I ordered a good supper for two, and she display'd an appetite after mine own heart. When we had supp'd, I asked her name and address. Her name was Kennedy. I was astonished to find that she was one of the girls whom Lord Pembroke had assessed at six guineas. I concluded that it was best to do one's own negotiating, or at any rate not to employ a nobleman as an agent.

On another occasion, Casanova treated two girls to the opera.

I took them to the performance at Covent Garden, where the castrato Tenducci surprised me by introducing his wife to me; I thought he was joking, but it was true... Having already had two children, he laughed at those who said that, being a castrato, he could not have any.

Did you know?

? Later rebuilt, the original piazza dated from the 1630s and was modelled on the one at Livorno in Italy. The flower and fruit market began in 1670 and by the 1830s was the main wholesale supplier for London. It moved out in 1974 and the site is now occupied by tourist cafés and art and craft shops.

? There are two museums near the piazza, both useful on a rainy day. The Theatre Museum (7 Russell Street) tells the story of English theatre from Shakespeare's time onwards. It has plenty of hands-on exhibits for children, and a make-up artist who can give them a scar or a bloody wound to keep them happy.

? The London Transport Museum lives in the old flower market on the piazza. It has multilingual touch screens, a replica horse bus and a real underground train from 1863 for children to sit in.

ST PAUL'S CHURCH, COVENT GARDEN
G B Shaw

5

This is where **George Bernard Shaw** set the opening scene of his play *Pygmalion*, which later became the musical *My Fair Lady*:

> London at 11.15pm. Torrents of heavy summer rain. Cab whistles blowing frantically in all directions. Pedestrians running for shelter into the portico of St Paul's church (not Wren's cathedral but Inigo Jones's church in Covent Garden vegetable market), among them a lady and her daughter in evening dress. All are peering out gloomily at the rain, except one man with his back turned to the rest, wholly preoccupied with a notebook in which he is writing.

The man is Henry Higgins, a Professor of Phonetics. It was here that he met Eliza Doolittle, the impoverished flower girl from the market, anxious to improve herself. She asked him to help her talk like a lady, and the rest is theatrical history – one of the most successful plays and musicals of all time.

Did you know?

? *Pygmalion* opened on April 11 1914 and was an immediate success, although Shaw regarded it as 'a shameless potboiler'. He modelled Eliza partly on Nell Gwyn, who began by selling oranges around these same streets, but ended up as mistress of Charles II and mother of a duke.

? Mayfair was, and still is, a very rich part of London for upper-class ladies. Flower girls pronounced it 'Myfair'. Hence *My Fair Lady*.

? Make a musical out of *Pygmalion*? 'I absolutely forbid any such outrage?' said G B Shaw. *My Fair Lady* was not performed until several years after his death.

? St Paul's church was completed in 1633. **Claude Duval**, a stylish French highwayman noted for his success with women, was buried in the central aisle after his execution in 1670. The stone above his grave says it all:

Here lies Du Vall: Reader, if male thou art,

Look to thy purse; if female, to thy heart.

? In the middle of theatreland, the church is a favourite with the acting profession. Many famous stars have got married or attended memorial services here. The entrance is not from the piazza, but from the churchyard at the other end.

10 HENRIETTA STREET
Jane Austen

6

Of all **Jane Austen**'s brothers, Henry was her favourite. He worked as a banker at 10 Henrietta Street. After his wife's death, he lived here too, in the rooms above the bank. Jane Austen and her niece came to stay with him in September 1813, soon after he had moved in.

> Here I am, my dearest Cassandra, seated in the Breakfast, Dining, sitting room… Fanny will join me as soon as she is dressed & begin her Letter… We arrived at a quarter past 4 & were kindly welcomed by the Coachman, & then by his Master, and then by William, & then by Mrs Perigord, who all met us before we reached the foot of the Stairs. Mme de Bigeon was below dressing us a most comfortable dinner of Soup, Fish, Bouillee, Partridges & an apple Tart, which we sat down to soon after 5, after cleaning & dressing ourselves & feeling that we were most commodiously disposed of. The little adjoining Dressing-room to our apartment makes Fanny & myself very well off indeed, & as we have poor Eliza's bed our space is ample in every way.

The breakfast/sitting-room was on the first floor, overlooking the street. Jane and Fanny's bedroom was on the second floor. After dinner, they went to the theatre to see Samuel Beazley's *Five Hours at Brighton*.

> At 7 we set off in a Coach for the Lyceum – were at home again in about 4 hours and ½ – had Soup & wine & water, & then went to our Holes… Of our three evenings in Town one was spent at the Lyceum & another at Covent Garden; – the *Clandestine Marriage* was the most respectable of the performances, the rest were Sing-song & trumpery.

Did you know?

? Jane was in London to talk business with her brother. *Pride and Prejudice* had just come out, to huge acclaim. She had completed *Mansfield Park* and was about to start on *Emma*. She wanted Henry to negotiate with the publishers on her behalf.

? Henry lived in Henrietta Street until March 1816, when his bank went bust after a sudden change in Government policy. Forced into bankruptcy, he had to move house in a hurry, as Jane told her publisher (John Murray, see page 149) on April 1: 'In consequence of the late sad Event in Henrietta St, I must request that if you should at any time have anything to communicate by Letter, you will be so good as to write by the post, directing to me (Miss J Austen) Chawton near Alton.'

? At the end of Henrietta Street, turning left into Bedford Street, stood *The Castle* tavern. The playwright **Richard Brinsley Sheridan** fought a duel there on May 4 1772. He and a Captain Mathews were in love with the same girl, so they hired a room in the pub and fought each other with swords. Sheridan won on that occasion, breaking Mathews' weapon. But honour was not satisfied, so they later fought another duel in which Sheridan was seriously wounded. He recovered eventually and married the girl.

? Taking the next left into Maiden Lane, **Charles Dickens** once worked across the road as a 12-year-old in a blacking factory. 'Next to the shop at the corner of Bedford Street in Chandos Place are two rather old-fashioned houses and shops adjoining one another. They were one then, or thrown into one, for the blacking business; and had been a butter shop. Opposite to them was, and is, a public-house, where I got my ale.' The pub was presumably O'Reilly's at 67 Chandos Place.

35 MAIDEN LANE
Edward VII and Lillie Langtry
34–35 Maiden Lane

7

He was the Prince of Wales, later to be **Edward VII**. She was **Lillie Langtry**, a beautiful young woman newly arrived from the Channel Islands. They were introduced in June 1877 and became lovers at once. But they found it hard to be alone, with so many people watching. Lillie had a flat in Eaton Place, but her husband was always there, keeping a wary eye on her. They needed to find somewhere else to go if they wanted to be alone.

One of the places they found was Rules restaurant. Edward often met Lillie here, in a private dining-room upstairs. Their table was by the lattice window on the first floor, overlooking the street. The affair continued for years, although Lillie was never particularly keen on the prince. 'He always smelt so *very strongly* of cigars' – and insisted on smoking them at mealtimes.

Did you know?

? Founded in 1798, Rules is London's oldest restaurant. Dickens and Thackeray were regulars in the 19th century.

? Just across the street from Rules, 10 Maiden Lane marks the site of *The White Wig*, one of the places where **Voltaire** stayed in 1727 during his exile from Paris. By his own account, he was once chased through the streets of

London by an English mob accusing him of being a frightful foreigner. He won them round by crying 'Brave Englishmen, am I not unhappy enough already in not having been born among you?' While in England, Voltaire attended Sir Isaac Newton's funeral in Westminster Abbey. It was he who first recorded the story of a falling apple inspiring Newton's interest in gravity.

27 SOUTHAMPTON STREET
David Garrick

8

Early in March 1737, two friends from Lichfield arrived in London together to seek their fortune. One was **Samuel Johnson**, a former schoolmaster hoping to make his way in the literary world. The other was **David Garrick**, once a pupil of Johnson's, but now intent on becoming a great actor.

Garrick was the first to find success. Within a few years he had taken London by storm and was living like a movie star. He controlled the Theatre Royal and had made enough money to buy a lavish house near by – 27 Southampton Street.

Johnson took much longer to get established. While Garrick enjoyed the high life, mixing with lords and ladies, Johnson was still poor and unknown, struggling to pay his bills. The two remained friends, but Johnson was jealous of Garrick's success. In 1752 he launched a bitter attack on Garrick, accusing him in a newspaper article of getting above himself now that he was famous. He described a visit he had made to see 'Prospero' at his home in Southampton Street.

> When I told my name at the door, the footman went to see if his master was at home, and, by the tardiness of his return, gave me reason to suspect that time was taken to deliberate. He then informed me, that Prospero desired my company, and shewed the staircase carefully secured by mats from the pollution of my feet. The best apartments were ostentatiously set open, that I might have a distant view of the magnificence which I was not permitted to approach; and my old friend receiving me with all the insolence of condescension at the top of the stairs, conducted me to a back room, where he told me he always breakfasted when he had not great company…
>
> While we were conversing upon such subjects as imagination happened to suggest, he frequently digressed into directions to the servant that waited, or made a slight inquiry after the jeweller or silversmith; and once, as I was pursuing an argument with some degree of earnestness, he started from his posture of attention, and ordered, that if Lord Lofty called on him that morning, he should be shown into the best parlour.

Relations were restored after Johnson had achieved success on his own account. Garrick died in 1779 and received a lavish funeral in Westminster Abbey. Johnson wept openly at the service, as did **Edmund Burke**.

Did you know?

? Garrick lived at 27 Southampton Street for 23 years. Besides Johnson and Burke, he was friendly with **Sir Joshua Reynolds** and **William Hogarth**, who painted a double-portrait of Garrick and his wife at home, Garrick sitting at his desk, Mrs Garrick reaching over his head to snatch his quill pen.

David Garrick's house

? Garrick the actor was a man of so many faces that neither Reynolds nor Hogarth was able to capture a true likeness. Reynolds hurled his palette to the floor in disgust. Hogarth painted several different faces on another canvas, then cut out the best one and sewed it into place.

? Today, a theatre, a street and a London club are all named after Garrick.

36 TAVISTOCK STREET
Thomas De Quincey

9

As a teenage dropout, **Thomas De Quincey** came to London and lived rough for a while, wandering the streets around Soho without a penny to his name. He later returned to his family and was sent to Oxford, where he first tried opium as a cure for toothache.

By 1821, after years of drug addiction, De Quincey was broke again, with a wife and child to support. He returned to London, at the age of 35, to try and make a living as a journalist. Taking a room at 36 Tavistock Street (then 4 York Street), he sat down to write a long article for the *London Magazine*. It was about his years of drug addiction, and he called it *The Confessions of an English Opium-Eater*.

The work went well, but De Quincey was dreadfully short of cash. A bill was due and the debt collectors were after him. He would be thrown into a debtors' prison if he couldn't pay up. In desperation, he wrote to his friend **Samuel Taylor Coleridge**, reminding him that he had lent him £300 years earlier and asking if there was any chance of getting it back.

'Dear De Quincey!' Coleridge replied. 'I conjure you to feel convinced that were it in my power to raise the money, you should not have received this melancholy History as an answer.' Coleridge was broke too and there was nothing he could do.

So De Quincey went into hiding. Carefully checking the street for debt collectors, he slipped out of the house on August 9 and vanished for the next eight days, taking his manuscript with him. The sooner he finished it, the sooner he would be able to pay his debts. He sat in coffee shops all day, writing his confessions over a cup of coffee bought on credit. But even then, he found it 'difficult to write at all: for it happened that the only coffee-rooms where I was known enough to expect credit, were those of great Coach-Inns.' And coaching inns were always very busy and noisy.

Yet De Quincey managed. He sneaked back to Tavistock Street on August 17 and six days later the first half of the book was done. It appeared in the *London Magazine*'s September issue and was an immediate success. The second half followed in October and De Quincey's fame was assured.

Did you know?

? Foolishly, De Quincey had sold the book outright to his publishers. They gave him a total of £62 for it, and that was all he ever got.

? The Quincy family from Boston, Massachusetts, were his American cousins.

26 WELLINGTON STREET
Charles Dickens
10

From 1859 until his death 11 years later, **Charles Dickens** worked several days a week here at the offices of his magazine *All The Year Round*. He lived here too for much of the time, in a little flat on the top floor. It's where he put the finishing touches to *A Tale of Two Cities* and *Great Expectations*.

The year 1859 was a bad one for Dickens. He had recently dumped his wife for a young actress, and had lost a lot of friends as a result. He wanted to begin his life afresh and did so by founding a weekly magazine, *All The Year Round*. To get the project off to a good start, he needed to write a weekly serial for it himself. He had an idea for a new story, but wasn't sure what to call it. *Buried Alive? The Doctor of Beauvais?* Perhaps *The Thread of Gold?*

In the end, he decided on *A Tale of Two Cities*. The first fully fledged issue of his new magazine appeared on June 4 1859, with the opening chapter of *A Tale of Two Cities* on the front page. Thereafter Dickens produced a chapter a week, working feverishly on the manuscript at his country home, then delivering it to Wellington Street and working through the next few days to bring the magazine out on time. He borrowed great chunks of the novel from *A History of the French Revolution* by his friend **Thomas Carlyle**, who sent a 'cartload' of books round to help Dickens with his research.

He borrowed the characters from life as well. Lucie Manette, the beautiful girl for whom Sydney Carton went to the guillotine, was closely modelled on Dickens' new actress friend – so closely that he sent her the weekly proofs for her comments. *A Tale of Two Cities* was published as a novel as soon as it was complete, and was dramatised as well – at the Lyceum Theatre, still there across the road, 50 yards down Wellington Street towards the Strand. For the play, Dickens changed the famous last words of the book ('It is a far, far better thing that I do…') to the distinctly less dramatic 'Farewell Lucie, farewell life!'

Did you know?

? Among the contributors to *All The Year Round* was Dickens' old friend **Wilkie Collins**, whose novels *The Moonstone* and *The Woman in White* were first serialised in the magazine. Dickens privately thought *The Moonstone* 'wearisome beyond endurance', but the public did not agree. Crowds gathered in the street outside No 26 whenever a new instalment went on sale.

? Dickens loved Covent Garden. Earlier in his life, he had had offices at 16 Wellington Street (since demolished), where he wrote of his enthusiasm for this part of London. 'I have never outgrown the whole region of Covent Garden... There is a fine secrecy and mystery about the Piazza – how you get up to those rooms above it, and what reckless deeds are done there... I have not outgrown the two great Theatres... Even as I write in my commonplace office I behold, from the window, four young ladies with peculiarly limp bonnets, and of a yellow or drab style of beauty, making for the stage-door of the Lyceum Theatre, in the dirty little fog-choked street over the way...'

SOMERSET HOUSE
William Herschel, Lord Nelson

11

Somerset House was built in the late 18th century to house Government departments and learned societies. Among them was the Royal Society, composed of the country's most eminent scientists, which moved in at the end of November 1780.

A few months later, on April 26 1781, the society's members entered the vestibule off the Strand to hear an astonishing paper written by **William Herschel**, a German musician living in Bath. Herschel was a keen amateur astronomer in his spare time. Looking through a telescope in his back yard one evening, he had spotted something which no-one else had ever spotted before – another planet up there, the first to be identified since the days of the Greeks and the Romans.

To begin with, Herschel was unsure of what he had found. The object was moving through the heavens, so it wasn't a star. But it might have been a comet, and Herschel said as much in his paper to the Royal Society:

> On Tuesday the 13th of March, between 10 and 11 in the evening, while I was examining the small stars in the neighbourhood of H Geminorum, I perceived one that appeared visibly larger than the

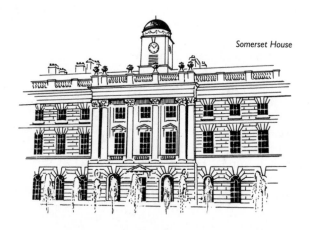

Somerset House

rest: being struck with its uncommon magnitude, I compared it to H Geminorum and the small star in the quartile between Auriga and Gemini, and finding it so much larger than either of them, suspected it to be a comet.

But it was a planet, as other astronomers quickly confirmed. A debate raged for years as to what it should be called. Herschel wanted to call it the Georgian planet in honour of George III, who was now funding his work. A French astronomer suggested Herschel, a German Hypercronius. In the end, they settled on Uranus, the father of Saturn in ancient mythology.

Did you know?

? Herschel's paper was read by his friend, Sir William Watson, while he himself stayed in Bath. Under George III's patronage, Herschel soon gave up music teaching and spent the rest of his life happily polishing mirrors and building bigger telescopes to look for another planet.

? The Royal Society moved to Piccadilly in 1857. Its old rooms are now part of the Courtauld Gallery, one of the world's great collections of Impressionist art. **Van Gogh**'s *Self-Portrait with Bandaged Ear* is here, as well as **Manet**'s *Bar at the Folies Bergères* and one of the two versions of *Le Déjeuner sur l'Herbe*. There are also works by **Renoir**, **Monet**, **Degas**, **Pissarro**, **Cezanne**, **Toulouse-Lautrec**, **Rubens**, **Goya**, **Van Dyck**, **Bruegel**, **Botticelli**, **Veronese** and **Tintoretto**.

? Somerset House also has a rotating exhibition of treasures on loan from the Hermitage Museum in St Petersburg, in the South Building facing the river.

In the 18th century, the buildings on the west side of the courtyard were occupied by the Royal Navy's Sick and Hurt office. Rear-Admiral **Sir Horatio Nelson** paid them a visit in 1797 to claim long overdue compensation for the loss of his arm and eye on active service. Unfortunately, he had failed to bring a medical certificate with him, so his claim to be minus an arm was met with considerable scepticism. Nelson may have terrified the French, but he was no match for an English bureaucrat.

Perhaps on the same trip, Nelson called in at Richard Thresher's hosiery shop, 152 Strand, just by the entrance to Somerset House, to order some uniform stockings. Thresher commiserated with him for the loss of his arm.

'Lucky for you it wasn't my leg,' Nelson is said to have replied.

12 BUCKINGHAM STREET
Samuel Pepys

12

> For Samuel Pepys Esqr at his
> lodging in Yorke-streete
>
> 8 June 1684
>
> Sir…
>
> Mr Flamsteed has lately advertized me of an eclipse of the moone
> which will happen the 17th of this month about 3 in the morning,
> and wished I would give you notice of it, that if your leasure
> permitted he might have the honor of your company, and I should
> readily waite upon you.
>
> Your most humble and faithfull servant
>
> John Evelyn

Samuel Pepys lived in York Buildings, Buckingham Street for many years, first at No 12 (still there) and then at No 14 (since rebuilt). As well as being a diarist, naval administrator and Member of Parliament, he was also President of the Royal Society and took a keen interest in science. His fellow members included **Sir Isaac Newton**, **Sir Christopher Wren**, the diarist **John Evelyn** and the Astronomer Royal, **John Flamsteed**. Pepys held open house for the society on Saturday nights, giving the members a chance to meet each other over a drink and browse through his magnificent library, one of the finest in London.

He also held musical evenings for his particular friends. John Evelyn attended one at No 14 on April 19 1687.

> I heard the famous Singer the Eunuch Cifacca, esteemed the best in
> Europe & indeede his holding out & delicatnesse in extending & loosing
> a note… was admirable. For the rest, I found him a meere wanton,
> effeminate child; very Coy, & prowdly conceited to my apprehension.
>
> This was before a select number of some particular persons whom
> Mr Pepys (Secretary of the Admiralty & a greate lover of Musick)
> invited to his house, where the meeting was, & this obtained by
> peculiar favour & much difficulty of the Singer, who much disdained
> to shew his talent to any but Princes.

Did you know?

? On July 17 1688, Evelyn came round again to watch the fireworks celebrating the birth of a son to James II. 'We stood at Mr Pepys' Secretary of the Admiralty to greate advantage for the sight, & indeede they were very fine, & had cost some thousands of pounds about the pyramids and statues &c.' But the birth of a Catholic heir to the throne led to the rapid departure of James II. Pepys had risen in the king's service, so James' fall meant his fall too. He never held public office again.

? Pepys' library is now at Magdalene, his old Cambridge college.

43 VILLIERS STREET
Rudyard Kipling

13

Staring out of the window one foggy day in 1890, **Rudyard Kipling** thought he was dreaming when he saw a man kill himself on the pavement opposite. But it was really happening, as the blood quickly showed.

Kipling was only 23 when he moved into Villiers Street the previous autumn, but already making a name for himself as a writer. His *Plain Tales from the Hills* had caused a stir in India, enough for Kipling to give up his job and sail for England in the hope of repeating his success on a larger stage. He was short of cash when he arrived, so he took a dingy flat at No 43 and lived very modestly until the earnings started to flow from his pen.

> My rooms were small, not over-clean or well-kept, but from my desk I could look out of my window through the fan-light of Gatti's Music-Hall entrance, across the street, almost on to its stage. The Charing Cross trains rumbled through my dreams on one side, the boom of the Strand on the other, while, before my windows, Father Thames under the Shot Tower walked up and down with his traffic.

> At the outset I had so muddled and mismanaged my affairs that, for a while, I found myself with some money owing me for work done, but no funds in hand…I had nothing to pawn save a collection of unmarked shirts picked up in all the ports; so I made shift to manage on what small cash I had in pocket.

> My rooms were above an establishment of Harris the Sausage King, who, for tuppence, gave as much sausage and mash as would carry one from breakfast to dinner… another tuppence found me a filling supper.

Like many colonials, though, Kipling was taken aback by London's gloomy weather. 'Once I faced the reflection of my own face in the jet-black mirror of the window-panes for five days. When the fog thinned, I looked out and saw a man standing opposite the pub where the barmaid lived.

> Of a sudden his breast turned dull red like a robin's, and he crumpled, having cut his throat. In a few minutes – seconds it seemed – a hand-ambulance arrived and took up the body. A pot-boy with a bucket of steaming water sluiced the blood off into the gutter, and what little crowd had collected went its way.

Did you know?

? Kipling often frequented Gatti's music hall across the street (no longer there). 'The smoke, the roar, and the good-fellowship of relaxed humanity at Gatti's set the scheme for a certain sort of song. The Private Soldier in India I thought I knew fairly well. His English brother (in the Guards mostly) sat and sang at my elbow any night I chose… the outcome was the first of some verses called *Barrack-Room Ballads*.' Kipling worked on the ballads in Villiers

Street with a note pinned on his door: 'To publishers: a classic while you wait'.

? Kipling later wrote *The Jungle Book* as well (Walt Disney had nothing to do with it). He won the Nobel Prize in 1907.

CRAVEN STREET
36 Craven Street – Benjamin Franklin

14

Newly arrived from the colonies, a young American got a shock when he called unexpectedly at 36 Craven Street in 1767. His fellow American **Benjamin Franklin** lived on the top two floors. The young man didn't know anyone in London, so he thought he would introduce himself to Franklin and bring him all the latest news from home.

But when he reached the second floor, he saw that the door was slightly ajar – and there was Franklin, in a blue-green suit with gilt buttons, energetically kissing a young woman on his knee. History does not record her name, but it certainly wasn't Mrs Franklin. She was 3,000 miles away, in Philadelphia.

Franklin had been living at No 36 (then No 7) since 1757. He was a professional lobbyist for the Pennsylvania Assembly. He needed to be near Parliament, so Craven Street suited him very well. 'I lodge in Craven Street near Charing Cross,' he wrote to his wife. 'We have four rooms, furnished, and everything about is pretty genteel.' Franklin's bedroom was the second-floor front, with another room behind for his electrical experiments (it was he who fitted the lightning conductors on St Paul's cathedral). His son William lived above, complaining of 'the Watchman's hoarse Voice calling Past two aClock and a Cloudy Morning'.

Did you know?

? From Franklin's memoirs: 'I found at my door in Craven-street, one morning, a poor woman sweeping my pavement with a birch broom; she appeared very pale and feeble, as just come out of a fit of sickness. I ask'd who employ'd her to sweep there; she said, "Nobody, but I am very poor and in distress, and I sweeps before gentlefolks' doors, and hopes they will give me something." I bid her sweep the whole street clean, and I would give her a shilling; this was at nine o'clock; at 12 she came for the shilling.'

? Franklin left No 36 in October 1772 and moved a few doors up the street to another house, number unknown. It was there, on January 29 1775, that the former Prime Minister **William Pitt**, Earl of Chatham, called round for urgent discussions on the gathering crisis in America. Chatham had been too grand and too busy to receive Franklin in the past, but the situation in America was so grave – the colonists were talking openly of independence – that now he was calling on Franklin himself. The neighbours gaped in awe as the great man arrived and went in. 'He stayed with me near two hours, his equipage waiting at the door; and being there while people were coming from Church, it was much taken notice of, and talked of, as at that time was every little circumstance that men thought might possibly any way affect American affairs. Such a visit from so great a man, on so important a business, flattered not a little my vanity.'

? A few days later, watched by Franklin in the gallery, Chatham made a speech in the House of Lords calling for reconciliation with the American colonists. But he was ignored and war became inevitable. Franklin left Craven Street in March and sailed reluctantly for America to join the rebels. He was one of the signatories to the Declaration of Independence on July 4 1776.

32 Craven Street – Heinrich Heine

A few doors down from Benjamin Franklin, the German poet **Heinrich Heine** lived here in 1827, during a four-month stay in England. As a Jew, barred from the professions in Germany, he was in London to see how the English lived. He later published his *Letters from England*, a collection of political reporting from a land where liberty and the freedom of the individual were taken seriously.

Unfortunately, Heine did not like what he saw. He loathed London and found the English insufferable. Heine was a hero among intellectual liberals on the Continent, but in London nobody had heard of him. 'It is snowing outside,' he complained in a letter home. 'There is no fire in my chimney... It is damp and uncomfortable. No-one understands me here, and no-one understands German.'

Heine failed to take the town by storm, and for the rest of his life thought of England as a place 'where machines behave like human beings and human beings like machines'. But he did at least find love in London. Her name was Kitty Clairmont, and she lived in Regent's Park. Heine abandoned her at the end of his stay, yet remembered her eight years later when he was arranging the poems of the 'Kitty Cycle' to be set to music:

> Kitty stirbt! Und kalt gebettet
> Liegt sie bald im Kirchhofsgrunde.
> Und sie weiss es! Doch fur andere
> Sorgt sie bis zur letzten Stunde.
> (Kitty is dying! And coldly bedded
> She will lie soon in the churchyard.
> And she knows it! Yet it's for others
> That she cares until her last hour.)

25 Craven Street – Herman Melville

> I commence this Journal at 25 Craven Street, Strand, at 61/2 pm on Wednesday Nov 7th 1849 – being just arrived from dinner at a chop House, and feeling like it.

On his first visit to England, the American novelist **Herman Melville** was here to see the country and find an English publisher for his work. He needed money to continue his travels on the Continent, so it was a disappointment when the first publishers he approached failed to come up with the goods:

> Upon my arrival in Craven Street, found the letter which I expected from Mr Colbourne. The letter simply declines my proposition (£200 for 1st 1000 copies) & on the ground, practically, of the cursed state of the copyright matter.

Socially, however, Melville was a success. His long hair and green coat marked him out as an oddity in London, but the invitations were soon flowing thick and fast.

> Found that Mr Rogers had called – 'a gentleman from St James who came in his coach' – as the chambermaid expressed it. Also was handed – with a meaning flourish – a note sealed with a coronet. It was from Mr Rutland – the Duke of Rutland I mean – inviting me to visit Belvoir Castle.

Unfortunately, Melville felt unable to return such hospitality at Craven Street.

> While sitting in my room reading the *Opium Eater* by the fire I am handed Mr George Atkinson's card – the girl (pursuant to my directions) having told him at the door that I was 'not in'. I am obliged to employ this fashionable shift of evasion of visitors – for I have not a decent room to show them – but (& which is the cause) I can not in conscience ask them to labour their way up to the 4th storey of a house… Have just this moment finished the *Opium Eater*. A most wondrous book.

Melville sailed for home on December 24 and later wrote *Moby Dick*. Sales were so bad that he was forced to give up writing altogether and take a job as a customs officer. He didn't become a famous American author until many years after his death.

WHAT NOW?

The Sherlock Homes pub (10–11 Northumberland Street) is in the next street. It used to be called the Northumberland Arms and stood next to the Turkish baths used by Sherlock Holmes and Dr Watson in *The Adventure of the Illustrious Client*. The pub now has a faithful re-creation of Holmes and Watson's sitting room and a collection of memorabilia associated with Conan Doyle's fictional detective.

Trafalgar Square (see page 40) lies just beyond. The National Gallery on the north side of the square contains a mind-boggling collection of art: **Titian, Rembrandt, Giotto, da Vinci, Caravaggio, Rubens, Vermeer, Van Dyck, Velázquez, Van Gogh, Renoir** and others.

Round the side of the National Gallery (to the right as you face it), the National Portrait Gallery contains original portraits of famous Brits from the time of **Richard III** and **William Shakespeare** right up to **Princess Diana** and beyond. All the most interesting characters from this guide are in there somewhere.

Nearest public lavatory Charing Cross station

✏ Charing Cross station, Embankment

WHERE TO EAT

At Covent Garden The Royal Opera House does lunch, as does 8 Russell Street (where Boswell met Dr Johnson). Rules restaurant at 35 Maiden Lane still looks much as it did when Edward VII and Lillie Langtry dined there (and Dickens and Thackeray). Dickens' old office at 26 Wellington Street is now the Charles Dickens Coffee House. Covent Garden market provides plenty of fast food, and Somerset House offers the expensive Admiralty restaurant or a cheaper café on the river terrace. Further along, the shop below Kipling's old flat now sells bagels instead of sausages and mashed potato.

Other restaurants near by:

Bertorelli's 44a Floral Street. Famous old Italian restaurant. Does smart dinners for opera-goers, also quick pizzas for lunch.
Calabash 38 King Street. African food, cheap, cheerful and interesting.
Joe Allen 13 Exeter Street. Wide choice of dishes, very popular with actors.
Livebait 21 Wellington Street. Very good seafood.
Simpson's 100 Strand. Smart and expensive. Collar and tie required, but worth it if you like that sort of thing.

At Trafalgar Square The National Gallery has a good restaurant. There are a few cafés along Whitehall towards the Houses of Parliament. But your best bet is to head up towards Leicester Square or Piccadilly, with the delights of Soho beyond.

Soho

WALK AT A GLANCE

Features Traditionally full of foreign immigrants, Soho has some of the best restaurants in London. Parts of it are a red-light district late at night.
Time Allow 1 hour.
Length 1 mile.
● Piccadilly Circus, Leicester Square, Tottenham Court Road, Oxford Circus

1 **Wardour Street**
   • the Rolling Stones get their act together
   • Simon calls Garfunkel up on stage.

2 **Gerrard Street**
   • Lord Bolingbroke calls on John Dryden
   • James Boswell joins Dr Johnson's Club
   • Edmund Burke reflects on the French Revolution.

3 **Charing Cross Road**
   • Helene Hanff buys secondhand books.

4 **Old Compton Street**
   • Richard Wagner loses his dog
   • Verlaine and Rimbaud meet Eleanor Marx.

5 **Denmark Street**
   • the Rolling Stones record their first album
   • Casanova catches his girl with another man.

6 **Frith Street**
   • Mozart plays the piano
   • John Logie Baird invents television.

7 **Dean Street**
   • Karl Marx watches his daughter die.

8 **Poland Street**
   • Shelley works on his poetry.

9 **Carnaby Street**
   • Bob Dylan and the Stones get their gear.

10 Beak Street
- Canaletto tries to sell his paintings.

11 Regent Street
- Tchaikovsky is dazzled
- Oscar Wilde meets the Marquess of Queensberry.

33 WARDOUR STREET
The Rolling Stones

South of Shaftesbury Avenue, opposite Gerrard Street

1

Few bands had a less auspicious start than the **Rolling Stones**. They first got together in 1962, but fans were interested in jazz then, not 'jungle music'. They did get the occasional gig – at Sidcup Art College Christmas dance – but more than once found themselves playing to an audience of only six. They were so short of money that they sometimes had to steal potatoes to survive.

They couldn't find a regular drummer either, or a bass player. Nobody wanted to play with them full-time, or even part-time, except for fun. And it wasn't any fun when there were more people in the band than in the audience.

So it was a dispirited group that presented itself at the Flamingo Jazz Club (then at 33 Wardour Street) on January 14 1963. After expenses, the Rolling Stones made about 25 pence each for their performance that evening, and were received in stony silence by an audience that had come to hear jazz rather than R&B. The group's appearance did nothing to help. At a time when pop

groups all wore identical suits and ties, the Stones turned up on stage in their street clothes. They were quite used to being banned from dances because of their tight trousers, or from work for wearing a shirt that was pink rather than white. And when they grew their hair long, they were asked to leave hotels as well, and refused service in pubs and cafés.

But their gig at the Flamingo was memorable, because it was the first time that all five Rolling Stones – **Mick Jagger**, **Keith Richards**, **Brian Jones**, **Bill Wyman** and **Charlie Watts** – appeared on stage together. Their line-up was complete at last and they were beginning to get their act together, even if the audience that night didn't appreciate it. The face of rock music was about to change for ever.

The Stones played the Flamingo again on January 28, but were not invited back thereafter. They took three of the Flamingo's metal stools with them when they left, piling their equipment into the back of the van at the end of another unsuccessful gig. They would give it a year, they decided, and if they hadn't made it by then they would abandon hope and get themselves proper jobs. Nobody in Wardour Street gave the Rolling Stones a dog's chance as they climbed gloomily into their van and drove away into the obscurity that surely awaited them.

Did you know?

? In the autumn of 1964, another band failed to show up, so the Flamingo's manager got an unknown American to fill in at short notice. **Paul Simon** tried out a song he had just written, *The Sound of Silence*. It seemed to go down well, so he called his friend **Art Garfunkel** up on stage. The two of them sang *Benedictus* in perfect harmony and the audience was thunderstruck.

? Wardour Street was full of music clubs in the 1960s, including the Marquee Club (**Stones**, **Beatles**, **David Bowie**, **Jimi Hendrix**, **Rod Stewart**, **Eric Clapton**), which moved from Oxford Street in 1964. **Bob Dylan** was having a drink at Les Cousins during his 1965 tour when word of his presence spread through Soho. Dylan escaped his fans by hijacking a taxi in Wardour Street, with a blonde in it, and heading back to the Savoy Hotel – taking the blonde with him.

GERRARD STREET
9 Gerrard Street – Turk's Head tavern

A convivial man, **Samuel Johnson** liked nothing better than to sit up late, discussing literature with his friends. In 1764, he and the artist **Sir Joshua Reynolds** decided to form a dining club for the purpose. They held the inaugural meeting in a first-floor room of what was then the Turk's Head tavern, at 9 Gerrard Street.

> Soon after his return to London, which was in February, was founded that CLUB which existed long without a name, but at Mr Garrick's funeral became distinguished by the title of THE LITERARY CLUB. Sir Joshua Reynolds had the merit of being the first proposer of it, to which Johnson acceded; and the original members were, Sir Joshua Reynolds, Dr Johnson, Mr Edmund Burke, Dr Nugent, Mr Beauclerk, Mr Langton, Dr Goldsmith, Mr Chamier, and Sir John Hawkins.

> They met at the Turk's Head, in Gerrard-street, Soho, one evening in every week, at seven, and generally continued their conversation till a pretty late hour.

In 1773, **James Boswell** was proposed for membership. He was on tenterhooks, waiting to hear if he had been elected:

> In a short time I received the agreeable intelligence that I was chosen. I hastened to the place of meeting, and was introduced to such a society as can seldom be found. Mr Edmund Burke, whom I then saw for the first time, and whose splendid talents had long made me ardently wish for his acquaintance; Dr Nugent, Mr Garrick, Dr Goldsmith, Mr (afterwards Sir William) Jones, and the company with whom I had dined.

> Upon my entrance, Johnson placed himself behind a chair, on which he leaned as on a desk or pulpit, and with humorous formality gave me a Charge, pointing out the conduct expected from me as a good member of this club.

The club continued to meet at the Turk's Head until 1783, when it became a private house. They then moved to a pub in Sackville Street, and thereafter to Dover Street and St James'.

Did you know?

? By 1810 the club had had 76 members, including **David Garrick, Adam Smith, Oliver Goldsmith, Charles James Fox, Sir Joseph Banks, R B Sheridan, Edward Gibbon, George Canning** and **Humphrey Davy** – a very distinguished list.

• Now a Chinese supermarket, 9 Gerrard Street still has many of its original fittings behind the modern partitions.

37 Gerrard Street – Edmund Burke

Coming home from a dinner party in January 1790, the Irish Member of Parliament **Edmund Burke** decided not to go to bed at once, but to stay up, 'late as it was', and read a pamphlet about the revolution in France. The pamphlet approved of the events across the Channel, arguing that radical change in France was long overdue. But Burke was not so sure. He wondered where it would all end, with ancient institutions suddenly overturned and mob rule in the streets.

Burke was so disturbed by the pamphlet that he sat down in the next few days to pen a reply. *Reflections on the Revolution in France* took him most of the year to write and was published on November 1 1790. It was an immediate sensation on both sides of the Channel.

'I tremble for liberty, from such an example to kings,' he warned. 'I tremble for the cause of humanity… Patience will achieve more than force. Good order is the foundation of all things.'

But his words went unheeded in Paris. The Terror began in 1793 and thousands lost their lives. Burke's worst fears, gloomily prophesied from Gerrard Street, had come to pass.

Did you know?

? Burke was the leading political thinker of his day. His *Reflections* helped to change public opinion in England, which had largely favoured the French Revolution in its early stages. George III read the book with approval, as did Queen Marie-Antoinette of France. She was so moved that she burst into tears halfway through and had to stop reading.

? Burke did some of his best work at night. A neighbour saw him regularly, from across the street. 'Many a time when I had no inclination to go to bed at the dawn of day, I have looked down from my window to see whether the author of the *Sublime and Beautiful* had left his drawing-room, where I had seen that great orator during many a night after he had left the House of Commons, seated at a table covered with papers, attended by an amanuensis who sat opposite to him.'

? Slightly altered over the years, No 37 eventually fell into disrepair and had to be demolished in 2001. At time of writing, English Heritage was pressing for the new building to be an exact replica of the original.

43 Gerrard Street – John Dryden

One summer morning in 1697, the young aristocrat **Henry St John** called at No 43 to see his friend **John Dryden**. He found the former Poet Laureate looking tired and drawn. 'I have been up all night,' Dryden explained. 'My musical friends made me promise to write them a musical ode for their feast of St Cecilia. I have been so struck with the subject which occurred to me, that I could not leave it till I had completed it. Here it is, finished at one sitting.'

The ode was *Alexander's Feast*, 'the finest and noblest ode that had ever been written in any language', according to one contemporary critic. It was an astonishing achievement, if Dryden really did write it in one night. The work was set to music by Jeremiah Clarke and played with great success around London. Dryden received £40 for it, money he badly needed in his old age.

He wrote much of his most famous poetry at No 43, sitting at his desk 'in the ground room next the street'. By his own account, he was 'in my declining years; struggling with wants, oppress'd with sickness, curb'd in my genius, liable to be misconstrued in all I write'. But he still had his friends, among them the playwright **William Congreve**, who often came round to see him. Dryden lived the rest of his life in the house and died here in 1700.

Did you know?

? Henry St John later became the statesman **Viscount Bolingbroke**. He looked after **Voltaire** (a fan of Alexander's Feast) during the latter's stay in England from 1727.

? There's some doubt about whether Dryden actually lived at No 43. It may have been next door at No 44. 'My House is in Gerrard Street,' he told a friend, 'the fifth door on the left hand side, comeing from Newport Street.' Either way, the house is a Chinese supermarket now.

? As a boy, **Charles Dickens** used to visit his uncle in Gerrard Street. Mr Jaggers, Pip's lawyer in *Great Expectations*, also lived here. 'He conducted us to Gerrard Street, Soho, to a house on the south side of that street, rather a stately house of its kind, but dolefully in want of painting, and with dirty windows… We all went into a stone hall, bare, gloomy, and little used. So, up a dark brown staircase into a series of three dark brown rooms on the first floor.'

84 CHARING CROSS ROAD
Helene Hanff   3
Corner of Shaftesbury Avenue

Later filmed with **Anne Bancroft** and **Anthony Hopkins**, the correspondence between New Yorker **Helene Hanff** and Frank Doel of the booksellers Marks and Co began on October 5 1949:

> Gentlemen –
>
> Your ad in the *Saturday Review of Literature* says that you specialize in out-of-print books… I am a poor writer with an antiquarian taste in books and all the things I want are impossible to get over here except in very expensive rare editions, or in Barnes & Noble's grimy, marked-up schoolboy copies.
>
> I enclose a list of my most pressing problems. If you have clean secondhand copies of any of the books on the list, for no more than $5.00 each, will you consider this a purchase order and send them to me?
>
> Dear Madam…
>
> We have managed to clear up two thirds of your problem. The three Hazlitt essays you want are contained in the Nonesuch Press edition of his *Selected Essays* and the Stevenson is found in *Virginibus Puerisque*. We are sending nice copies of both these by Book Post and we trust they will arrive safely in due course.

Gentlemen –

The books arrived safely…Now then. Brian told me you are all rationed to 2 ounces of meat per family per week and one egg per person per month and I am simply appalled… I am sending a small Christmas present to Marks and Co. I hope there will be enough to go round, he says the Charing Cross Road bookshops are all quite small.

Dear Miss Hanff,

Just a note to let you know that your gift parcel arrived safely today and the contents have been shared out between the staff… I should just like to add that everything in the parcel was something that we either never see or can only be had through the black market. It was extremely kind and generous of you to think of us in this way.

Frank Doel, for Marks and Co.

The correspondence continued until 1969, when Frank Doel died. Helene Hanff paid her first visit to England two years later. She went straight to Charing Cross Road to find No 84 no longer in business.

The two large rooms had been stripped bare…The window letters which had spelled Marks and Co had been ripped off the window, a few of them were lying on the window sill, their white paint chipped and peeling.

I started back downstairs, my mind on the man, now dead, with whom I'd corresponded for so many years. Halfway down I put my hand on the oak railing and said to him silently: 'How about this, Frankie? I finally made it'.

Did you know?
? No 84 is now a restaurant, but Charing Cross Road is still the place for secondhand books.
? Compulsory food rationing from World War II continued well into the 1950s. Deprived of cake and sweets, the British were never healthier.

OLD COMPTON STREET
Richard Wagner

4

The pub is no longer there, but most of Old Compton Street remains as it was when **Richard Wagner** and his wife stayed here during their first trip to England in August 1839. Wagner was 26, a struggling composer, so poor that his passport had been confiscated as surety for his debts. He and his wife had been smuggled to England by a crew of sailors who thought they were criminals fleeing the law.

The Wagners arrived at London Bridge and took a cab to Soho with Robber, their Newfoundland dog, sitting across their knees.

The sights we saw surpassed anything we had imagined, and we arrived at our boarding-house in Old Compton Street agreeably stimulated by the life and the overwhelming size of the great city…

I found my knowledge of English quite inadequate when it came to conversing with the landlady of the King's Arms. But the good dame's social condition as a sea-captain's widow led her to think she could talk French to me, and her attempts made me wonder which of us knew least of that language. And then a most disturbing incident occurred – we missed Robber, who must have run away at the door instead of following us into the house.

Our distress at having lost our good dog after having brought him all the way there with such difficulty occupied us exclusively during the first two hours we spent in this new home on land. We kept constant watch at the window until, of a sudden, we joyfully recognised Robber strolling unconcernedly towards the house

from a side street. Afterwards we learned that our truant had wandered as far as Oxford Street in search of adventures.

The Wagners stayed in London for a week. Wagner had earlier sent his overture *Rule Britannia* to Sir John Smart, president of the Philharmonic Society, without receiving any reply. He spent several days trying to contact Smart, only to find that he wasn't in London at all. No-one was interested in the Wagners or their music, so they did a bit of sightseeing – including their first train ride – and then departed for Paris on August 20.

Did you know?

? When he got home, Wagner found the only copy of *Rule Britannia* returned to him, with a carriage fee of seven francs to pay. He didn't have the money, so he told the postman to take it away again and never learned what happened to it.

? In 1872, the French poets **Paul Verlaine** and **Arthur Rimbaud** lived briefly at 5 Old Compton Street during their English sojourn after the fall of the Paris commune. On November 1, they met Karl Marx's daughter Eleanor at a socialist lecture in a room above the pub at 6–7 Old Compton Street.

4 DENMARK STREET
Casanova, the Rolling Stones
5

La Charpillon was only 17, but already she had had countless lovers. Among them was **Giacomo Casanova**, who had foolishly sent her some incriminating letters that she refused to give back. The girl lived with her mother in Denmark Street (Casanova didn't say which number). One evening late in 1763, he decided to go round there and force them to return his property to him.

> I put two pistols in my pocket and proceeded to the wretched woman's abode… I was furious by the time I arrived, but when I passed by the door I saw a handsome young hairdresser, who did La Charpillon's hair every Saturday evening, going into the house.
>
> I did not want a stranger to be present at the scene I intended to make, so I waited at the corner of the street for the hairdresser to go… I waited on; eleven struck, and the handsome barber had not yet gone. A little before midnight, a servant came out with a lamp, I suppose to look for something that had fallen out of the window. I approached noiselessly; stepped in and opened the parlour-door, which was close to the street. I saw La Charpillon and the barber stretched out on the sofa making 'the beast with two backs', as Shakespeare calls it.
>
> When the slut spotted me, she gave a shriek and unhorsed her gallant, whom I thrashed with my cane until he escaped in the confusion. While this was going on La Charpillon, half-naked, remained crouched behind the sofa, trembling lest the blows should begin to descend on her.

The hairdresser fled, clutching his trousers. So did La Charpillon, spending the night with a friend near Soho Square. Casanova stayed to smash a mirror and some chairs and a china service that he had given her. Then he too stormed into the night, intending to drown himself in the river without further ado.

He was still suicidal a few days later. He bought as many lead balls as his pockets would hold and set off for Westminster Bridge. But he met a friend

on the way who invited him to an orgy instead. The friend and two pretty girls stripped off all their clothes and danced naked. Casanova was so dispirited he could only sit and watch as his friend had both of them.

Did you know?
? Need it be said? Casanova was Italian.

Nowadays, Denmark Street is full of music offices. It was at Regent Sound, a tiny recording studio at No 4 little bigger than a hotel room, that the **Rolling Stones** recorded their first album in 1964. The studio was a rundown place with stained walls and egg boxes on the ceiling to baffle the sound. It was intended for advertising jingles and demo tapes rather than master recordings. It had no mixers either, so sound could only be recorded in mono. What you heard was what you got.

This was perfect for the Stones. Cigarettes in hand, they all crowded in and went to work. *Not Fade Away* was recorded on January 10. Other tracks followed, in batches of two or three, for the rest of the month. By February 4, the Stones had had enough and were barely talking to each other, let alone playing together. **Mick Jagger** forgot the words to *Can I Get A Witness?* and had to run to Savile Row and back to get a copy from the publishers. He was out of breath when he returned, and sounds it on the recording.

Gene Pitney had arrived by then, bringing a bottle of brandy to lighten the mood. The Stones got stuck into the drink while Jagger and **Phil Spector** sat on the staircase outside studio reception and wrote the lyrics to *Little By Little* in ten minutes flat. They recorded it straight away, along with *Now I've Got A Witness* and a couple of obscene songs for private listening. Pitney played the piano, Spector played a half-dollar coin against the empty brandy bottle. Cool, or what?

Did you know?
? **Keith Richards** on Regent Sound: 'We did our early records in a room insulated with little egg cartons. It was a little demo studio, a tiny little back room and it was all done on a two-track Revox.'

FRITH STREET
22 Frith Street – John Logie Baird

Evicted from his previous office for causing an explosion, the amateur inventor **John Logie Baird** moved to Frith Street in 1924 and rented two small rooms on the second floor of No 22 to continue his experiments. Baird was an electrical engineer, trying to find a way of 'seeing by wireless' that he was certain would change the world if he could only make it work. He called it television.

His equipment was not impressive. Baird had no money and had to make do with whatever bits and pieces he could find.

> It was weird and wonderful... I was amazed at what he had improvised out of the most unpromising material. String, cardboard and pieces of rough wood with Meccano parts, bits of bicycles and strange scraps of Government surplus stores all combined to make a television machine which introduced me to television as an official fact.

Baird had managed to produce some very patchy TV images of a ventriloquist's dummy, but the breakthrough came in 1925 when he replaced his filament with a much faster neon lamp.

> At that time I was working very intensively in a small attic laboratory in the Soho district of London. Things were very black; my cash resources were almost exhausted and as, day by day, success seemed as far away as ever I began to wonder if general opinion was not after all correct, and that television was in truth a myth.
>
> But one day – it was, in fact, the first Friday in October – the dummy's head suddenly showed up on the screen not as a mere smudge of black and white, but as a real image with details and graduations of light and shade. I had got it! I could scarcely believe my eyes and felt myself shaking with excitement.
>
> I ran down the little flight of stairs to Mr Cross' office and seized by the arm his office boy, William Taynton, hauled him upstairs, and put him in front of the transmitter. I then went to the receiver, only to find the screen a blank. William did not like lights and whirring noises and had withdrawn out of range. I gave him 2s 6d and pushed his head into position.
>
> This time he came through and on the screen I saw the flickering but clearly recognisable image of William's face – the first face to be seen on television – and he had to be bribed with 2s 6d for the privilege of this distinction!

It was another three months before Baird gave the first public demonstration of his invention. On Tuesday, January 26 1926, a group of 40 scientists, including Nobel laureate **Sir William Bragg**, gathered at Frith Street in full evening dress and queued in batches of six to climb the stairs to Baird's tiny rooms at the top.

I could hear their footsteps echoing as they climbed, and their mutterings. Inside they had to find their way over a litter of cables and other equipment.

In one room was a large whirling disc, a most dangerous device, had they known it, liable to burst at any minute and hop round the room with showers of broken glass... The whole assembly here were given an opportunity to be televised and I was certainly gratified by the interest and enthusiasm. The audience were for the most part men of vision and realised that in these tiny flickering images they were witnessing the birth of a great industry.

Unfortunately for Baird, a rival TV system was later adopted in preference to his own. He was the first person to give a public demonstration of television, but his is not the system in use today.

Did you know?

? In his early days, Baird was so desperate for money that he approached the *Daily Express* and requested press coverage for his ideas. But the assistant editor was not impressed by Baird's claim to have invented a method of seeing by electricity. He went to the news room and selected a burly reporter: 'For God's sake, Jackson, go down to the reception room and get rid of a lunatic who is down there. He says he's got a machine for seeing by wireless. Watch him carefully, he may have a razor hidden.'

? Television sets were first marketed in the 1930s, but didn't sell well in the years leading up to World War II. The Government encouraged their manufacture anyway, calculating that the screens would prove useful for another British invention that the public didn't yet know about – radar.

? Baird's original apparatus and the dummy's head are now in the Science Museum, South Kensington.

20 Frith Street – W A Mozart

Known then as Thrift Street, this was the address of the **Mozart** family during their stay in England 1764–65. It's not the actual house – that was rebuilt in 1858 – but it's still worth a look, since you're in the street anyway.

Young Wolfgang and his sister were on a concert tour of Europe, organised by their father. They had mixed success in London – several appearances at Court, several highly profitable concerts, but also sluggish ticket sales and even a few gigs in pubs, as if they were just ordinary travelling musicians. At Frith Street, Wolfgang composed duets to play with his sister, and in May 1765 his father announced them to the public:

Mr Mozart, the father of the celebrated young musical Family, who have so justly raised the Admiration of the greatest Musicians of Europe, proposes to give the Public an Opportunity of hearing these young Prodigies perform both in public and private, by giving on the 13th of this month a Concert, which will be chiefly conducted by his son, a boy of Eight years of Age, with all the overtures of his own composition.

Tickets may be had at 5s each of Mr Mozart, at Mr Williamson's in Thrift Street, Soho, where Ladies and Gentlemen will find the Family at home every day in the week from 12 till 2 o'clock, and have an opportunity of putting his talents to a more particular proof by giving him anything to play at sight, or any Music without a Bass which he will write upon the Spot without recurring to his Harpsichord.

The Mozarts went home in August, after a 15-month stay. Wolfgang never returned to England, but retained happy memories. In later life, he exulted in British military victories and sometimes referred to himself as a dyed-in-the-wool Englishman.

Did you know?

? Although 20 Frith Street has been rebuilt, the Mozarts also lived for a time at 180 Ebury Street, Belgravia, where Wolfgang composed his first symphony. That house is still there (see page 164).

28 DEAN STREET
Karl Marx

7

A refugee from the failed revolution in Prussia, **Karl Marx** was virtually penniless in 1850. He had a wife and four children, but no job and no income. He was entirely dependent on handouts from his friend **Friedrich Engels**, whose family had a textile business in Manchester.

At the end of the year, the Marxes moved into two miserable rooms on the top floor of 28 Dean Street. The whole family – along with the maid – slept in one tiny room. The other was full of broken furniture, dirty plates, and Marx's books and manuscripts piled high on a table overlooking the street. There was no lavatory or running water. A Prussian police spy was shocked at Marx's life there:

He leads the existence of a real bohemian intellectual. Washing, grooming and changing his linen are things he does rarely, and he likes to get drunk… He has no fixed times for going to sleep and waking up. He often stays up all night, and then lies down fully clothed on the sofa at midday and sleeps till evening, untroubled by the comings and goings of the whole world.

In fact, Marx was greatly irritated by the activities of his Prussian watchers. He and Engels had complained about them to the *Spectator*:

Really, Sir, we should never have thought that there existed in this country so many police spies as we have had the good fortune of making the acquaintance of in the short space of a week. Not only that the doors of the houses where we live are closely watched by individuals of a more than doubtful look, who take down their notes very coolly every time one enters or leaves it; we cannot make a single step without being followed by them wherever we go. We cannot get into an omnibus or enter a coffee house without being favoured with the company of at least one of these unknown friends.

The Marxes lived at No 28 for five years. It was only ten minutes' walk from the Reading Room of the British Museum, where Marx was preparing the ground for *Das Kapital*. He wrote about the exploitation of workers by day, then came home at night to the family maid whom he had got pregnant, and his wife as well. Their life was such a mess that when one of the children died, there wasn't even enough money for a coffin.

When she died we left her lifeless little body in the back room, went into the front room and made our beds on the floor. Our three living children lay down by us and we all wept for the little angel whose livid, lifeless body was in the next room.

But later came salvation. Marx's wife was a Prussian baroness. Her uncle died in 1855 and then her mother, leaving them enough money to move out to Kentish Town and live in a proper house. The Marxes moved at once and never lived in Soho again.

Did you know?

? For the rest of his life, Marx remembered Soho with horror, associating it with poverty and the death of three of his children. 'The region round Soho Square still sends a shiver down my spine if I happen to be anywhere near there.'

? Soho was the nursery of world Communism in the 1840s. The early Communists were refugees from Prussia. Disguised as the German Workers' Educational Association, they held their meetings in a room above the Red Lion pub, still there at 20 Great Windmill Street (near Piccadilly).

15 POLAND STREET
Percy Bysshe Shelley
Corner of Noel Street

Headstrong and impulsive, **Percy Bysshe Shelley** was thrown out of Oxford in 1811 for writing a pamphlet on *The Necessity of Atheism*. His friend Thomas Jefferson Hogg was thrown out too. Together the two young men set off for London and tramped around Soho looking for somewhere to live.

It wasn't easy. Shelley was a poet and very choosy about where he lived. He had rejected several places before they came to No 15, on the corner of Noel Street.

A paper in a window announced lodgings; Shelley took some objection to the exterior of the house, but we went in, and this time auspiciously.

There was a back sitting-room on the first floor, somewhat dark, but quiet… The walls of the room had lately been covered with trellised paper; in those days it was not common. There were trellises, vine-leaves with their tendrils, and huge clusters of grapes, green and purple, all represented in lively colours. This was delightful; Shelley went close up to the wall and touched it: 'We must stay here; stay for ever!'

There was some debate about a second bedroom, and the authorities were consulted below; he was quite uneasy, and eyed the cheerful paper wistfully during the consultation. We might have another bedroom; it was upstairs. That room, of course, was to be mine. Shelley had the bedroom opening out of the sitting-room; this also was overspread with the trellised paper. He touched the wall and admired it.

'Do grapes really grow in that manner anywhere?'

'Yes, I believe they do!'

'We will go and see them then, soon; we will go together!'

Hogg returned to his family after a few weeks, leaving Shelley by himself. On April 18 he wrote:

This place is a little solitary, but as a person cannot be quite alone when he has even got himself with him, I get on pretty well. I have employed myself in writing poetry, and as I go to bed at eight o'clock, time passes quicker than it otherwise might.

But the idyll did not last. Shelley's father wanted to know what he was going to do with his life now that he had been expelled from Oxford. Shelley briefly contemplated medicine, but then eloped on a whim with a schoolfriend of his sisters. They got married in Edinburgh on August 28. Shelley was just 19, his bride 16. The marriage didn't last.

Did you know?

? Shelley later became a leading Romantic poet. He drowned off Italy in 1822 in a boating accident that caught the popular imagination. He was still only 29.

? Shelley's second wife was **Mary Godwin**, the author of *Frankenstein*. She wrote it in 1816, when the Shelleys and Lord Byron were in Geneva, competing with each other to see who could write the best supernatural story.

? Also with them in Geneva was Byron's doctor friend, **John Polidori**. His contribution was *The Vampyre* – a forerunner of Dracula – which was published under Byron's name to increase sales. Polidori lived and died in Soho at 38 Great Pulteney Street (near Golden Square).

CARNABY STREET
The Rolling Stones

9

It's a pathetic sight now, but there was a time in the mid-1960s when the clothes of Carnaby Street ruled the fashion world. The mini-skirt had just been invented in London, sending shock waves from Los Angeles all the way to Vladivostock. Parents across three continents forbade their daughters to wear them. The daughters wore them anyway, and the parents were forced to concede that the torch had passed to a new generation. It wasn't long before daughters stopped trying to dress like their mothers, and mothers started trying to dress like their daughters instead.

Men's fashions went crazy too, and shops all over the world were renamed Carnaby Street in emulation. The **Rolling Stones** came here on Saturday, May 4 1963 to buy tight black jeans, black roll-neck sweaters and Cuban high-heeled boots from Anello & Davide. 'The London group with the slightly wild look' came again at the end of June for blue leather waistcoats and black and white dog-tooth jackets. **Bob Dylan** came too, and the **Beatles**, and the **Who**, and everyone else. Carnaby Street was where it was at in the swinging sixties – fab gear for groovy people.

The scene was at its grooviest in 1967, with 'flower power' and the summer of love still to come. Hippies with bells round their necks wafted along the street, blowing bubbles and handing out flowers to passers-by to wear in their hair. People of both sexes were dressed in all the colours of the rainbow, a visual feast that subsequent generations have never managed to emulate. 'Psychedelic' was the word on everyone's lips, though no-one was quite sure what it meant. If London was the heart of the swinging sixties, then Carnaby Street was the very heart of London. But that was then, before the circus moved on. Carnaby Street just sells tourist junk now.

41 BEAK STREET
Canaletto

10

Famed for his paintings of his native Venice, **Antonio Canal** arrived in London in May 1746 hoping to cash in on his reputation with the English aristocracy. They were already big buyers of his Venetian work, but a war in

Europe meant that fewer of them were travelling to Venice, so now Canaletto (as he was known) was coming to them instead.

He was almost 50 when he arrived, 'a covetous greedy fellow' with a strong appreciation of his own worth. 'It's said he has already made himself easy in his fortune and likewise that he has brought the most part to putt into the Stocks here for better security, or better interest than abroad.'

Canaletto settled in Beak Street, known then as Silver Street. He found plenty of work to begin with, but commissions began to slacken off after a while, partly because of a conspiracy by English painters and art dealers to belittle his talents. So Canaletto painted a picture of his own and offered it for sale from his Soho rooms on July 25 1749:

> SIGNOR CANALETTO hereby invites any Gentleman that will be pleased to come to his House, to see a Picture done by him, being *A View of St James' Park*, which he hopes may in some Measure deserve their Approbation. The said View may be seen from Nine in the Morning till Three in the Afternoon, and from Four till Seven in the Evening, for the Space of fifteen Days from the Publication of this Advertizement. He lodges at Mr Richard Wiggan's, Cabinet-Maker, in Silver-Street, Golden Square.

Business picked up again and Canaletto prospered. Apart from a quick trip back to Venice to invest his earnings in property, he stayed in London for nine years. His paintings of the city are easily the best record of what London looked like 250 years ago.

Did you know?

? The view of St James' Park advertised by Canaletto is almost certainly the one now owned by **Andrew Lloyd Webber**.

CAFÉ ROYAL, 68 REGENT STREET
Oscar Wilde and the Marquess of Queensberry 11

Ornately modelled on the boulevard cafés of Paris, the Café Royal was the height of fashion at the end of the 19th century. **Oscar Wilde** used to lunch here several times a week, often with his boyfriend **Lord Alfred Douglas**. They were doing just that on April 1 1894 when they spotted Lord Alfred's father, the **Marquess of Queensberry**, lunching alone at another table.

Queensberry disapproved of Wilde and had forbidden his son to see him. To avoid a scene, Lord Alfred invited him over to their table and introduced him to Wilde. The meeting went well and Queensberry was momentarily charmed. 'I don't wonder you are so fond of him,' he told his son at the end of the meal. 'Mr Wilde is a wonderful man.'

Later that day he had second thoughts. In a letter to his son, he voiced his doubts in no uncertain terms.

> Your intimacy with this man Wilde. It must either cease or I will disown you and stop all money supplies... to my mind to pose as a

thing is as bad as to be it. With my own eyes I saw you both in the most loathsome and disgusting relationship as expressed by your manner and expression...

No wonder people are talking as they are. Also I now hear on good authority that his wife is petitioning to divorce him for sodomy and other crimes. Is this true, or do you not know of it?

It was true. Queensberry later destroyed Wilde's career and his son never forgave him.

Did you know?

? On Monday, March 25 1895, as his court case against Queensberry was reaching its climax, Wilde held a crisis meeting at the Café Royal with Lord Alfred, the American **Frank Harris**, and **George Bernard Shaw**. Harris and Shaw advised Wilde to drop the case and flee to Paris, but Douglas advised him to fight on. Wilde foolishly took his advice and lost the case. The strain clearly shows in **Toulouse-Lautrec**'s portrait of him, done a few days before he went to prison.

? Among the many other authors who have frequented the Café Royal are **John Buchan** ('I went home, dressed, dined at the Café Royal, and turned into a music-hall'), **D H Lawrence**, **George Orwell** and **Sir Arthur Conan Doyle**. The latter set a Sherlock Holmes story here: 'Mr Sherlock Holmes, the well-known private detective, was the victim this morning of a murderous assault... The event seems to have occurred about 12 o'clock in Regent Street, outside the Café Royal... The miscreants who attacked him escaped from the bystanders by passing through the Café Royal and out into Glasshouse Street behind it.'

? On a working visit to London, **Peter Ilich Tchaikovsky** was very taken with this part of the city. 'Walking in Regent Street, one sees so many carriages with such sumptuous, expensive accoutrements, that the eye is fairly dazzled. It makes Paris look like a village.'

WHAT NOW?

Shopping? Soho is bordered by Oxford Street to the north and Regent Street to the west, both very good for clothes. Charing Cross Road to the east is full of bookshops (Foyle's alone has 30 miles of shelves and 630,000 titles in stock). Piccadilly lies to the south, and the British Museum is only ten minutes' walk from Karl Marx's old flat in Dean Street.

Nearest public lavatories Soho Square, Oxford Circus, Piccadilly Circus Underground, corner of Shaftesbury Avenue and Charing Cross Road, corner of Broadwick Street and Berwick Street

● Oxford Circus, Piccadilly Circus, Leicester Square, Tottenham Court Road

WHERE TO EAT

Soho has always been full of foreigners and is accordingly a gastronomic delight. Whatever you like to eat, you will find it here somewhere. The restaurants in Gerrard Street are almost exclusively Chinese, but the rest of Soho is very diverse. Parts of it are a red-light area late at night, but playgoers can eat here quite safely after the theatre. Apart from the places already mentioned in the walk, try:

Chinatown
Jen 7 Gerrard Street. Hong Kong food.
Lee Ho Fook 4 Macclesfield Street. Chinese barbecue.
Fung Shing 15 Lisle Street. Gourmet Chinese.
Tokyo Diner 2 Newport Place. Japanese fast food, with explanatory notes.

Rest of Soho
Bar Italia 22 Frith Street. Television was first demonstrated upstairs.
Andrew Edmunds 46 Lexington Street. Wine bar cum bistro.
Busaba eathai 106 Wardour Street. Unpretentious Thai food, but you may have to share a table.
Café Espana 63 Old Compton Street. Good Spanish cooking.
Kulu Kulu 76 Brewer Street. Sushi on a conveyor belt.
Mezzo 100 Wardour Street. Space for 600 diners, often full!
Pollo 20 Old Compton Street. Traditional Italian.
Randall & Aubin 16 Brewer Street. Champagne and oyster bar.
The Red Fort 77 Dean Street. Upmarket Indian curry.
Kettner's 29 Romilly Street. Oscar Wilde dined at Kettner's with Lord Alfred Douglas in October 1892. Wilde used to go upstairs with his rentboys afterwards, as did Lillie Langtry with Edward VII. Nowadays, though, Kettner's is an upmarket pizza house cum champagne bar.
Golden Lion 51 Dean Street. Gay pub, formerly frequented by Noel Coward. In the 1980s, mass murderer Dennis Nilsen used to pick up young men here before dismembering them. Nilsen was distantly related to Virginia Woolf, but disclaimed the connection on the grounds that she was mad.

Mayfair

WALK AT A GLANCE

Features One of the richest and smartest neighbourhoods in central London, with shops and homes to match.
Time Allow an hour for the walk, more for shopping along Bond Street and Oxford Street.
Length 1½ miles, if you return to your starting point.
● Green Park, Piccadilly Circus, Oxford Circus, Bond Street

1 Dover Street
 • Lord Queensberry leaves his card for Oscar Wilde.

2 Albemarle Street
 • John Murray burns Lord Byron's memoirs.

3 Burlington House
 • the Duke of Wellington has a ball
 • Lord Byron avoids Lady Caroline Lamb
 • Charles Darwin has an idea.

4 Savile Row
 • The Beatles perform impromptu on the roof of Apple Corps
 • Richard Brinsley Sheridan dies a pauper's death.

5 New Bond Street
 • Lord Nelson mourns the loss of his arm.

6 Brook Street
 • George Frederick Handel composes *The Messiah*
 • Jimi Hendrix takes a trip.

7 Hanover Square
 • Prince Talleyrand negotiates the treaty that will trigger World War I
 • Queen Victoria listens to Felix Mendelssohn.

8 Stratford Place
 • Martin Van Buren is recalled to America from his sick bed.

9 Berkeley Square
 • Lord Clive of India cuts his throat.

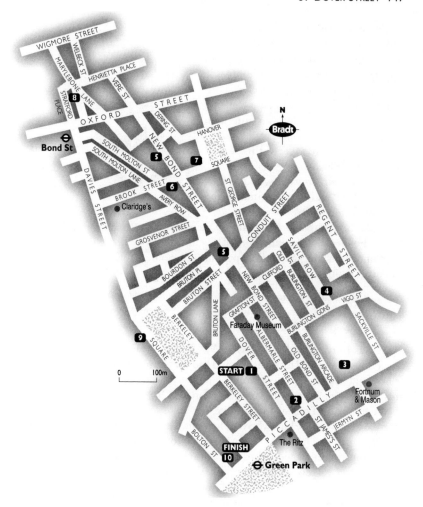

10 Bolton Street
- Sir Walter Scott calls on Fanny d'Arblay
- John Singer Sargent calls on Henry James.

37 DOVER STREET
Oscar Wilde

1

Oscar Wilde was at the height of his powers on February 28 1895. After a long run of successes, his latest and most enduring play, *The Importance of Being Earnest*, had opened a fortnight earlier to rave reviews from the critics. As he strolled along Dover Street that Thursday morning, there wasn't a playwright in the English-speaking world who wouldn't have changed places with him for a share of his professional success.

Wilde was heading for the Albemarle, his club at No 37 (now part of a bank). As soon as he arrived, the hall porter handed him a card left by the **Marquess**

of Queensberry ten days earlier. It was addressed 'To Oscar Wilde posing Somdomite' (Lord Queensberry could not spell). Most of the writing was illegible, but the message was clear. Lord Queensberry was publicly accusing Wilde of homosexuality, a crime then punishable by imprisonment.

No 37 Dover Street

'Who else has seen this card?' demanded Wilde.

'No-one, sir. It was I who put it in the envelope and I don't understand what is written on it.'

Wilde should have torn the card up there and then. Instead, he hurried back to his hotel with the intention of fleeing to Paris. But the manager had impounded his luggage until he paid his bill. So he wrote a note to his friend Robert Ross instead:

> Bosie's father has left a card at my club with hideous words on it. I don't see anything now but a criminal prosecution. My whole life seems ruined by this man.

Bosie was **Lord Alfred Douglas**, one of Wilde's boyfriends. The Marquess of Queensberry objected to the liaison and had made it his business to destroy Wilde if he could. The only way of stopping him that Wilde could see was to sue the marquess for libel. It was unwise, particularly as Queensberry had been careful to accuse him only of *posing* as a sodomite, but Wilde felt he had to do something to stop the man plaguing him wherever he went. Otherwise it would go on for ever.

Wilde sued and lost. He in turn was tried for sodomy and sentenced to two years' imprisonment with hard labour. He fled abroad after his release and died in poverty a few weeks after his 46th birthday.

Did you know?

? **Frédéric Chopin** lived at 48 Dover Street (since rebuilt) during his last visit to England in 1848. He had moved from Bentinck Street to be closer to Piccadilly. 'At last I have good lodgings; but no sooner have I settled in than my landlord now wants to make me pay twice as much… It's true that I have a large and splendid drawing room and can give my lessons there, but so far I have only five pupils. I don't know what I shall do.'

? 'Piccadilly…well, I was there half an hour ago, and have never seen anything more beautiful in my life' – **Felix Mendelssohn**.

50 ALBEMARLE STREET
John Murray, publisher

2

'Mad, bad and dangerous to know,' **Lord Byron** was the most famous poet of his day, a dashing aristocrat and a huge best seller. He was published by John Murray and came to see him regularly when he was in London.

Sir Walter Scott met him here on April 7 1815.

> It was in the spring of 1815, that, chancing to be in London, I had the advantage of a personal introduction to Lord Byron… We met for an hour or two almost daily, in Mr Murray's drawing room, and found a great deal to say to each other.

Both poets walked with a limp, clumping arm in arm together down the stairs. Byron died later in Greece, on a romantic mission to fight the Turks. He left his memoirs to Murray, but they were so scandalous – Byron was bisexual, and perhaps incestuous – that Murray declined to publish them. Instead, on May 17 1824, he burned them in the drawing-room fireplace on the first floor, a disaster for historians and poetry lovers alike.

Did you know?

? Another of Murray's authors was the young **Benjamin Disraeli**. Murray took so long to respond to a novel Disraeli had sent him that the future Prime Minister gave up in despair: 'As you have had some small experience in burning manuscripts perhaps you will be so kind as to consign [mine] to the flames.'

? Other Murray authors included the poets **Southey** and **Coleridge**, the novelist **Jane Austen**, the naturalist **Charles Darwin** (who worried that the *Origin of Species* wouldn't sell), and **Herman Melville**, who came to dinner on November 23 1849: 'I have just returned from Mr Murray's, where I dined agreeably to invitation. It was a most amusing affair. Mr Murray was there in a short vest & dress-coat, looking quizzical enough – his footman was there also, habited in small clothes & breeches, revealing a despicable pair of sheepshanks… At dinner, the stiffness, formality & coldness of the party was wonderful. I felt like knocking all their heads together.'

? Further along Albemarle Street, the Royal Institution at No 21 houses the laboratory (now a small museum) where **Michael Faraday** pioneered the use of electro-magnetism in the early 19th century.

BURLINGTON HOUSE
Charles Darwin, Lord Byron, the Duke of Wellington 3
Burlington House is now the Royal Academy of Arts

In the summer of 1814, it seemed that the Napoleonic Wars were over at long last. France had been defeated, Napoleon had been exiled to Elba, and Europe was at peace for the first time in a generation. On July 1, the members of Wattier's Club celebrated by inviting 1,700 people to a ball at Burlington House in honour of the newly ennobled **Duke of Wellington**.

Among the guests were **Lord Byron**, dressed as a monk, and his rejected lover **Lady Caroline Lamb**, dressed (in the hope of getting him back) as a boy. The dandy **Beau Brummell** was there too, and the hooker **Harriette Wilson**, her identity concealed behind a mask. The garden was tented for the occasion and the rooms expensively decorated. There were singers, jugglers, rope dancers, balloon rides and Grimaldi the clown to provide entertainment. Supper was served at 1.30am, and the dancing continued until seven o'clock that morning, followed by breakfast at eight.

Yet Lord Byron, for one, did not enjoy it very much. Lady Caroline was plaguing him with her attentions, refusing to accept her rejection. She was mentally unstable, so he feared trouble.

> I was obliged to talk to her, for she… passed before where another
> person and myself were discussing points of Platonism so frequently
> and remarkably as to make us anticipate a scene. As she was masked
> and dominoed, and it was daylight, there could be little harm… Not
> all I could say could prevent her from displaying her green *pantaloons*
> every now and then.

Harriette Wilson caught Byron alone and upbraided him for his ill-treatment of Caroline. 'Such contempt as you have lavished on poor Lady Caroline Lamb would kill me.' Yet Byron was not apologetic. 'Is there any sort of comparison to be made between you and that mad woman?' The affair was over, whether Caroline liked it or not. She accepted the inevitable after a while and went back to her long-suffering husband (later Prime Minister **Lord Melbourne**).

Did you know?

? In those days, Burlington House was the London home of the Duke of Devonshire. Now, it houses the Royal Academy of Arts (there is usually a good exhibition on) and various learned societies as well.

Among the learned societies which meet at Burlington House is the Linnean. It was in the Reynolds Room (first floor, front) that 30 members gathered on Thursday, July 1 1858 for a natural history meeting at which two last-minute contributions had been hastily added to the agenda.

The contributions were from **Charles Darwin** and **Alfred Russel Wallace**. Between them, they had come up with one of the most

Burlington House

revolutionary scientific ideas of the 19th century – that organisms fight for survival and only the fittest make it. Each had been working on the idea unknown to the other. When Darwin's friends realised this, they arranged for the two men to go public together at the Linnean Society meeting.

Neither was there in person. Wallace was in Malaysia. Darwin was at home in Kent. His baby son had died three days earlier and he was too upset to talk about his work. Their papers were read out by the society's secretary to an audience that had come to hear something totally different. The meeting went on too long and the talks were rushed. The audience completely failed to grasp the significance of what they were being told.

Darwin published *The Origin of Species* in 1859, but it wasn't until years later that his theory of natural selection became widely accepted. The Linnean Society members had been in at the birth of evolution, although only a few of them had realised it at the time.

Did you know?

? The meeting was attended by the society's president, Thomas Bell, who was not impressed by Darwin's paper. He later observed that his year in office had not 'been marked by any of those striking discoveries which at once revolutionize, so to speak, the department of science on which they bear'. Oops!

? The Reynolds Room is open to the public only between one and two every afternoon, and only by guided tour. Arrive on time to be sure of a place.

? Access to Savile Row, the next stop on the walk, is easiest via the Burlington Arcade (outside and to the left, as you face Burlington House). The Duke of Devonshire had the arcade built in 1819 to stop people throwing rubbish into his garden.

SAVILE ROW
3 Savile Row – The Beatles

4

Savile Row is famous for its bespoke tailoring. Crowned heads come to Savile Row for their handmade suits, as do the aristocracy and Hollywood stars. So it was a shock, in the summer of 1968, when The Beatles suddenly arrived as well, setting up the headquarters of their new business venture at No 3. Before anyone knew it, the street was full of girls with flowers in their hair, crowding the opposite pavement and shrieking every time they spotted one of the 'fab four'. The gentlemen's outfitters of Savile Row had never seen anything like it in their lives.

Apple Corps occupied all five floors of No 3. A doorman in a grey morning coat was supposed to deter intruders, but the girls quickly learned to arrive by taxi and march in as if they had an appointment. They learned too that they had

rivals for The Beatles' affections. **Yoko Ono**, **John Lennon**'s Japanese girlfriend, was booed and hissed whenever she went in to Apple. So was **Linda Eastman**, **Paul McCartney**'s new girlfriend, when she came out with Paul on her arm, holding him tight so everyone would know that he belonged to her now.

The girls across the street waited on the pavement from early in the morning until late every night. Two blind ones from Texas were invited in to touch John Lennon (no wonder he thought The Beatles were bigger than Christ). Hell's Angels from San Francisco stood outside with their motorbikes, sharing the pavement with wild-eyed hippies with bells round their necks who were planning to start a new life in the south seas… only they had no bread, man, and could The Beatles help them out? The beautiful people, the not so beautiful, and the frankly half-witted all stood there, gazing adoringly at the building that housed the objects of their affections.

Inside, the basement had been turned into a recording studio. It was not as good as Abbey Road, but it is where *Let It Be* was recorded, the album pieced together in circumstances that were far from ideal. And it was on the roof of No 3, one January afternoon in 1969, that The Beatles were filmed together for almost the last time, playing tracks from the album. **Ringo Starr** wore a red plastic raincoat for the occasion, **George Harrison** green trousers, and John Lennon a short ladies' coat. They all gave it their best as a bearded Paul McCartney sang *Get Back* across the rooftops while stunned neighbours climbed onto their fire escapes to listen.

The impromptu concert was the last straw for Savile Row's tailors. No warning had been given, so they sent for the police and asked for the noise to be silenced. The Beatles broke up the following September when John Lennon declared that he had had enough. Nobody really believed him as he got into his white Rolls-Royce and drove off down Savile Row, but he meant what he said and never played with the group again. The Beatles were history… and so were the 1960s.

Did you know?

? Before he left, John held a short ceremony on the roof at which he formally changed his middle name from Winston (he was born the year Churchill became Prime Minister) to Ono. A Commissioner of Oaths was there to make it legal.

? Next door to The Beatles, the tailors Gieves and Hawkes are what Savile Row is really all about – quality tailoring to the highest standards. Lord Nelson was a customer and died in one of their uniforms.

14 Savile Row – Richard Brinsley Sheridan

At the end of a riotous dinner party in October 1815, three cheerful drunks returned to Savile Row and made their way unsteadily to bed. One was **Richard Brinsley Sheridan**. The others were **Lord Byron** and his friend Douglas Kinnaird, who were seeing the old playwright safely to his door.

> Kinnaird and I had to conduct Sheridan down a damned corkscrew staircase, which had certainly been constructed before the discovery of fermented liquors, and to which no legs, however crooked, could possibly accommodate themselves. We deposited him safe at home, where his man evidently used to the business, waited to receive him in the hall.

The man was indeed used to it. Sheridan had been a brilliant dramatist once, but he hadn't written anything for years, preferring to spend his time as a Member of Parliament instead. But he had recently lost his parliamentary seat and been thrown into prison for debt. He owed so much that all he could do was get drunk as often as possible and try to forget the creditors hammering on his door.

'I am absolutely undone,' he complained to a friend. 'They are going to put the carpets out of the window, and break into Mrs Sheridan's room and *take me* – for God's sake let me see you.'

Sheridan's health collapsed under the strain. His wife too was dying of cancer. Another friend came to see them and

> found him and Mrs Sheridan both in their beds, both apparently dying, and both starving… They had hardly a servant left. Mrs Sheridan's maid she was about to send away, but they could not collect a guinea or two to pay the woman's wages. When Mr Vaughan entered the house, he found all the reception rooms bare, and the whole house in a state of filth and stench that was quite intolerable.

> Sheridan himself he found in a truckle bed in a garret with a coarse blue and red coverlet, such as one sees as horse-cloths over him; out of this bed he had not moved for a week, not even for the occasions of nature, and in this state the unhappy man had been allowed to wallow.

Vaughan did his best for the Sheridans, but the bailiffs were unsympathetic. They broke into the house to seize the remaining furniture and would have removed Sheridan as well if his doctor hadn't threatened to indict them for murder. Sheridan was left alone and died miserably in his garret on July 7 1816.

Did you know?

? In Sheridan's most famous play, *The School for Scandal*, the hero cheerfully sells off the family portraits to pay his debts. So did Sheridan in real life. His Gainsboroughs went first and then – most painfully of all – the portrait of his late first wife by Reynolds.

23 Savile Row – English Heritage

Further along Savile Row, the headquarters of English Heritage is worth a visit for anyone interested in the country's past, as readers of this guide surely are. English Heritage has 460,000 members, but needs many more to help fund conservation work and protect the nation's heritage. Above all, it needs to maintain the ceaseless fight against property developers, who would cheerfully allow all of England's historic buildings to rot if it meant they could be demolished and replaced with office blocks.

For a small joining fee, you can become part of the fight. In return, you get free admission to more than 400 historic attractions, and reduced-price entry to many more. You receive a quarterly magazine, and access to a wide range of books and videos detailing every aspect of English Heritage's activities, from painstaking restoration work using traditional techniques to re-enactments of medieval jousting tournaments to amuse the kids.

Look in now, telephone: free 0870 333 1181, email: members@english-heritage.org.uk or write to English Heritage, Membership Department, PO Box 570, Swindon, SN2 2YR.

103 AND 147 NEW BOND STREET   5
Lord Nelson

Both are on the west side of New Bond Street. Going from 147 to 103 you will pass Brook Street, with the homes of Handel and Jimi Hendrix a few yards to the left, and of Talleyrand to the right

The year 1797 was a mix of good and bad for Rear-Admiral **Sir Horatio Nelson**. Good because his heroic exploits against the French were at last bringing him the recognition he craved; bad, because he had recently lost his right arm in battle, to add to the eye that he had already lost in the service of his country.

So it was a distinctly gloomy Nelson who took lodgings at 147 New Bond Street on his return to England. With only one arm and one eye, he was convinced that his career was at an end. His arm was very sore, taking months to heal. To cap it all, he was accused of being unpatriotic in October because he failed to put lighted candles in the windows to celebrate a minor victory by Admiral Duncan against the Dutch:

> One night, during this state of suffering, after a day of constant pain, Nelson retired early to bed, in hope of enjoying some respite by means of laudanum. He was at that time lodging in Bond Street; and the family was soon disturbed by a mob knocking loudly and violently on the door. The news of Duncan's victory had been made public, and the house was not illuminated.

> But when the mob were told that Admiral Nelson lay there in bed, badly wounded, the foremost of them made answer: "You shall hear no more from us tonight"; and, in fact, the feeling of respect and sympathy was communicated from one to another with such effect, that, under the confusion of such a night the house was not molested again.

Nelson changed lodging soon afterwards, moving up the street to No 103. His arm was healing at last and the navy was going to re-employ him. He went to sea again in 1798, defeating the French at the battle of the Nile – a feat of seamanship without parallel in modern naval warfare. He was given a pension as a result, created Lord Nelson of the Nile, and showered with gifts from monarchs all over Europe.

Did you know?

? On December 8 1797, Nelson quietly left a note of thanksgiving at St George's, Hanover Square, his local church, for the healing of his arm. 'An officer desires to return thanks to Almighty God for his perfect recovery from a severe wound, and also for the many mercies bestowed on him.'

? His next stop was the navy's Sick and Hurt Office at Somerset House (see page 120), to claim compensation for the loss of his arm. But he had forgotten to bring a doctor's certificate, so the clerk refused to believe him!

BROOK STREET
23 Brook Street – Jimi Hendrix

6

South side, just off New Bond Street

Like his next door neighbour, **Jimi Hendrix** was an immigrant who had come to London to further his musical career. The obscure American arrived in 1966, carrying everything he possessed in his guitar case – one Fender Stratocaster, a jar of face cream and a change of clothes. He promptly formed the Jimi Hendrix Experience and became a star almost at once.

In 1968 and 1969, Hendrix lived much of the time at No 23, the home of one of his many girlfriends. He was impressed to discover that Handel had once lived next door. He sent his girlfriend out to buy all Handel's music and was determined to do his composing here, just as Handel had done. And just as Handel had felt close to God with his 'Hallelujah Chorus' (in the *Messiah*), so Hendrix felt good when he was performing: 'When I get up on stage – well, that's my whole life. *That*'s my religion.'

A lady journalist interviewed him here for an underground newspaper.

I was very surprised that, when I got to his flat in Mayfair, he opened the door in the nude. I followed his naked torso up the stairs to the first floor. As soon as he got into the room, he got into bed. Quite a strange way to start an interview with a famous pop star – or anyone else, come to that!

Most of the interview was conducted with Jimi in bed and me sitting on the side of the bed. And on his bedside table was the biggest collection of alcohol and drugs, I mean there were three

Nos 23 and 25 Brook Street

> different types of hash, grass, amyl nitrates, pills and lots of different kinds of bourbon and whisky. We just helped ourselves…

> Then at one point he offered me some amyl nitrate and we both went out of our skulls… It was quite clear all along that if I wanted to go to bed with him, I could have just got inside. He never touched me, but it was 'understood', free and easy.

The drink and drugs took their toll. Hendrix was in the flat of another girlfriend when he overdosed in the early hours of Friday, September 18 1970. An ambulance rushed him to hospital, but he was dead on arrival. The Jimi Hendrix experience was over – at only 27.

Did you know?

? London was where it was at, in the swinging sixties. Hendrix loved the city. 'You know what really turns me on about London, just watching the girls go by – it's a fantastic city for girl watchers. They're all so beautiful and so many different nationalities.'

25 Brook Street – George Frederick Handel

> Yesterday morning [April 11 1735] my sister and I went with Mrs Donellan to Mr Handel's house to hear the first rehearsal of the new opera *Alcina*. I think it the best he ever made… 'tis so *fine* I have not words to describe it… Whilst Mr Handel was playing his part, I could not help thinking him a necromancer in the midst of his own enchantments.

Better known for his *Water Music*, **George Frederick Handel** moved into No 25 in July 1723 and remained here for the next 36 years. It is where he composed the *Messiah* and many other works. He liked to work at home, with his creature comforts around him. He held rehearsals here as well, and sold tickets to subscription concerts between the hours of 9am and 3pm.

Like his patron, George I, Handel was a German immigrant who had come to England to further his career. He was a bachelor with few interests beyond music, although he did amass a large collection of paintings, including two Rembrandts. He had a huge appetite, but, when he was composing, food left outside his door remained untouched for hours. Nothing ever came between Handel and his work.

Disaster struck him in 1752.

> We hear that George Frederick Handel Esq, the celebrated Composer of Musick was seized a few Days ago with a Paralytick Disorder in his Head, which has deprived him of Sight.

Handel gamely continued playing and composing, but his best years were over. He sought consolation in religion, often attending church at St George's, Hanover Square (just across New Bond Street), and died at home on the morning of April 14 1759.

Did you know?
? The music Handel composed for the coronation of George II in 1727 has been played at every coronation since.

? So many people wanted to attend the first performance of his *Messiah* in 1742 that gentlemen left their swords at home for the evening and ladies wore dresses without hoops to make more room.

? His house is now a small museum.

21 HANOVER SQUARE
Prince Talleyrand
Corner of Brook Street

7

For as long as anyone could remember, **Prince Talleyrand** had been one of the leading statesmen of Europe. He survived the French Revolution, served Napoleon faithfully, served the French monarchy as well, and managed to remain at the centre of politics for more than 40 years without ever losing his head or his job. In 1830, he came to London as French ambassador and crowned a glittering career as one of the most outstanding diplomats the capital had ever seen.

The centre of it all was the French embassy at 21 Hanover Square. Talleyrand's entertaining was legendary, his invitations the most sought after in London. 'Our dinners are a success,' reported his niece, who acted as his hostess. 'They mark an epoch in London's gastronomy, but the cost is ruinous.' Yet Talleyrand ignored the expense in the belief that good cooking was essential for diplomacy – especially French diplomacy.

His biggest success in London was the treaty which separated Belgium from the Netherlands, establishing it as a country in its own right. Talleyrand worked tirelessly on the treaty with his friend, the **Duke of Wellington**. He worked so hard that he was often still up at four or five o'clock in the morning and became seriously ill as a result. But he was so important to the negotiations that the conference continued at his bedside, the delegates making their way to Hanover Square to carry on the discussions in his sick room.

At long last the treaty was signed. Belgium became independent in 1831, its borders guaranteed by Britain and France. Talleyrand did not live to see Kaiser Wilhelm dismiss the treaty as 'a scrap of paper' in 1914, when he launched his troops into Belgium. But Britain and France honoured their obligations and declared war on Germany. Belgium remained independent – but millions died in the war that followed.

Did you know?
? From **Charles Greville**'s diary: 'During the period of his embassy in England I lived a good deal with Talleyrand, his house being always open to me, and I dined there *en famille* whenever I pleased. Nothing could be more hospitable, nothing more urbane and kind than he was... still retaining his faculties unimpaired, and his memory stored with the recollections of his extraordinary and eventful career, and an inexhaustible mine of anecdotes.'

? The Hanover Square music rooms have vanished under an office block now, but they were a great favourite with **Felix Mendelssohn** during his many visits to London. **Queen Victoria** came to hear him conduct his Scottish symphony on April 26 1847 and then to play Beethoven's G-major piano concerto as soloist.

7 STRATFORD PLACE
Martin Van Buren

8

Nicknamed 'Little Magician' for his political skills, **Martin Van Buren** resigned from the US cabinet in 1831 in order to prepare a bid for the presidency. Before running, though, he needed to distance himself from Washington for a while. So he sailed for England in August to serve a spell as the American ambassador in London.

There was no official embassy at the time. Van Buren rented Stratford Place because it was big enough for his needs without being too expensive. He hired seven servants and a carriage, but was careful to keep within his official budget, which was modest by the standards of other London embassies. 'I pay £300 for my carriage and about 2,600 dollars for my servants including their board in the house,' he reported home. 'We go, however, upon notions of strict economy.'

Van Buren did well in London. William IV liked him, as did the Government. He saw a lot of Prince Talleyrand, even persuading the Frenchman to speak English, something he usually refused to do. He was friendly also with the American author **Washington Irving**, who moved in with the Van Burens for a while.

But disaster struck on the morning of Monday, February 20 1832. Van Buren was ill in bed when his valet brought him the mail from America. His appointment as ambassador had not been ratified by the Senate – on the casting vote of the Vice-President. Van Buren got out of bed at once and dragged himself downstairs to join Irving and his secretary at the breakfast table. They had read the news in the morning papers and were anxiously wondering what Van Buren's reaction would be.

The king was holding a reception that evening. Van Buren forced himself to go, even though he was ill. He needed to show his face at Court, to reassure people that the United States still had an ambassador, albeit rejected by his own government.

In fact, everyone was very sympathetic. The English fully understood that Van Buren's rejection was political, rather than any reflection on his abilities. They went out of their way to be kind to him in the months that followed, pressing invitations on him before his return home. Van Buren sailed back to America in June 1832 and won the presidency four years later.

Did you know?
? Just opposite Bond Street Underground, Van Buren's old house is close to Selfridge's, D H Evans and John Lewis, Oxford Street's biggest department stores.

45 BERKELEY SQUARE
Lord Clive of India   9

Almost forgotten now, **Robert Clive** was once a great British hero – the soldier and administrator who added India to the British Empire. He made a fortune in the process and then came home to buy himself a country estate and a seat in the House of Lords.

But he also made enemies, who accused him of using British might to enrich himself at the Indians' expense. A parliamentary inquiry was held in 1773, at which Clive defended himself vigorously. He was more or less exonerated, but the strain proved too much for his sanity. He killed himself at his London home on Tuesday, November 22 1774.

> Lord Clive had long been ill – in a very nervous state – and had been warned by his physician against taking laudanum, but he would and did take it. Mr and Mrs Strachey and Miss Ducarel were at Lord Clive's house in Berkeley Square. Lord Clive went out of the room, and not returning, Mr Strachey said to Lady Clive, 'You had better go and see where my lord is.' She went to look for him and at last, opening a door, found Lord Clive with his throat cut. She fainted, and servants came. Patty Ducarel got some of the blood on her hands and licked it off.

Patty Ducarel had been with Clive minutes earlier:

> At about noon or a little later, she came into his room and said: 'Lord Clive, I cannot find a good pen; will you be so good as to make me one'. 'To be sure', replied he, and, taking a penknife from his waistcoat pocket, he moved towards one of the windows and mended the pen. The lady took it back with thanks and left the room… The weapon with which he killed himself was seen to be the same penknife.

Did you know?
? The Clive family did not want his suicide known. There was no post-mortem. Instead, his body was rushed out of the house that same afternoon and taken to his estate in Shropshire. He was buried next day in an unmarked grave so that the body could not be exhumed. To this day, no-one knows exactly where the grave lies.

3 BOLTON STREET
Henry James

10

> I have an excellent lodging in this excellent quarter – a lodging whose
> dusky charms – including a housemaid with a dark complexion, but a
> divine expression and the voice of a duchess – are too numerous to
> repeat.

Henry James moved into Bolton Street on December 12 1876. The American
was 33 and had been in France for the past year. His first novel had just been
published and he was determined to earn his living as a writer. He crossed the
Channel on December 10 and two days later had rented a cramped apartment
on the first floor of 3 Bolton Street, with a window looking out across the
street. It was a modest place, but James was perfectly content.

> When I first took up my abode in Bolton St, I had very few friends,
> the season was of the darkest and wettest; but I was in a state of deep
> delight. I had complete liberty, and the prospect of profitable work; I
> used to take long walks in the rain. I took possession of London; I felt
> it to be the right place.

James quickly made so many friends in London that he was able to dine out
almost every night. His flat was convenient for the clubs and theatres, and he
soon found work as well. He wrote *The Europeans* at Bolton Street, then *Daisy
Miller*, *Washington Square* and *The Portrait of a Lady*. He started writing soon
after he got up, then ate breakfast – he loved the English idea of bacon, eggs,
tea and toast – in the middle of the morning. He worked for another few hours
afterwards, before going out for the rest of the day, or spending the evening at
his club.

His rooms were too small for entertaining, but James did occasionally
receive visitors. His fellow American, **John Singer Sargent**, who later
painted his portrait, came to see him in July 1884, bringing the French writer
Paul Bourget with him. Bourget dedicated his most famous novel, *Cruelle
Enigme*, to James, who had introduced him to literary London and dined him
out at his club.

James' social life was so hectic that he actually enjoyed the solitude when
the social season was over and his friends returned to their country estates for
the rest of the year. London was so quiet then that James could hear the
policeman's boots creaking along Bolton Street as he lay in bed. And he loved
the sound of the postman rapping on the door in the morning, bringing the
correspondence that he so enjoyed. James stayed in Bolton Street until 1885,
when the death of his parents prompted him to move to a bigger apartment in
Kensington. He became a British citizen in 1915 and died a year later.

Did you know?

? Famous for her graphic description of a mastectomy without anaesthetic ('I
then felt the Knife rackling against the breast bone – scraping it!'), **Fanny
d'Arblay** (née **Burney**) moved to 11 Bolton Street in 1818, after the death

of her husband. In 1826, a neighbour brought **Sir Walter Scott** round to see her. They had not met before, and the old lady had not heard of Scott's lameness: 'When he limped towards a chair, she said "Dear me, Sir Walter, I hope you have not met with an accident?" He answered, "An accident, madam, nearly as old as my birth".'

WHAT NOW?

Go shopping in Bond Street or Oxford Street, stroll down to Piccadilly Circus, or cut across Green Park to Buckingham Palace. It's a longish walk to Apsley House (the Duke of Wellington's old home) at Hyde Park Corner, but you can easily take the Underground (one stop from Green Park). The house is now a museum, of interest both to military buffs – it has plenty of Napoleonic memorabilia – and lovers of early 19th-century grandeur. The present Duke of Wellington still keeps a private flat on the top floor.

Nearest public lavatories Green Park and Piccadilly Circus Undergrounds

⊖ Green Park and Piccadilly Circus

WHERE TO EAT

There are fast food places and cafés everywhere. The Ritz is just across the road, if you are Fred Astaire (and properly dressed). Also consider:

The Mirabelle 56 Curzon Street. Very up-market, with excellent food in elegant surroundings.

Chor Bizarre 16 Albemarle Street. Up-market Indian food, at an up-market price.

Mulligan's 13 Cork Street. Bar upstairs, restaurant downstairs. Good Irish food, but a wider menu as well.

The Square 6 Bruton Street. Good all-round food.

Sartoria 20 Savile Row. Once a tailor's shop, but now part of Sir Terence Conran's empire.

Momo 25 Heddon Street. Up-market Moroccan, advisable to book.

Rasa W1 6 Dering Street. Indian, non-smoking, vegetarian, but very good.

Le Caprice Arlington Street. Very fashionable, so book well in advance.

Sotheby's 34 New Bond Street. The famous auction house has a café as well. Afternoon tea the way the English do it, wines chosen by Sotheby's wine department, a strict ban on smoking and mobile phones. And plenty of *objets d'art* to bid for, if you want to browse around while you're there.

Belgravia

WALK AT A GLANCE

Features Too central to be a suburb, Belgravia is a very rich
residential area, full of embassies and smart hotels.
Time Allow ³/₄ hour.
Length I mile.
⊖ Victoria, Sloane Square

1 **Ebury Street**
  • Ian Fleming escapes a horsewhipping
  • Mozart composes his first symphony
  • Vita Sackville-West disguises herself as a man.

2 **Eaton Square**
  • Laurence Olivier prays for Vivien Leigh
  • Benjamin Disraeli and the Duke of Wellington call on Prince
    Metternich.

3 **Eaton Place**
  • W M Thackeray comes to hear Chopin play.

4 **Cadogan Place**
  • William Gladstone and Lord Macaulay call on William Wilberforce
  • King William IV sneaks round the back to avoid Mrs Jordan.

5 **Sloane Street**
  • Oscar Wilde is arrested for indecency.

EBURY STREET
22 Ebury Street – Ian Fleming
1
Victoria Station end of the street

In the days before World War II, there was only one thing for an English
gentleman to do if he discovered that his wife or his sister was being mistreated
by a cad – call round with a horsewhip and give the fellow a thrashing he
would never forget.

It was on just such a mission that Fitz Wright rang the bell at 22B one
weekend in the late 1930s. His sister Muriel was a beautiful model, one of the
first upper-class women to enter the profession. She was seeing a young man

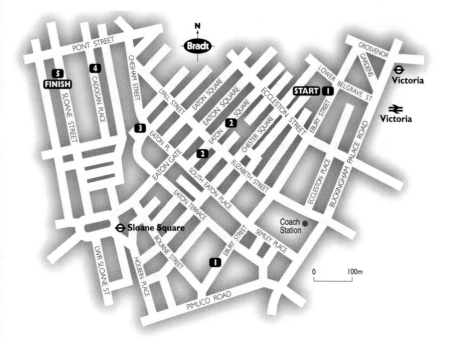

named **Ian Fleming**, who had been at Eton with Wright. Fleming's attitude to women was to treat them like dirt, but Wright wasn't having that where his sister was concerned.

Fleming had lived at 22B since 1936. It was one of four flats in a converted school. He lived at the top in a cramped apartment with a single large room, where he entertained countless girls to a dinner of champagne and sausage. After dinner, he produced his collection of French pornography – pictures of schoolmistresses standing over manacled men with whips in their hands. Then he invited them to join him in his bedroom at the end of the balcony.

Fleming was not a nice man. The sex and sadism of the James Bond novels accurately reflected his own life. He liked his women to be 'cowering slaves', sometimes whipping them so hard that towels had to be used to staunch the blood. He saw them as inferior beings, to be used and discarded at will.

It was at Ebury Street that Fleming first thought of writing a thriller. There would be a villain sitting in an armchair, and a hero who was a mix of Bulldog Drummond and the more sophisticated characters of Geoffrey Household's novels. Fleming did nothing about it until after World War II, in which he served in naval intelligence. Then he sat down early in 1952 and in a few short weeks wrote *Casino Royale,* with its extraordinary flagellation scene, the first of a long line of James Bond novels.

Did you know?

? Fleming wasn't in when Fitz Wright came to horsewhip him. Forewarned, he had taken Muriel to Brighton for the weekend.

? He bought the flat from **Sir Oswald Mosley**, leader of the British Union of Fascists. Mosley too was a compulsive womaniser. He lived with his family a few hundred yards away, but claimed he needed this flat as well to work and hold political meetings. In fact, he used it for adulterous liaisons. The bed was on a raised dais in Mosley's time, behind a curtained alcove, with warm air available at the touch of a button. Women often fell for Mosley, even if they disliked his politics.

180 Ebury Street – W A Mozart
Sloane Square end of the street

For a few weeks in the summer of 1764, the **Mozart** family rented this country house near Chelsea, two miles from London, while Wolfgang's father Leopold fought a mysterious illness that threatened to kill him. The Mozarts had been living in Soho, but they moved out to Chelsea because it was much healthier, offering Leopold his best chance of survival.

He wrote home on August 9:

> I am now in a spot outside the town, where I have been carried in a sedan chair, in order to get more appetite and fresh strength from the good air. It has one of the most beautiful views in the world.
> Wherever I look, I see only gardens and in the distance the finest castles; and the house in which I am living has a lovely garden.

The Mozarts stayed seven weeks in Ebury Street while Leopold slowly recovered. The children were forbidden to play the piano while he was ill, so young Wolfgang spent the time composing his first symphony instead. His father's appetite improved, but the local cooking was not up to much.

> We had our food sent to us at first from an eating-house; but as it was so poor, my wife began to do our cooking and we are now in such good trim that when we return to town next week we shall continue to do our own housekeeping. Perhaps too my wife, who has become very thin, will get a little fatter.

The family moved back to Soho on September 25, taking Mozart's first symphony with them.

182 Ebury Street – Harold Nicolson and Vita Sackville-West

Famous for the gardens they created at Sissinghurst castle, **Harold Nicolson** and **Vita Sackville-West** enjoyed one of the more unconventional marriages of the early 20th century. Both were bisexual and cheated on each other with members of their own sex. Their most testing moment came in 1918 when Vita fell in love with her childhood friend **Violet Keppel** (later Mrs Trefusis).

Vita dressed as a man for the affair. After dark one evening, she slipped out of the house in men's clothes with a khaki bandage round her head (a common sight during World War I) and went for a stroll along Piccadilly, smoking a cigarette and calling herself 'Julian'. She and Violet attracted so little attention that they repeated the experiment and lived together more or less openly for a while. But the affair did not last. Violet married Denys Trefusis while still seeing Vita, and for some considerable time relations between all four were difficult. But then the two women returned to their husbands and resigned themselves to married life – and gardening.

Vita later fell in love with **Virginia Woolf**, whom she met in December 1922. She immediately asked her to dinner at Ebury Street. Virginia came round and the two rapidly became close, although Woolf was never very passionate. Vita's parents lived at Knole, a magnificent stately home in Kent. Virginia often stayed there with her and later put the whole experience of Vita and Knole into her novel *Orlando*.

Did you know?

? No 182 Ebury Street belonged to Vita's mother, Lady Sackville. She also bought the Mozarts' old house next door and built connecting doors between the two. The architect **Edwin Lutyens** added a large dining-room in the garden, later destroyed in the bombing of 1940.

EATON SQUARE
54 Eaton Square – Vivien Leigh
South side of the square

2

For the last ten years of her life, the actress **Vivien Leigh** occupied a large flat here whenever she was in London. She and **Laurence Olivier** moved in in 1956, just as their marriage was breaking up. Vivien Leigh kept the flat after the divorce and died here in 1967.

The flat was lavishly appointed, as befitted a pair of superstars. There were flowers everywhere, Aubusson rugs, paintings and sketches by Degas, Cellini and Augustus John. The *pièce de résistance* was the four-poster in the bedroom, a faithful reproduction of Scarlett O'Hara's bed at Tara in *Gone with the Wind*, Vivien Leigh's most famous film.

She was already sick when she moved in. She was being treated for manic depression, a debilitating mental illness that sometimes led her to strip her clothes off in public, or have sex with the taxi-driver who had brought her home. Her marriage collapsed under the strain, although Olivier remained a good friend to the end. He gave her a Rolls-Royce as a parting gift, before going off to film *Spartacus* with Kirk Douglas and Tony Curtis.

Her other friends remained loyal as well. The playwright **Terence Rattigan** lived next door. **Noel Coward** and **Michael Redgrave** came round to see her. There were often fans outside, delivering bunches of the flowers she loved. Vivien went to Atlanta in 1961 for the centenary of the American Civil War and was mobbed on Peachtree Street by filmgoers who thought of her only as Scarlett O'Hara.

She was 53 when she died of tuberculosis. Her body was found on the bedroom floor late one night. Laurence Olivier was in hospital with cancer, but he came round early next morning, sneaking in by a side-entrance in the basement to avoid the reporters and photographers besieging the front door. 'Looking for the last time at that beautiful dead face... I stood and prayed for forgiveness for all the evils that had sprung up between us.'

That evening, Saturday, July 8 1967, all the theatres in the West End extinguished their front-of-house lights for an hour in tribute.

Did you know?

? Born in Darjeeling, Vivien Leigh was probably part-Indian. If they had known it, most American states of the redneck South would have required the woman who brought Scarlett O'Hara and Blanche DuBois to the screen to sit in the back of the bus and use the 'coloured' washroom, as being not good enough to mix with pure white folks!

44 Eaton Square – Prince Metternich
South side of the square

For more than 40 years, **Prince Metternich** was ambassador, Foreign Minister and Chancellor of Austria, one of the great European statesmen of his day. After Napoleon's defeat in 1815, he had been a leading architect of the peace treaty that brought stability to Europe for the next 30 years.

But his dislike of Napoleon and the excesses of the French Revolution had turned him into a reactionary, distrustful of any political change. He firmly opposed democracy in his own country and paid the price in 1848, when he was forced to flee the revolution in Austria and seek refuge in England.

Metternich was 75 when he arrived, and very short of money. He moved into No 44 in May and was immediately swamped with distinguished visitors coming to pay their respects. The **Duke of Wellington**, his old ally from 1815, called almost every day, although he himself was 79. **Benjamin Disraeli** called too, to learn statesmanship from a master. So did **Lord Palmerston**, an old enemy of Metternich's, coming to salute his foe. And so did the future **Kaiser of Prussia**, keen to see his father's old friend.

Metternich was touched.

> If I still had responsibilities of state, I could scarcely do justice to their performance in view of the great number of friends, old and new, who now visit our small drawing-room. People have offered to lend me whole castles and other country estates... We could not have been better received in London, if I had been John Bull in person.

Metternich admired the freedoms enjoyed by the English, but felt that similar liberties on the Continent would lead to mob rule. Unable to afford Eaton Square, he moved out in September and went to Brighton, before returning eventually to Austria. He died in 1859.

Did you know?
? Eaton Square is *Upstairs, Downstairs* territory, for anyone who remembers the 1970s soap opera.

99 EATON PLACE
Frédéric Chopin
Corner of West Eaton Place

After an early career as a singer, Adelaide Kemble married an industrialist and settled down in Eaton Place. But she retained her interest in music and it was at her London home, on June 23 1848, that **Frédéric Chopin** gave his first public performance after fleeing to England from the revolution in France.

Chopin was not a happy man. He had recently split from his mistress, the writer George Sand, and he was dying of consumption. He would much rather have been in Paris, where his heart lay. But there was no work in Paris during the revolution, so he had been forced to seek a living in England whether he wanted to or not.

He complained,

> I am not yet used to this London air and this endless round of
> visits, dinners and soirees is very hard on me. I have been spitting
> blood these last few days... The weather has been horrible and
> that does me no good at all... If only London were not so black
> and the people not so heavy and dull, and if only there were no
> sooty smell or fogs.

Chopin's first concert was not particularly successful either. **William Makepeace Thackeray** found the time to come, although he was within a week of completing *Vanity Fair*. So did **Jenny Lind**, the Swedish 'nightingale'. But Chopin was too frail to attempt anything strenuous on the piano. The reception he received was polite, rather than ecstatic. In his view, the English were philistines anyway, who did not take music seriously enough.

> These English are so different from the French... They are good and
> kind souls, but so eccentric that I quite understand that if I stayed
> here I myself could become petrified or turned into a machine.

Chopin returned to France in November and died the following year.

CADOGAN PLACE
44 Cadogan Place – William Wilberforce

All his life, **William Wilberforce** campaigned for the abolition of slavery. A committed Christian and a Member of Parliament, he saw it as his sacred duty to get the necessary legislation through Parliament. In 1807, he succeeded in getting the slave *trade* abolished in all parts of the British Empire, but the abolition of slavery altogether continued to elude him.

Wilberforce was dying in 1833 when he came to London to see his doctor. He stayed with his cousin at 44 Cadogan Place and closely followed the events at Westminster, where a bill for the abolition of slavery was having its second reading in the House of Commons.

Many people came round to keep him abreast of developments. Among them were the historian **Lord Macaulay** and a rising young politician named **William Gladstone**, who called in on Thursday, July 25. 'Went to breakfast with old Mr Wilberforce... Heard him pray with his family. Blessing and honour are upon his head.'

The bill was passed on July 26, with substantial compensation for the slave owners. Wilberforce was delighted. 'Thank God that I should have lived to witness a day in which England is willing to give 20 millions sterling for the Abolition of Slavery'. His life's work was complete. He died three days later, in the early hours of Monday, July 29.

He was buried in Westminster Abbey. The cortège from Cadogan Place was immense – a long row of carriages, and a vast crowd of mourners who accompanied the coffin along the pavement. Even among Londoners not attending the funeral, one in three wore tokens of mourning that day. West Indian slaves mourned as well, and so did free African-Americans in New York.

Did you know?

? A year later, on July 31 1834, more than 800,000 British slaves were set free. A shameful chapter in the nation's history was over.

? Among those Members of Parliament who voted against the abolition of slavery was... William Gladstone. His family fortune came from slavery.

? Wilberforce's son Sam inherited his Christian zeal. As Bishop Wilberforce, he was later a prominent opponent of Charles Darwin's decidedly non-Christian ideas about the origin of species.

30 Cadogan Place – Dora Jordan

For almost 20 years, **Dora Jordan** lived happily with the royal Duke of Clarence (later **William IV**) in a big country house near Hampton Court. She was an Irish actress of modest origin; he was a younger son of George III. Dora bore him ten children and there was never a cross word between them.

But then William decided to get married. He needed some legitimate children to ensure the royal succession and he had grown tired of Dora, who had put on weight over the years. So he dumped her in 1811 and told her to move out. Dora gathered her things together and took a lease on 30 Cadogan Place, a terrible comedown after what she had grown used to with the duke.

She was devastated at losing William. She took her mind off it by busying herself with the move, leaving herself no time to brood.

> If it was not for the bustle of endeavouring to get the house ready for the dear little ones, I should be found hanging some morning in my

garters… I would not remain a week in the Kingdom, so disgusted
am I with the whole affair.

William did at least feel guilty about his behaviour. He delivered the youngest
five children to the new house on February 7 1812, sneaking round to the back
door to avoid meeting their mother. He was a loving father and sorry to part
with the younger children. But they should stay with their mother until they
were old enough to rejoin him in high society.

Dora returned to the stage to support herself. The audience at Covent
Garden gave her a rapturous reception that brought tears to her eyes. They
were in no doubt as to who was the injured party in the breakup.

But money continued to be a problem. Dora could not really afford
Cadogan Place, particularly after her remaining children left home. Once her
12-year-old son had gone to sea with the navy, and her 15-year-old had joined
his regiment in France, there was little reason for her to stay. In 1815, she
called in an auctioneer to value the contents of the house. The man robbed
her blind, buying the furniture for a fraction of its true worth. Dora went to
France to escape her creditors and died miserably in 1816. William became
king in 1830.

Did you know?

? Dora was universally liked, as William Hazlitt observed. 'Her face, her tears,
her manners were irresistible. Her smile had the effect of sunshine, and her
laugh did one good to hear it… She was all gaiety, openness and good nature.
She rioted in her fine animal spirits.'

CADOGAN HOTEL, SLOANE STREET
Oscar Wilde

5

Corner of Pavilion Street

Time was fast running out for **Oscar Wilde** on the afternoon of April 5 1895.
He had lost a libel action that morning against the **Marquess of
Queensberry**, during which he had been revealed as an active homosexual, a
crime then punishable by two years in prison. It was only a matter of hours
before the police came and took him away.

The playwright holed up in the Cadogan Hotel
while he pondered his next move. His friends
Robbie Ross and Reggie Turner urged him to
escape to France while there was still
time. The authorities were
deliberately delaying his arrest for a
few hours to give him a chance to
get away. A half-packed suitcase lay on
the bed. All he had to do was catch the boat
train for Dover and make his escape before
the police arrived with a warrant for his
arrest.

But Wilde refused to go. He was not the kind to run away. A combination of inertia and an Irish desire for martyrdom prompted him to stay and face the music instead. 'I shall stay and do my sentence, whatever it is,' he insisted to his friends. **Lord Alfred Douglas** arrived and pleaded with him to go, but Wilde was adamant. He would take the rap and to hell with the lot of them.

The men in bowler hats arrived at ten past six. A waiter showed them to Wilde's room on the first floor (then 120, now 118). He had been drinking all afternoon and was unsteady on his feet as they entered. 'We have a warrant here, Mr Wilde, for your arrest on a charge of committing indecent acts.'

Wilde went quietly. 'If I must go, I will give you the least possible trouble.' He asked if he would be given bail. The detectives didn't think so. They led him outside and took him in a cab to Bow Street police station. He was found guilty as charged and given the maximum sentence of two years' imprisonment with hard labour.

Did you know?

? Even Wilde's sworn enemy, the Marquess of Queensberry, wanted him to escape to France. 'I will not prevent your flight, but if you take my son with you, I will shoot you like a dog.'

? The boat train to Dover was packed for days after Wilde's arrest. Homosexuals left the country in droves, most heading for France, where it wasn't a crime.

? During his prison sentence, Wilde was transferred to Reading Gaol by train. A jeering crowd recognised him on the platform at Clapham Junction and taunted him for half an hour. One man spat in his face. 'For a year after that was done to me, I wept every day at the same hour and for the same space of time.'

WHAT NOW?

Harrod's department store is 400 yards from the Cadogan Hotel. Go north along Sloane Street, turn left at Hans Crescent. Harrod's have a dress code, so if you have a backpack, they will ask you to take it off and carry it in your hand.

Harvey Nichols department store is at the end of Sloane Street, on the corner of Knightsbridge, with Hyde Park beyond.

The Science Museum, the Natural History Museum and the Victoria & Albert Museum are half a mile from the Cadogan Hotel. Go west along Pont Street, continue up Beauchamp Place, turn left along the Brompton Road towards Cromwell Gardens.

Peter Jones department store is at Sloane Square, 500 yards south from the Cadogan Hotel along Sloane Street. The store stands on the corner of the King's Road, where the beautiful people used to hang out in the 1960s. The King's Road is not as fashionable as it used to be, but still worth a look.

South of Sloane Square, Lower Sloane Street leads to Royal Hospital Road on the right. The Royal Hospital was designed by Sir Christopher Wren in the 17th century to house the old soldiers known as Chelsea Pensioners. Next to it, the National Army Museum is worth a visit for anyone interested in the British army (but don't confuse it with the Imperial War Museum, south of the river on Lambeth Road, a real 'must see' for war enthusiasts).

Nearest public lavatories Sloane Square, Victoria railway station

⊖ Knightsbridge, Sloane Square, Victoria

WHERE TO EAT
Harrod's department store is full of restaurants, as are the streets around it. There are plenty of boulevard places along the King's Road. Otherwise:

Zafferano 15 Lowndes Street. Very good Italian food, but you probably need to book.

Osteria d'Isola 145 Knightsbridge. Italian again. Two restaurants at the same address, one smart and formal, the other less so.

The Fifth Floor Harvey Nichols, corner of Knightsbridge and Sloane Street. Up-market fashion store with several eating places attached. The Fifth Floor is smart, expensive and very fashionable, but the store also has a café, sushi bar and more.

Bloomsbury and the British Museum

WALK AT A GLANCE

Features Once famed for its literary connotations, Bloomsbury is a residential area dominated by the British Museum and University College.
Time Allow half an hour for the walk, anything up to 3 hours for the British Museum.
Length I mile.
⊖ Tottenham Court Road, Russell Square, Euston Square, Warren Street, Goodge Street

1 Bedford Square
- Virginia Woolf meets Winston Churchill
- Lytton Strachey falls for Nijinsky
- Lady Ottoline Morrell is betrayed by D H Lawrence.

2 Gower Street
- Charlie Chaplin comes to tea
- Maynard Keynes is disturbed by a Zeppelin raid.

3 British Museum
- Casanova and the Mozarts look round
- Karl Marx writes *Das Kapital*
- Lenin takes Gorky on a guided tour.

4 Russell Square
- Charles Dickens passes through
- George Orwell offers *Animal Farm* to T S Eliot.

5 Gordon Square
- Virginia Woolf moves in, the Bloomsbury Group follow
- Lydia Lopokova dances
- Pablo Picasso fails to dress
- Lytton Strachey gets his cocoa.

6 Woburn Walk
- W B Yeats discovers sex
- Maude Gonne looks somewhat out of place.

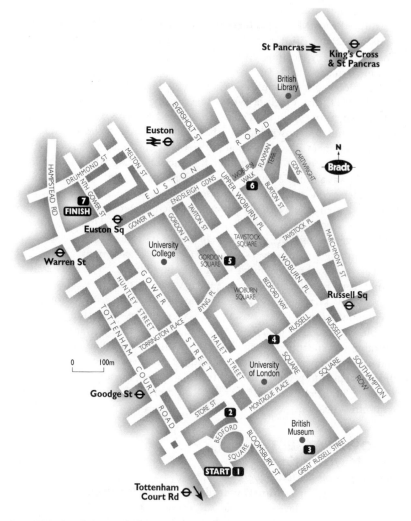

St Pancras ⇌

King's Cross
& St Pancras

British
Library ●

Euston ⇌ Ө

N

Bradt

7
FINISH

Euston Sq Ө

Warren St

EVERSHOLT ST

EUSTON ROAD

ENDSLEIGH GDNS

UPPER WOBURN PL

WOBURN WALK

FLAXMAN TERR

BURTON ST

CARTWRIGHT GDNS

HAMPSTEAD RD

DRUMMOND ST

NTH GOWER ST

MELTON ST

GOWER PL

TAVITON ST

GORDON ST

6

University
College ●

GORDON
SQUARE **5**

TAVISTOCK
SQUARE

TAVISTOCK PL

WOBURN PL

MARCHMONT ST

Russell Sq Ө

GOWER STREET

HUNTLEY STREET

BYNG PL

WOBURN
SQUARE

BEDFORD WAY

4

RUSSELL SQUARE

RUSSELL SQUARE

TOTTENHAM COURT ROAD

TORRINGTON PLACE

MALET STREET

University
of London ●

SOUTHAMPTON ROW

0   100m

Goodge St Ө

STORE ST

MONTAGUE PLACE

2

BLOOMSBURY ST

British
Museum ●

3

GREAT RUSSELL STREET

START 1

**Tottenham
Court Rd** Ө ↓

7   **North Gower Street**
     • Giuseppe Mazzini's maid meets his mummy.

44 BEDFORD SQUARE
Lady Ottoline Morrell
South side

1

Soon after his election to Parliament in 1906, Philip and **Lady Ottoline Morrell** acquired this handsome town house in what was then a Bohemian part of London. Morrell went off to the House of Commons every day while Lady Ottoline established a literary salon in the two drawing-rooms on the first floor. Her Thursday evening parties soon became a magnet for all the artists and writers of her generation. Everyone came, from **Henry James**, **Augustus John**, **Bertrand Russell** and **Max Beerbohm** to **Hilaire Belloc**, the future Prime Ministers **Herbert Asquith** and **Ramsay MacDonald**, the poets **Yeats** and **Eliot**, and the Russian ballet stars **Sergei Diaghilev** and **Vaslav Nijinsky** (fighting off the advances of **Lytton Strachey** in a purple suit and orange stock).

The Bloomsbury set came as well. It was at one of the Morrells' parties, on May 18 1911, that **Virginia Woolf** met a rising politician named **Winston Churchill**, 'very rubicund all gold lace and medals on his way to Buckingham Palace'. Churchill was going to a ball, but he dined at the Morrells first, entertaining them all with his political gossip at the dinner table.

It was here too that Lady Ottoline first met **D H Lawrence** in December 1914. He was a miner's son and she was the sister of a duke, but they took to each other at once. Lawrence was fascinated by the possibility of a working man having an affair with an aristocrat, a theme later explored in his most notorious novel, *Lady Chatterley's Lover*. Ottoline introduced him to her friends and did everything in her power to help further his career. Lawrence rewarded her by putting her in a novel – not *Lady Chatterley's Lover*, but *Women in Love*.

'I have got a long way with my novel,' he told her on May 24 1916. 'It comes very rapidly and is very good'. What he didn't say was that the character of Hermione Roddice was closely based on Lady Ottoline, and deeply unflattering. 'She was rich... yet macabre, something repulsive. People were silent when she passed, impressed, roused, wanting to jeer.' Ottoline was mortified when she read the manuscript. She moved heaven and earth to prevent its publication, and for whatever reason *Women in Love* did not appear in print until 1921. It was another 12 years, when both were seriously ill, before she and Lawrence could bring themselves to be civil to each other again.

3 GOWER STREET
John Maynard Keynes

2

No 3 is just off Bedford Square

During World War I, **John Maynard Keynes** lived briefly in a ground floor flat at No 3, while working as an economist at the Treasury. **Dora Carrington**, then an art student, lived above him, while the top floor was occupied by the writer **Katherine Mansfield** and her future husband John Middleton Murray.

In September 1915, Keynes and his secretary, Miss Chapman, were at work one night when a German air raid began:

> As I write, Zeppelin bombs are dropping all around, about one every minute and a half I should say, and the flashes and explosions are terrifying. I am much more frightened than I thought I should be. Miss Chapman is sitting with me in the dining room, which we have decided is safest – I don't know why. She doesn't seem in the least nervous and spends her time soothing Rex [a dog]. I daresay we shall find in the morning that the bombs have not been within a mile of us; but it does seem very near.

Did you know?

? In later years, **Lady Ottoline Morrell** sold her grand house in Bedford Square and moved around the corner to a more economical 'doll's house' at 10 Gower Street (across the road from Keynes). Her parties were not as lavish as before, but she did have **Charlie Chaplin** to tea late in 1931. All the servants found an excuse to enter the drawing-room and gape at the movie star as he sat there wondering what to make of **Lytton Strachey** and **Augustus John**.

BRITISH MUSEUM
Great Russell Street **3**

The British Museum opened to the public in 1759 and has been on the same site ever since, although the present building dates only from the 1840s. It was very popular from the start, with foreigners as well as native Londoners. **Giacomo Casanova** came to see it in 1763 ('He had to go to the Museum, and my curiosity to see the famous collection which is such an honour to England made me accompany him'). The **Mozart** family came a year later, as Wolfgang's older sister noted in her diary:

> British museum, where I saw the library, antiquities, all sorts of birds, fish, insects and fruits; a special bird called a basson, a rattlesnake, a film of bark and hair from the fibre of a bark; a Chinese shoe, a model of the tomb in Jerusalem; all sorts of things that grow in the sea, stones, indian balsam, the globe of the world and the globe of the heavens, and all sorts of other things.

Less impressed was **Vladimir Ilich Lenin**, who brought **Maxim Gorky** to see the museum in 1907.

> One of those present told how, while showing them the treasures, Lenin 'called this Museum a hoard of colossal wealth plundered by Britain from its colonies. He said that this establishment was invaluable for studying the entire process of the development of capitalism.'

SOME OF THE MUSEUM'S HIGHLIGHTS

Egyptian mummies Coffins, funerary equipment, 2,000-year-old portraits that could have been done yesterday.

Rosetta Stone An ancient tablet discovered in Egypt in 1799. It has a long inscription on it in three languages – Greek, demotic and Egyptian hieroglyph. Hieroglyphs had been a mystery until then, but the parallel text in Greek enabled scholars to make a start on deciphering the code.

Rameses II Statue of the Egyptian pharoah, so imposing that it inspired **Percy Shelley** to write one of his most intriguing poems in 1818. 'My name is Ozymandias, king of kings: Look on my works, ye Mighty, and despair!'

Oxus treasure Gold bracelets, models of chariots and horses from the Near East, 400BC.

Mausoleum of Halikarnossos Ancient Greek sculptures from one of the Seven Wonders of the World.

Parthenon sculptures Known also as the Elgin marbles, because Lord Elgin retrieved them from the Parthenon, which had fallen into disrepair, and gave them to the museum for safekeeping in 1816. The Greek government now wants them back, but the British won't oblige, for fear of setting a precedent.

> It was not the museum that attracted Lenin, but 'the world's richest library', Krupskaya stresses.

Be that as it may, the museum does have more than six million items from all over the globe. It is one of the world's great collections and can overwhelm a first-time visitor. If you're not sure how to proceed, you could begin by taking the museum's highlights tour. This lasts 90 minutes and provides a quick glimpse of some of the treasures on offer. After that, you can proceed on your own or come back another day.

Reading Room
Museum courtyard

For almost 150 years, the round Reading Room had a copy of virtually every book printed in the English language, and many others as well. Countless famous people came to consult works that they couldn't find anywhere else. Among them was **Karl Marx**, who came almost every day for nearly 30 years. He wrote several books in the Reading Room, including *Das Kapital* between 1863 and 1865. The desk at which he wrote is still there today.

Which desk was it? That's a question that **Lenin** asked on May 10 1905, when he brought a party of Bolsheviks here on a pilgrimage. The answer is that Marx did not reserve a particular seat and sat wherever he could find a

Portland vase Beautifully crafted Roman cameo glass from the 1st century AD.

Roman gladiator's helmet Forget Hollywood, this is the real thing.

Lindow Man The top half of an ancient Briton, preserved in a peat bog until his discovery in 1978. He had been ritually strangled in prehistoric times and still has the rope round his neck to prove it. There's only half of him because he had been sliced in two by a peat-cutting machine before the driver noticed. He is known, for obvious reasons, as Pete Marsh.

Neolithic trackway The oldest in Europe. A section of wooden road built across a Somerset marsh around 3,800BC.

Sutton Hoo ship burial Anglo-Saxon longship from around AD625. Excavated in 1939, it contained a hoard of treasure, including a terrifying iron helmet.

Lewes chessmen Set of walrus ivory chess pieces, used by Vikings in the Outer Hebrides.

Voyages of discovery Vancouver's collection from northwest America in the 17th century, **Captain Cook**'s from the South Seas in the 18th.

And of course much, much more...

place. The books he used were shelved on open access near rows K to P, so he probably sat there rather than anywhere else.

As for Lenin himself, the answer is much easier. Under an assumed name, he reserved a seat to study the 'land question' and sat usually at L13.

Did you know?

? Built in what was then the museum courtyard, the Reading Room was opened in 1857 to house an ever-increasing flow of books that could no longer be accommodated elsewhere. The idea was that books should be available on reasonable demand to anyone who wanted to read them, including poor people seeking to improve themselves by self-education.

? Today, the courtyard has been glassed over and the books – all 12 million of them – have been moved to the British Library, a state-of-the-art new building at St Pancras that opened in

British Museum

1998.The Library houses **Magna Carta** and many other interesting manuscripts (see list at end under *What now?*, page 184).

? Among the distinguished foreigners who have worked in the Reading Room: **Louis Blanc, Friedrich Engels, Washington Irving, Muhammad Ali Jinnah, Minakata Kumegusu, Giuseppe Mazzini, Samuel Morse, G V Plekhanov, Ezra Pound, Mario Praz, Arthur Rimbaud, José Rizal, Gertrude Stein, Hippolyte Taine, Leon Trotsky, Mark Twain, Simone Weil, Sun Yat-Sen.**

? And the Brits: **Sam Beckett, Rupert Brooke, Wilkie Collins, Joseph Conrad, Charles Darwin, Charles Dickens, Benjamin Disraeli, Sir Arthur Conan Doyle, George Eliot, Michael Faraday, W S Gilbert, Sir Henry Rider Haggard, Thomas Hardy, Gustav Holst, Aldous Huxley, Rudyard Kipling, George Orwell, Bertrand Russell, G B Shaw, Bram Stoker, W M Thackeray, Anthony Trollope, Evelyn Waugh, H G Wells, Oscar Wilde.**

24 RUSSELL SQUARE
T S Eliot
Corner of Thornhaugh Street

4

> By the waters of Leman I sat down and wept.

First published in 1922, *The Waste Land* established **T S Eliot**'s reputation as the most avant-garde poet of his generation. It was an astonishing jumble of words, the work of a deeply unhappy man whose personal life was in chaos. Eliot's wife was mentally ill and his marriage a disaster. It was in these unpromising circumstances that one of the most extraordinary poems of the 20th century was written.

From 1925 until his death 40 years later, Eliot worked as a publisher at Faber and Faber's office in Russell Square. His own office was on the second floor, with a picture of Virginia Woolf on the mantelpiece and a view of Woburn Square through the window. He and his wife lived separately from 1932, but she continued to plague him at the office because that was the only place she could be sure of finding him. She often turned up in a state of hysteria, weeping bitterly and demanding to see him, while the receptionists claimed that Eliot was out or in a meeting. Sometimes she stood outside with a sandwich-board proclaiming 'I am the wife that T S Eliot abandoned'. Faber's secretaries soon learned to distract her attention long enough for Eliot to slip outside and beat a hasty retreat.

His wife was committed to a mental hospital in 1938. Eliot continued to work at Faber, a restrained figure, known to his colleagues as 'the Pope of Russell Square'. He did however celebrate his American origins by letting off firecrackers in the board room on the Fourth of July.

During World War II, Eliot often slept at the office on Tuesday nights, when he was on fire-watching duty. The office was bombed, so he was sympathetic in June 1944 when a fellow author sent him a 'crumpled' manuscript to read. The author too had been bombed and had had to retrieve his dog-eared manuscript from the rubble of his living room. The author was **George Orwell**. The manuscript was *Animal Farm*.

Eliot rejected it at once. He didn't think much of a book about pigs. With Britain and Russia fighting the Germans, it was a bad time to be rude about Communism. Chastened, Orwell dusted the work off again and tried elsewhere. *Animal Farm* was published in August 1945 and has never been out of print.

Did you know?

? Faber may have rejected *Animal Farm*, but they had better luck with one of Eliot's own books, a collection of verse entitled *Old Possum's Book of Practical Cats*. Get rid of the clunky title, bring in Andrew Lloyd Webber to write the score… before long, they had a hit musical on their hands.

? T S Eliot won the Nobel Prize in 1948.

? He was not responsible for the following palindrome, allegedly uttered by an American visitor to Russell Square: 'Was it Eliot's toilet I saw?'

? As a boy, **Charles Dickens** used to pass through the square on his way to work at a blacking factory: 'I see myself coming across Russell Square from Somers Town, one morning, with some cold hotch-potch in a small basin tied up in a handkerchief…'

GORDON SQUARE
46 Gordon Square – Virginia Woolf, J M Keynes
East side of the square

Bloomsbury was the name given to the self-regarding band of aesthetes who lived in this part of London in the early decades of the last century. The first to arrive was the writer **Virginia Woolf** (then Miss Stephen), who moved in to No 46 in 1904 with her three siblings. Her brother had been a member of the Apostles at Cambridge and continued to host Thursday evening discussions at No 46. From these Thursday and then Friday gatherings the Bloomsbury Group slowly evolved.

Virginia's room was at the top of the house, overlooking the plane trees in the square.

> We take chairs and sit on our balcony after dinner, and watch the servant girls giggling with waiters in the shade of the trees. Really Gordon Square with the lamps lit and the light on the green is a romantic place.

Virginia lived here until 1907, when her sister **Vanessa** got married and took over the whole house. She then moved to Fitzroy Square with her surviving brother.

A ROUGH GUIDE TO THE BLOOMSBURY GROUP IN GORDON SQUARE

No 37 Painter **Duncan Grant** occasionally lived here with **Vanessa Bell** (Virginia Woolf's sister) after she left her husband, **Clive Bell**.

No 41 James Strachey (brother of Lytton) lived with his wife **Alix** on the top floor. **Lytton Strachey**, the artist **Dora Carrington** and her husband **Ralph Partridge** also had rooms. In 1922, Russian ballet dancer **Lydia Lopokova** occupied the ground-floor flat before her marriage to **Maynard Keynes**. The whole house shook when she practised her *entrechats* (a leap while drumming your heels together).

No 42 Oliver Strachey (Lytton's brother) lived here with his daughter Julia in 1925.

No 46 Virginia Woolf arrived in 1904 with her siblings **Thoby, Adrian** and **Vanessa Stephen**. The first three moved out when Vanessa married **Clive Bell** in 1907. **Maynard Keynes** later moved in and lived with his friend, **Duncan Grant**. Grant subsequently left Keynes and went off with Vanessa. Keynes stayed and married **Lydia Lopokova**. **Lytton Strachey** felt left out.

No 50 Adrian Stephen (brother of Virginia Woolf) lived here after his marriage. Their sister Vanessa moved in with her children in 1919. Virginia often came to stay.

No 51 Lytton Strachey's family lived here from 1919 to 1963. Lytton lived on the second floor until 1928, in a ground-floor flat thereafter.

A later occupant of No 46 was the economist **John Maynard Keynes**, easily the most distinguished of all the Bloomsbury Group. He took over the lease in 1916, although Vanessa and her husband still retained rooms in the house. Bloomsbury's parties were so avant garde by then that Keynes was once rumoured to have made love to Vanessa on a sofa in front of everybody – hard to believe, since Keynes was in love with the artist **Duncan Grant**, and it was Grant who eventually went off with Vanessa!

In 1919, Keynes gave a party here for **Sergei Diaghilev**'s Russian ballet company, which was doing a season in London. Among the guests were **Pablo Picasso** (who didn't bother with evening dress) and the company's prima ballerina **Lydia Lopokova**, whom Keynes later married.

Did you know?

? Virginia Woolf, revisiting No 46 in 1908: 'It was a spring evening. Vanessa and I were sitting in the drawing room… Suddenly the door opened, and the long sinister figure of Mr **Lytton Strachey** stood on the threshold. He pointed his finger at a stain on Vanessa's white dress. "Semen?" he said. Can one really say it? I thought, and we burst out laughing. With that word all the barriers of reticence and reserve went down... Sex permeated our conversation. The word bugger was never far from our lips.'

? Virginia Woolf again: 'Gordon Square is like nothing so much as the lion's house at the zoo. One goes from cage to cage. All the animals are dangerous, rather suspicious of one another, and full of fascination and mystery. I'm sometimes too timid to go in at 46 Gordon Square and trail along the pavement, looking in at the windows.'

50 Gordon Square

This is where **Virginia Woolf**'s brother **Adrian Stephen** lived after his marriage. He was joined in 1919 by their sister Vanessa, who had returned to London so that her boys could go to school. She and the children occupied the top two floors. Virginia Woolf was a frequent visitor, often staying the night after parties.

She attended a party at No 46 early in January 1923 and then went to bed at No 50, only to be woken later by the cries of a woman. Putting her false teeth in to investigate, she discovered that Vanessa's husband was making noisy love to his mistress next door.

At another party at No 50, the Bloomsbury Group simulated copulation on stage with a performance of Schnitzler's *La Ronde*. **Ralph Partridge**'s groans were so realistic that everyone felt slightly sick. **Leonard Woolf** went home afterwards and thought seriously of committing suicide.

At yet another party here, a young man fell off the roof and was killed. Perhaps he had had enough of the Bloomsbury Group.

Did you know?

? From 1924 to 1939, Virginia Woolf's London base was 52 Tavistock Square (100 yards east of Gordon Square), where she lived with her husband Leonard and ran the Hogarth Press. The house was bombed in 1940 and the site is now occupied by the Tavistock Hotel.

51 Gordon Square – Lytton Strachey

This was the Strachey family home from 1919 to 1963. Their most eminent son was **Lytton Strachey**, the homosexual biographer who refused compulsory military service to fight in World War I. Asked by a tribunal what he would do if he saw a German soldier attempting to rape his sister, he memorably replied: 'I should try and come between them'.

To begin with, Lytton only stayed here during the university term, occupying his sister's second-floor room while she was away at Cambridge.

After his mother's death in 1928, he took over her ground-floor rooms and turned them into a self-contained flat. An Italian visitor was not impressed.

> It would be hard to imagine a house more middle-class and more
> 19th century. Victorian lithographs adorned the walls of the entrance
> hall, and the maid wore a crest of tulle; by the side of the twin pillars
> was to be found the classic tablet listing the various members of the
> family with the captions 'In' and 'Out'.

Lytton's personal rooms were just as bad.

> It was as if one had stepped into a page of a Victorian novel. A Louis
> Philippe divan, a few books on a windowsill, a small desk, more lady-
> like than one would associate with an extremely successful author…
> Behind the muslin by the windows, the pale green of the trees of
> Gordon Square could be discerned in the setting sun.

One of the servants brought Strachey a cup of cocoa every midday without fail. His enemies tartly observed that he was never far from a cup of tea or a glass of lemonade. He retired to the country at weekends, living in a bizarre threesome with the artist **Dora Carrington** and her husband **Ralph Partridge**. He died of cancer in 1932 and Carrington shot herself seven weeks later.

5 WOBURN WALK
W B Yeats

6

He won the Nobel Prize in 1923, but for much of his life **W B Yeats** was penniless, an impoverished Irish poet struggling to make ends meet as best he could. In 1896,

he moved into two rooms on the top floor of 5 Woburn Walk (then 18 Woburn Buildings). The 30-year-old Yeats had never had a place of his own before, but he had fallen in love with a married woman and wanted somewhere to be alone with her. He lost his virginity to her soon after moving in, but found the experience so stressful that the relationship soon fizzled out.

A friend came to see him in October 1900:

> Not far from Woburn Place, you turn down a side street and come to
> a long, narrow door, next to a cobbler's shop, on the post of which is
> a tiny brass plate, beneath a bell inscribed with the name 'W B Yeats'.
> You ring and wait until you hear steps coming down some squeaking,
> creaking stairs; the door opens and there is Mr Yeats waiting to
> receive you with all the courtesy and stateliness of the grand school…
> You shake his long bony hand delicately – it might break, it feels so
> brittle – and follow his long, thin figure, dressed in black, up the
> narrow wooden staircase, which goes winding round and round, until
> the topmost storey is reached.

Here you are ushered into a large room hung about with Blake's engravings of Dante, a Rossetti, some Beardsleys, and others of a mystical character. The window overlooks the tops of the little shops opposite and a tree or two, for the street is a poor one, where humble folk live and work and children swarm, where there is no carriage-way and foot passengers alone can pass, it is so narrow. A street of the poor, and so in harmony with the tender, sad strain of so much of Yeats' poetry.

Yeats later rented more rooms in the house and held regular Monday evening parties for his friends. Everyone came, from **G B Shaw** and **Lady Gregory** (who secretly left money for Yeats behind the teapot), to the young **Rupert Brooke** and **Ezra Pound**. A particular guest was **Maud Gonne**, the Irish revolutionary:

No taxis or motor cars then, and her chariot was an old four-wheeler. It was her first visit to that strange slummy little court behind St Pancras Church… It was a wretched wet black winter's night, and Yeats had arranged a small party to meet her and darted out of his doorway in the rain to receive his guest at the end of the court. As she dismounted in dismay, a tall stately figure in green gown, a gold torque round her neck, a troop of dirty little urchins had gathered from nowhere attracted by this lovely 'lidy' and called out shrilly for half-pennies.

Gonne was fond of Yeats, yet always refused to marry him. Instead, he married George Hyde-Lees in October 1917 and briefly set up home with her at Woburn Walk. But the German Zeppelin raids were so heavy that the newly-weds moved to Oxford after a few weeks and never returned.

Did you know?

? Woburn Walk has smartened up since Yeats' time. It's very pretty and quaint – the nicest street on this walk. You can sit outside Yeats' house and have a coffee while the world passes by.

? The British Library (Magna Carta etc) is a few hundred yards away, across the Euston Road.

183 NORTH GOWER STREET
Giuseppe Mazzini

7

Opposite Euston Street

Sentenced to death at home, the Italian republican **Giuseppe Mazzini** fled abroad to Switzerland, then to England after the Swiss refused to tolerate him any longer. He lived in England for a total of 25 years – most of his remaining life – ending up more English than the English themselves. He even missed the bad weather when at last he was allowed to return to his native land!

The President of Young Italy arrived in 1837 and for the first three years lived at 183 North Gower Street (then 9 George Street). He shared the house with several other Italians and kept warm by going to the British Museum, where he made friends with **Antonio Panizzi**, a fellow refugee under sentence of death. Sir Anthony Panizzi, as he later became, was on the museum staff and was largely responsible for the design of the round Reading Room. He had abandoned his revolutionary principles by 1837 and was embarrassed by Mazzini's republicanism. Mazzini even wore a moustache, clear sign of a dangerous radical, and refused all requests to shave it off.

He tried to support himself by journalism, but worked also as an importer of olive oil, salami, pasta, antiques, even an Egyptian mummy. The mummy was intended for the museum, but was so badly damaged on arrival that Mazzini kept it at home. It frightened away one of his servants, who swore she had seen it move and declined to stay in the house a moment longer.

Mazzini made many English friends, among them the novelist George Meredith, the historian Thomas Carlyle, and the philosopher John Stuart Mill, who invited him home to dinner. Mazzini could not afford the cab fare, so he had to walk four miles there and four miles back – a long way to go for English cooking ('a bit of fish or chicken which I do not like'). He made friends with other Italians as well, starting a school for Italian children and receiving free opera tickets from Italian singers in the cast.

Mazzini left North Gower Street in 1840 and moved to Chelsea. He did not live to see an Italian republic, but he did at least prepare the way for Cavour and Garibaldi to establish a united Italy.

WHAT NOW?

The British Library, 96 Euston Road (next to St Pancras railway station), is an unprepossessing building from the outside, but splendid within. You can have lunch there while admiring its treasures, which include:

Lindisfarne Gospels Decorated book-paintings from the 7th century.

Anglo-Saxon Chronicle Earliest known history of England written in English, 9th century.

Magna Carta Charter of concessions wrested from King John in 1215.

Codex Sinaiticus Earliest complete manuscript of the New Testament, Greek, 4th century.

Million Charms of Empress Shotoku Buddhist mantras printed in Japan in the 8th century.

Sultan Baybars' Koran Produced in Cairo, 1304.

Golden Haggadah Hebrew service-book from 1320.

Beowulf Only surviving medieval manuscript of this Old English poem, 11th century.

Gutenberg Bible Earliest full-scale work printed in Europe with moveable type, 1454–55.

Leonardo da Vinci's notebook Written in mirror writing, right to left.

Lady Jane Grey's prayerbook Carried by her to the scaffold (see page 67), with her own writing in it.

Shakespeare's First Folio Collected edition of 36 plays, half never published before, 1623.

The Duke's Plan of New York Map of the city, 1664.

Mozart's Thematic Catalogue A list of his compositions, in his own hand, 1791.

Nelson Memorandum Nelson's strategy for Trafalgar, in his own hand, 1805.

Jane Eyre A fair copy in Charlotte Brontë's handwriting, 1847.

Alice's Adventures Under Ground Autograph manuscript and drawings by Lewis Carroll, 1862–64.

The Beatles The lyrics to *I want to hold your hand*, by Paul McCartney.

Also near by is Dickens House, where **Charles Dickens** wrote *Oliver Twist* and most of *Nicholas Nickleby*. The house is open to the public at 48 Doughty Street, just under half a mile east from Russell Square, along Guilford Street.

Nearest public lavatories Russell Square, British Museum, Euston railway station

✪ Tottenham Court Road, Russell Square, Euston Square, Warren Street, Goodge Street

WHERE TO EAT

Fancy a Virginia Woolfburger? Try the Virginia Woolf Burger Bar and Grill at the Hotel Russell, Russell Square. The British Museum has two cafés and a restaurant that stays open in the evenings Thursday–Saturday. Across the road from the front entrance, the Museum Tavern often played host to **Karl Marx** (who once smashed five gaslights along the Tottenham Court Road after a boozy night out). Otherwise try:

Malabar Junction 107 Great Russell Street. Indian food from Kerala, served up from two separate kitchens, one strictly vegetarian.
The Mandeer 8 Bloomsbury Way. Indian vegetarian, cheap but good.
Wagamama 4 Streatham Street. Japanese, but everybody has to sit together.

The City

WALK AT A GLANCE

Features Heavily bombed during the Blitz, London's financial district has been rebuilt in a variety of styles, but still has enough old buildings to make a walk worthwhile.

Time Allow one hour for the City, longer if you continue across the river towards Shakespeare's Globe.

Length ½ mile.

Θ Bank, Mansion House

1 Guildhall
- Lady Jane Grey is sentenced to death
- Frédéric Chopin gives his last concert
- Herman Melville is shocked by the poverty.

2 Mansion House
- Charles Dickens looks in at the food
- Marshal Soult receives a rapturous welcome.

3 Royal Exchange
- Voltaire is impressed, and so are the Mozarts.

4 Cornhill
- Ebenezer Scrooge counts his money
- the Brontë sisters reveal their sex to a startled publisher.

5 George & Vulture inn
- Charles Dickens invites his friends to dinner, as does Mr Pickwick.

6 Monument
- Thomas Farriner accidentally burns London down
- Samuel Pepys looks on in horror.

GUILDHALL
Lady Jane Grey, Frédéric Chopin, Herman Melville
Gresham Street

Lady Jane Grey was only 16 when her father had her proclaimed Queen of England after the death of her cousin Edward VI. She ruled for nine difficult days and then stood down in favour of Queen Mary, the legitimate successor.

Mary kept her locked in the Tower of London until November 13 1553, when she was summoned to the Guildhall to stand trial on a charge of high treason.

Several others were tried at the same time. They were brought from the Tower on foot, winding their way through the streets while a sympathetic crowd watched in silence. An executioner's axe was carried in front of them as a brutal reminder of the penalty for treason.

It was a grim procession that arrived at the Guildhall. **Thomas Cranmer**, Protestant Archbishop of Canterbury, came first, walking immediately behind the axe. Jane's 17-year-old husband, **Lord Guildford Dudley**, came next, and then Jane herself, with her two gentlewomen following behind. She was so small that the others towered over her as they entered the hall and took their places for the trial.

> The lady Jane was in a black gowne of cloth, tourned downe; the cappe lyned with fese velvett, and edget about with the same, in a French hoode, all black, with a black byllment, a black velvet boke hanging before hir, and another boke in hir hande, open.

Jane was asked how she pleaded. In as firm a voice as she could manage, she admitted her guilt. There was never any doubt what the sentence would be. Archbishop Cranmer was later burned at the stake. Jane and her husband trudged despondently back to the Tower and were beheaded there the following February (see page 67).

Did you know?

? The City of London has been governed from the Guildhall for more than 800 years. The walls, porch and crypt of the present building date from 1430, but the roof has been replaced several times since then, notably after the Great Fire of 1666 and the Blitz of 1940, which left the interior completely gutted.

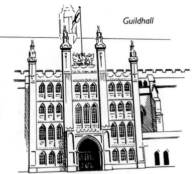

Guildhall

? The hall is used for important civic functions, such as state banquets and the annual installation of a new Lord Mayor of London. The **Tsar of Russia** and the **King of Prussia** were the City's guests at the Guildhall during the peace celebrations of 1814. **Frédéric Chopin** gave his last English recital in a side room on November 16 1848, raising money for Polish refugees. The Guildhall museum has a very rare example of **William Shakespeare**'s signature, attached to the property deed when he bought a house in Blackfriars. It is kept in the strong room and is not normally on show to the public.

In 1849, the American novelist **Herman Melville** visited the Guildhall during a business trip to London. He came the day after the annual Lord Mayor's show, when it was customary to distribute leftover food to the poor. Melville was one of many 19th-century observers shocked by the huge gulf between rich and poor in the world's most prosperous city.

> I pushed my way thro cellars and anti-lanes into the rear of the Guildhall, with a crowd of beggars who were going to receive the broken meats & pies from yesterday's grand banquet. Within the hall… were old broken tables set out with heaps of fowls hams &c &c pastry in profusion.

> We found ourselves in a rear-blind-walled place in the open air. I looked around amazed. The spot was grimy as a back-yard in the Five Points. It was packed with a mass of lean, famished, ferocious creatures, struggling and fighting for some mysterious precedency, and all holding soiled blue tickets in their hands…

> It was just the same as if I were pressed by a mob of cannibals on some pagan beach. The beings round me roared with famine. For in this mighty London misery but maddens.

MANSION HOUSE
Marshal Soult

Mansion House Place

Completed in 1753, the Mansion House is the official residence of the Lord Mayor of London. Its sumptuous state apartments – drawing-rooms, salon, conference room, ballroom and 90-foot-long Egyptian hall – are the first port of call for foreign dignitaries making a formal visit to the City.

On Tuesday, July 3 1838, a legendary foreigner came to pay a courtesy call on the mayor before going on to a reception at the Guildhall. He was **Marshal Soult**, the French general who had fought the English in Spain during the Napoleonic Wars. He had fought them at Waterloo as well, breakfasting with Napoleon before the battle. There wasn't an Englishman in the City that day who didn't want to get a look at Soult if he could.

The great man was in England for the coronation of Queen Victoria. He had caused a stir when he arrived at Westminster Abbey, the congregation breaking into spontaneous applause as he strode up the nave. It was the same in the City, and everywhere else he went during his three-week stay. Soult had once been England's sworn enemy, the man who had chased the British army all over Spain. Yet he was mobbed by enthusiastic crowds in London, as a puzzled Charles Greville noted in his diary:

> It is really curious to see the manner in which Soult has been received
> here, not only with every sort of attention and respect by persons in
> the most respectable ranks in life, members of all the great trading
> and commercial bodies, but with enthusiasm by the common people;
> they flock about him, cheer him vociferously, and at the review in the
> park he was obliged to abandon both his hands to be shaken by those
> around him. The old soldier is touched to the quick at this generous
> reception.

Did you know?

? The Mansion House stands at the heart of the City of London, the capital's financial area (quite distinct from the rest of London). The City has been a powerful commercial centre since 1191, when its rights and privileges were first recognised by the monarchy. Its boundaries cover a square mile, centred on the Royal Exchange and the Bank of England. Even today, no monarch may enter the City without the Lord Mayor's permission, and no troops either.

? As a child in the 1820s, **Charles Dickens** roamed the streets of the City, dreaming of the day when he would no longer be poor and hungry: 'There was a dinner preparing at the Mansion House, and when I peeped in at a grated kitchen window, and saw the men cooks at work in their white caps, my heart began to beat with hope that the Lord Mayor, or the Lady Mayoress, or one of the young Princesses their daughters, would look out of an upper apartment and direct me to be taken in. But, nothing of the kind occurred. It

was not until I had been peeping in some time that one of the cooks called to me (the window was open) "Cut away, you sir!" which frightened me so, on account of his black whiskers, that I instantly obeyed.'

ROYAL EXCHANGE
Voltaire

3

Cornhill

The Royal Exchange has been the meeting place of City merchants since the 1560s, when it was founded as a rival to the great trading centre at Antwerp. The original building was destroyed in the Great Fire of 1666, and its successor burned down again in 1838, but the open central court still has the original Turkish paving stones from the 16th century. Traders from all over the known world gathered there to make deals and exchange goods, a great Babel of different tongues that was one of the great tourist attractions of the City.

Voltaire lived near the Royal Exchange in 1727, during his exile from Paris. He was particularly impressed at the religious tolerance, so different from France, where only the official religion was allowed.

> Take a view of the *Royal-Exchange* in *London*, a place more venerable
> than many courts of justice, where the representatives of all nations
> meet for the benefit of mankind. There the Jew, the Mahometan, and
> the Christian transact together as tho' they all profess'd the same
> religion, and give the name of Infidel to none but bankrupts…

The **Mozart** family were impressed as well, Wolfgang's father noting that the courtyard was bigger than the one at Mirabell, with so many different traders doing business in the arcade. The crowd was so large that it was impossible for the Mozarts to find a way through, and the trade directory was 'the thickness of two fingers'.

Did you know?

? The Royal Exchange is one of the four places in London where the death of a monarch is formally announced with the words 'The king is dead. Long live the king!'. After the death has been announced at St James' Palace and Charing Cross, the Earl Marshal's cavalcade proceeds towards the City

The Royal Exchange

boundary at Temple Bar. A poursuivant rides forward, escorted by two trumpeters, halting at a red cord stretched across the road. Trumpet calls are exchanged, after which the City Marshal rides forward from the City side and asks 'Who comes there?' 'His Majesty's Officers of Arms, who demand entry into the City of London, in order to proclaim His Royal Majesty King Charles the Third.' The barrier is opened to admit the poursuivant and trumpeters only. They present the order in council authorising the proclamation, which is read aloud by the Common Cryer and the Serjeant-at-Arms of the City. The Lord Mayor declares 'Admit the cavalcade'. The monarch's death is then announced at Chancery Lane and the Royal Exchange, after which the Lord Mayor raises his tricorn hat and calls for 'Three cheers for the king'.

? The Royal Exchange closed at the outbreak of war in 1939 and did not reopen again afterwards. Business today is conducted on computer screens and the Exchange building is used for offices.

? On the left of the Royal Exchange, as you face it, stands the Bank of England. Known as the Old Lady of Threadneedle Street, it was founded in 1694 and is the country's central bank, responsible for issuing bank notes, setting interest rates and keeping the economy under control. The bank also has huge reserves of gold, which it keeps under heavy guard in the vaults. The façade and surrounding wall of the bank date from the 1790s. Everything behind was rebuilt in the 1920s. The bank has a small museum, entered round the corner in Bartholomew Lane, with lectures and a film show.

32 CORNHILL
The Brontë sisters

4

When they first sat down to write fiction, the **Brontë** sisters – **Anne**, **Charlotte** and **Emily** – were forced to adopt pen names to avoid the Victorian prejudice against female novelists. It was Acton, Currer and Ellis Bell who parcelled up the manuscripts of *Wuthering Heights*, *The Tenant of Wildfell Hall* etc and posted them down to various publishers in London. The publishers never met the authors and assumed they were dealing with men rather than a hapless trio of spinsters living in a remote parsonage in Yorkshire.

They might never have been rumbled if it hadn't been for the success of *Jane Eyre* in America. Seeking to cash in on the success, an unscrupulous publisher tried to pass off the works of all three as by the same author. The Brontës were outraged. In July 1848, Anne and Charlotte hurried down to London to reveal the truth to Charlotte's publisher at Smith & Elder, 32 (formerly 65) Cornhill.

> We found 65 to be a large bookseller's shop in a street almost as bustling as the Strand. We went in, walked up to the counter – there were a great many young men and lads here and there. I said to the first I could accost 'May I see Mr Smith?' He hesitated, looked a little surprised, but went to fetch him. We sat down and waited awhile, looking at some books on the counter, publications of theirs well known to us, many of which they had sent to us copies as presents.

At last somebody came up and said dubiously 'Did you wish to see me, Ma'am?' 'Is it Mr Smith?' I said looking up through my spectacles at a young, tall, gentlemanly man. 'It is.' I then put his own letter into his hand directed to 'Currer Bell'. He looked at it, then at me, again, yet again. I laughed at his queer perplexity. A recognition took place. I gave my real name – 'Miss Brontë'.

We were both hurried from the shop into a little back room ceiled with a great skylight and only large enough to hold 3 chairs and a desk, and there explanations were rapidly gone into.

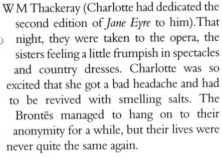

The publishers were thrilled by the Brontës. 'How long do you stay in Town?' they demanded. Smith invited them to stay at his own home and promised to introduce them to W M Thackeray (Charlotte had dedicated the second edition of *Jane Eyre* to him). That night, they were taken to the opera, the sisters feeling a little frumpish in spectacles and country dresses. Charlotte was so excited that she got a bad headache and had to be revived with smelling salts. The Brontës managed to hang on to their anonymity for a while, but their lives were never quite the same again.

Did you know?

? George Smith's recollection of the meeting: 'Two rather quaintly dressed little ladies, pale-faced and anxious-looking, walked into my room… This is the only occasion on which I saw Anne Brontë. She was a gentle, quiet, rather subdued person, by no means pretty, yet of a pleasing appearance. Her manner was curiously expressive of a wish for protection and encouragement, a kind of constant appeal which invited sympathy.'

? Smith introduced Charlotte to Thackeray in 1849. A carving on the bottom right door panel of No 32 (now Cornhill Insurance) depicts the meeting.

? Cornhill is also where Ebenezer Scrooge had his counting-house in **Charles Dickens'** *A Christmas Carol*. It was down an unnamed courtyard so foggy 'that although the court was of the narrowest, the houses opposite were mere phantoms… The ancient tower of a church, whose gruff old bell was always peeping slily down at Scrooge out of a gothic window in the wall, became invisible.'

THE GEORGE & VULTURE, GEORGE YARD
Charles Dickens
St Michael's Alley, off Cornhill

5

At the end of a narrow alleyway, the George & Vulture was established in 1600 and has been serving meals to City workers ever since. If it looks Dickensian, that's because Mr Pickwick made it his headquarters in 1830 after fleeing from his landlady, who was suing him for breach of promise. He brought his servant Sam Weller with him:

> Mr Pickwick and Sam took up their present abode in very good, old-fashioned, and comfortable quarters: to wit, the George and Vulture Tavern and Hotel, George Yard, Lombard Street.

Sam Weller was at the bar

> when a young boy of about three feet high… entered the passage of the George and Vulture, and looked first up the stairs, and then along the passage,

The George and Vulture

> and then into the bar, as if in search of somebody to whom he bore a commission; whereupon the barmaid, conceiving it not improbable that the said commission might be directed to the tea or table spoons of the establishment, accosted the boy with 'Now, young man, what do you want?' 'Is there anybody here named Sam?' inquired the youth, in a loud voice of treble quality.

After delivering his message,

> the young gentleman walked away, awakening all the echoes in George Yard as he did so, with several chaste and extremely correct imitations of a drover's whistle, delivered in a tone of peculiar richness and volume.

Did you know?

? **Charles Dickens** knew the George well. He gave a dinner here in 1834 for 34 of his friends and the inn still has the bill. It was at the George that Mr Pickwick was giving a dinner for the Pickwick Club, when his landlady's lawyers served a subpoena on them about the breach of promise.

? The inn can be reached from Cornhill, down St Michael's Alley, or from Lombard Street via George Yard.

MONUMENT
The Great Fire of London

6

Fish Street Hill at Monument Street

About 10pm on September 1 1666, at the end of another long hot day, **Thomas Farriner** closed down the oven of his bakery in Pudding Lane and prepared for bed. He was asleep soon after midnight, but woke again at 2am to discover that the house was on fire. The stairs were burning and the only escape was via the roof. Farriner managed to get his family out, but their maid was too scared to jump and died in the flames. The Farriners could only stand and watch as their house burned to the ground… and the house next door as

Monument

well, and the house after that, and all the other houses along the row, for as far as the eye could see.

The houses were made of wood, packed tightly together in a city that hadn't seen any rain for months. A high wind carried the flames from one rooftop to another and then to the warehouses along the wharf before anyone could stop them. It wasn't until four days later, when whole streets had been blown up with gunpowder to provide a firebreak, that the Great Fire of London was finally brought under control.

St Paul's Cathedral had burned down by then, 89 other churches, and more than 13,000 private houses – four-fifths of the entire city. Medieval London had ceased to exist.

Naturally the Farriner family claimed it was nothing to do with them. 'They are, as they swear, in absolute ignorance how this fire should come.' But nobody else was in any doubt. Once rebuilding was under way, a monument was erected to the disaster. It stands 202 feet high, and 202 feet west of the baker's shop in Pudding Lane where it all began. The monument marks the spot where the London that Shakespeare knew was destroyed for ever.

Samuel Pepys was asleep in his house at the Navy Office, just north of Tower Hill, when the fire broke out:

September 2 1666:

> Some of our maids sitting up late last night to get things ready against our feast today, Jane called us up, about 3 in the morning, to tell us of a great fire they saw in the City. So I rose, and slipped on my nightgown and went to her window… but being unused to such fires, I thought it far enough off, and so went to bed again and to sleep.

> About 7 rose again to dress myself… By and by Jane comes and tells me that she hears that above 300 houses have been burned down tonight by the fire we saw, and that it was now burning down all Fishstreet by London Bridge. So I made myself ready presently, and walked to the Tower and there got up upon one of the high places… and there I did see the houses at that end of the bridge all on fire…

So down, with my heart full of trouble, to the Lieutenant of the Tower, who tells me that it begun this morning in the King's bakers house in Pudding-lane... I down to the water-side and there got a boat and through bridge, and there saw a lamentable fire... Everybody endeavouring to remove their goods and flinging into the River or bringing them into lighters that lay off. Poor people staying in their houses as long as till the very fire touched them, and then running into boats or clambering from one pair of stair by the water-side to another...

Every creature coming away loaden with goods to save – and here and there sick people carried away in beds... The streets full of nothing but people and horses and carts loaden with goods, ready to run over one another, and removing goods from one burned house to another – they now removing out of Canning-street (which received goods in the morning) into Lumbard Streete and further... but little was or could be done, the fire coming upon them so fast...

A most horrid malicious bloody flame, not like the fine flame of an ordinary fire... It made me weep to see it. The churches, houses and all on fire and flaming at once, and a horrid noise the flames made, and the cracking of houses at their ruine.

September 4:

Now begins the practice of blowing up of houses in Tower-street, those next the Tower, which at first did frighten people more than anything; but it stopped the fire where it was done – it bringing down the houses to the ground in the same places they stood, and then it was easy to quench what little fire was in it.

Pepys' friend, **John Evelyn**, lived at Deptford. He walked to Southwark to view the fire from across the river:

I saw the whole South part of the Citty burning from Cheape side to the Thames, & all along Cornehill (for it likewise kindled back against the Wind) Tower-Streete, Fen-church-streete, Gracious Streete, & so along to Bainard Castle, and was now taking hold of St Paules-Church, to which the Scaffalds contributed exceedingly.

The Conflagration was so universal, & the people so astonish'd, that from the beginning... they hardly stirr'd to quench it, so as there was nothing heard or seene but crying out & lamentation, & running about like distracted creatures...

All the skie were of a fiery aspect, like the top of a burning Oven, & the light seene above 40 miles round about for many nights: God grant mine eyes may never behold the like, who now saw above ten thousand houses all in one flame, the noise & crakling & thunder of the impetuous flames, the shreeking of Women & children, the hurry of people, the fall of towers, houses & churches was like an hideous storme, & the aire all about so hot & inflam'd that at the last one was not able to approch it...

The poore Inhabitans dispersd all about St Georges, Moore filds, as far as higate, & severall miles in Circle, Some under tents, others under miserable Hutts and Hovells, without a rag, or any necessary utinsils, bed or board, who from delicatnesse, riches & easy accommodations in stately & well furnishd houses, were now reduc'd to extreamest misery & poverty...

I then went towards Islington, & high-gate, where one might have seene two hundred thousand people of all ranks & degrees, dispersed, & laying along by their heapes of what they could save from the *Incendium*, deploring their losse, & though ready to perish for hunger & destitution, yet not asking one penny for reliefe.

Did you know?

? As soon as the Great Fire was over, **Sir Christopher Wren** produced a very ambitious plan for rebuilding London. He wanted to clear the whole site and start again with a classical design of broad streets and wide piazzas, all radiating outwards from the twin focal points of St Paul's Cathedral and the Royal Exchange. London would have been as elegant as Paris if the plan had been accepted. But the cost was prohibitive and people were in a hurry to be rehoused. A better city arose from the ashes of the old, but a great opportunity was missed to make it even better still.

? Wren did at least design part of the Monument to the Great Fire. It has 311 steps, for anyone thinking of climbing to the top. **Charles Dickens** counselled against this in Martin Chuzzlewit: 'Two people came to see the Monument. They were a gentleman and a lady; and the gentleman said, "How much a-piece?" The Man in the Monument replied, "A Tanner". The gentleman put a shilling into his hand, and the Man in the Monument opened a dark little door. When the gentleman and lady had passed out of view, he shut it again, and came slowly back to his chair. He sat down and laughed. "They don't know what a many steps there is!" he said. "It's worth twice the money to stop here".'

WHAT NOW?

Mitre Square (see page 203), the nearest and best of **Jack the Ripper**'s murder sites, is just under half a mile away. Walk up Gracechurch Street and turn right along Fenchurch or Leadenhall Streets, or take the Underground from Monument to Aldgate.

If you feel like crossing the river, walk over London Bridge (no longer adorned with traitors' heads) to the south bank and continue along Borough High Street for 300 yards. On your left, **The George** (77 Borough High Street) is a wonderful old galleried inn, the last in London. It dates from 1676 and is mentioned in Dickens' *Little Dorrit*. Just beyond it, Talbot Yard marks the site of the Tabard Inn, where Chaucer's pilgrims assembled for their journey to Canterbury.

Back at the riverside, **The Anchor** on the south bank at Bank End, just west of the railway bridge, is a good place for lunch, with splendid views of the river. The inn was rebuilt in 1775. Oliver Goldsmith, James Boswell and Edmund Burke used to drink at the previous one in the 1760s.

From The Anchor, go west along Park Street, under Southwark Bridge Road. The remains of the **Rose Theatre** (a rival to Shakespeare's Globe) can be inspected at 56 Park Street, near Rose Alley. From there, follow the signs to the modern reconstruction of **The Globe** at New Globe Walk, Bankside, where they have a good permanent exhibition on 'Shakespeare's world'. Next door to the Globe, the Bankside power station has recently been converted into the **Tate Bankside Gallery of Modern Art** (a spillover from the other Tate Gallery, north of the river at Millbank). The gallery's collection is stunning.

Nearest public lavatory Monument

✪ Monument

WHERE TO EAT
Some of these places are shut on Saturdays and Sundays. With half a million people working here, the City is always very busy during the week. But only 5,000 people actually live in the City, so it tends to be a ghost town at weekends, and restaurants close accordingly.

1 Lombard, The Brasserie 1 Lombard Street. Very good, but full of business people in suits.

The Bell 29 Bush Lane. Said to have been a tavern since before the Great Fire of 1666.

Fuego 1a Pudding Lane. In the street where the Great Fire started, Fuego is a tapas bar and restaurant by day, a disco by night.

The Swan Ship Tavern Passage, 77–80 Gracechurch Street. Old and cramped, but atmospheric.

Lamb Tavern 10 Grand Avenue, Leadenhall Market. Very busy and popular at lunchtime. Leadenhall Market is fun.

Prism 147 Leadenhall Street. Expensive restaurant for City types, converted from a bank.

Jack the Ripper

WALK AT A GLANCE

Features This is a long walk if you do it all. It can be shortened by skipping the first two stops and beginning at No 3, Mitre Square (near Aldgate Underground). Remember though that Nos 2 to 4 (Henriques Street, Mitre Square, Goulston Street) all happened on the same dreadful night. If you're keen to follow in Jack's exact footsteps that night, then Henriques Street is the place to start.

Time Allow 2 hours.

Length I or 2 miles.

⊖ Whitechapel, Aldgate East, Aldgate

1 **Durward Street** (page 200)
   • Jack the Ripper kills his first victim just behind Whitechapel Underground.

2 **Henriques Street** (page 202)
   • he is about to disembowel Elizabeth Stride when he is disturbed.

3 **Mitre Square** (page 203)
   • he catches Catherine Eddowes and disembowels her instead.

4 **Goulston Street** (page 204)
   • he wipes his knife on a piece of Catherine's apron and drops it at Wentworth Dwellings.

5 **Commercial Street** (page 206)
   • he meets Mary Jane Kelly walking towards Thrawl Street.

6 **White's Row** (page 206)
   • he goes home with Mary Jane and carves her into little pieces.

7 **Hanbury Street** (page 201)
   • he chops up Annie Chapman in broad daylight.

Please note that the walk is organised differently from the others in this guide. The only way to make sense of Jack the Ripper is to read through the murders in chronological order and then plan the route that suits you best, either following the recommended trail or visiting the sites in whatever order is most convenient.

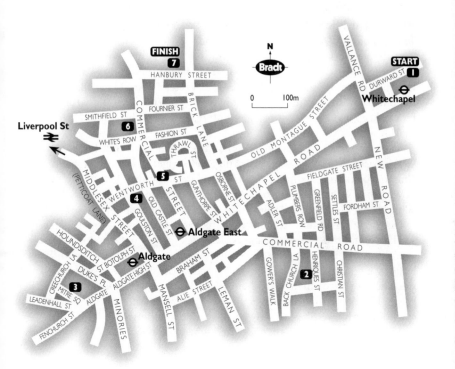

Background

In the autumn of 1888, a series of sensational murders took place in Whitechapel, in the poverty-stricken East End. Over a period of ten weeks, at least five women were brutally hacked to death by a sex maniac. All were prostitutes, and all but one were horribly mutilated, some beyond recognition. They were the victims of the most famous murderer in British history – **Jack the Ripper**.

Nobody ever discovered his identity. The murders were all the work of one man, but the police never came near to catching him. He rampaged through Whitechapel for ten dramatic weeks and then vanished without trace, disappearing as swiftly and silently as he had come. It seems highly probable that he took his own life after the last killing, unable to live with the horror of what he had done.

The East End has changed since the Ripper's day. A combination of slum clearance and German bombing has altered a couple of the sites beyond recognition. Some streets have had their names changed as well, after protests from local residents fed up with ghouls peering through their windows. But there's still plenty left, just as it was when Jack the Ripper prowled the shadows. For best results, try the walk alone at night, when the streets are deserted and you have only your own footsteps for company. It's highly atmospheric that way!

1ST MURDER
Mary Ann Nichols – Durward Street (formerly Buck's Row)
Turn left out of Whitechapel Underground

The Ripper's first victim was Mary Ann Nichols. A tiny woman of 43, she lodged in a doss-house at 18 Thrawl Street whenever she could afford it. In the small hours of August 31, however, she was flat broke. The manager threw her out at 1.40am because she didn't have the price of a bed. Mary Ann asked him to keep her a bed anyway and set off to earn the money, promising to be back as soon as she could.

Mary Ann was later seen at 2.30am on the corner of Osborn Street and the Whitechapel Road. 'She was very drunk and staggered against the wall.' The church clock was just striking the half hour as she steadied herself and turned down the Whitechapel Road towards Durward Street, just behind Whitechapel Underground. She was never seen alive again.

Her body was found in Durward Street at 3.40am by a carman going to work. 'He noticed a woman lying on her back on the footway (against some gates leading into a stable yard)'. She was wearing a brown ulster with brass buttons, a brown frock, grey woollen petticoat, flannel drawers, black woollen stockings, a pair of men's boots and a black straw hat trimmed with black velvet. Her dress had been pulled up above her knees and her throat had been cut from ear to ear. She had only been dead a few minutes.

The body was taken to the mortuary, where the police noticed that it had been disembowelled as well. They sent at once for the doctor.

> He arrived quickly and on further examination stated that her throat had been cut from left to right, two distinct cuts being on the left side. The windpipe, gullet and spinal cord being cut through, a bruise apparently of a thumb being on the right lower jaw, also one on left cheek.

> The abdomen had been cut open from centre of bottom of ribs on right side, under pelvis to left of the stomach; there the wound was jagged... Two small stabs on private parts appeared done with a strong bladed knife, supposed to have been done by some left handed person, death being almost instantaneous.

The doctor concluded that Mary Ann had been killed where she was found. But no-one had seen or heard a thing. The killer had come and gone completely undetected.

Did you know?

? At the time of Mary Ann's murder, the northern side of Durward Street consisted of tall, grim warehouses. The only building surviving from those days is the old school building on the south side, where Durward Street curls round into Winthrop Street. The stable yard lay between the school and a row of terraced houses where Kempton Court now stands.

? Mary Ann's body was found on the pavement in the gap between the end of Kempton Court and the wall leading to the old school building beyond.

2ND MURDER
Annie Chapman – 29 Hanbury Street.

Eight days later, the killer struck again. His second victim was Annie Chapman, a plump woman of 47, only five-foot tall. Evicted from her lodgings at 35 Dorset Street (now White's Row car park), she went out at 1.45am on September 8 to earn the money for a bed. She wasn't seen again until 5.30, when someone spotted her with a man outside another lodging house at 29 Hanbury Street.

The man was about 40, wearing a deerstalker hat. 'He may have been a foreigner. He looked what I should call shabby genteel.'

A few minutes later, another witness heard a woman saying 'No!' and the sound of something slumping against the fence in No 29's backyard. By 6.10, a body had been discovered there and reported to the police:

> I at once proceeded to No 29 Hanbury Street and in the back yard found a woman lying on her back, dead, left arm resting on left breast, legs drawn up, abducted, small intestines and flap of the abdomen lying on right side above right shoulder, attached by a cord with the rest of the intestines inside the body.

Annie was shabbily dressed in a black figured jacket, a brown bodice, a black skirt and an old pair of lace boots. Her uterus was missing, and part of the vagina and bladder. Whoever removed them evidently knew what he was looking for. Using a surgical knife, he must have worked for quite some time to carve her up – all of it in the early morning light, with 17 people asleep in the house only a couple of feet away.

Did you know?

? The killer had apparently pulled the brass rings from Annie's fingers and laid them out with a few coins at her feet – a well-known Masonic ritual. Was he a Freemason?

? Some reports insist that no coins were found. Had the evidence been removed by the police, many of whom were Masons?

? After this second murder, a medical magazine concluded that the murders were 'obviously the work of an expert – of one, at least, who had such knowledge of anatomical or pathological examinations as to be enabled to secure the pelvic organs with one sweep of the knife'.

? Alas, 29 Hanbury Street is no longer there. Truman's brewery stands on the site.

3RD MURDER
Elizabeth Stride – 40 Henriques Street (formerly Berner Street)

On September 30, the Ripper struck again. This time, he killed two women in one night. The first victim was Elizabeth Stride, a tall Swedish prostitute of 47. She lodged at 32 Flower and Dean Street and knew all about Jack the Ripper. She and her friends talked of little else.

Elizabeth was seen with several men in the hours before she died. One was a respectable-looking man of about 28, carrying a parcel and wearing a deerstalker hat. 'Complexion dark, small dark moustache; dress, black diagonal coat, hard felt hat, collar and tie'. He was seen with her in Henriques/Berner Street at 12.35am. She was dead 20 minutes later.

A steward at the International Working Men's Club found her body at 1am as he was driving his pony and trap into Dutfield's Yard (no longer there, see below). The horse shied at a heap of clothing on the ground just inside the gates. The steward lit a candle which immediately blew out. But he had seen enough to fetch help at once.

> The scene of the crime is a narrow court in Berner-street, a quiet
> thoroughfare running from Commercial-road down to the London,
> Tilbury and Southend Railway. At the entrance to the court are a
> pair of large wooden gates... There is a dead wall on each side of
> the court, the effect of which is to enshroud the intervening space
> in absolute darkness after sunset. Further back some light is thrown
> into the court from the windows of a workmen's club, which
> occupies the whole length of the court on the right, and from a
> number of cottages occupied mainly by tailors and cigarette makers
> on the left.

Elizabeth's throat had been cut, but she had not been mutilated. The pony and trap had disturbed the Ripper at his work. As soon as the coast was clear, he emerged from the shadows and hurried off, probably up Commercial Road, looking for someone else to kill...

Did you know?

? '1.10am. Body examined by the doctors mentioned who pronounced life extinct, the position of the body was as follows: – lying on left side, left arm extended from elbow, cachous [sic] lying in the hand, right arm over stomach, back of hand and inner surface of wrist dotted with blood, legs drawn up, knees fixed, feet close to the wall, body still warm...'

? Elizabeth was killed so quickly that she was still clutching a packet of cashew nuts when she was found.

? Dutfield's yard has gone. It lay on the west side of Henriques Street, in the open space just south of the SBL school 1903 building.

? A few days before the murder, **Dr Barnardo**, founder of the famous children's homes, had visited Elizabeth Stride's lodgings at 32 Flower and Dean Street (now the dog-leg part of Thrawl Street). 'One poor creature, who had evidently been drinking, exclaimed somewhat bitterly to the following effect: "We're all up to no good, and no-one cares what becomes of us. Perhaps some of us will be killed next!" And then she added: "If anybody had helped the likes of us long ago, we would never have come to this!" I have since visited the mortuary in which were lying the remains of the poor woman Stride, and I at once recognised her as one of those who stood around me in the kitchen of the common lodging house on the occasion of my visit.'

? Dr Barnardo's daughter later married **Somerset Maugham**, whose first novel *Liza of Lambeth* reflected his experience as a medical student working among street women in the 1890s. The publicity from Jack the Ripper ultimately did the East End a power of good, helping to expose the huge gap between rich and poor in England, the slums of Whitechapel right next door to the City of London, then the richest square mile in the world.

? While Jack the Ripper was at work in the East End, playgoers in the West End were flocking to see *The Strange Case of Dr Jekyll and Mr Hyde*, **Robert Louis Stevenson**'s drama about an apparently respectable doctor who murdered a prostitute and then committed suicide before the police could unmask him. In case you're wondering, Stevenson was in the South Seas during the Ripper murders.

? On a lighter note, the American singer **Paul Simon** lived with his English girlfriend in a third-floor flat at Dellow House, off Cable Street near the railway viaduct, before he was famous. They were joined in 1965 by **Art Garfunkel** and used to do their washing at the launderette on Commercial Road. Simon was thinking of these streets, where his girlfriend lived, when he wrote *Homeward Bound*.

4TH MURDER
Catherine Eddowes – Mitre Square

At the same time as Elizabeth Stride's throat was being cut in Henriques/Berner Street, Catherine Eddowes was being released from a cell at Bishopsgate police station. She had been arrested a few hours earlier for being drunk and disorderly, impersonating a fire engine in Aldgate High Street. The police had kept her in custody until she was sober enough to go home.

Catherine was 46, but looked much older. 'Goodnight, old cock,' she told the policeman, as she left the station. She lived at 6 Fashion Street, but didn't go that way after her release.

A woman answering her description was seen talking to a man in Church Passage (now St James' Passage, leading to Mitre Square) at 1.35am. At some point, a policeman stood at the end of the passage and shone his lamp into the dark, deserted square, but saw nothing amiss. Another policeman had patrolled the square from Mitre Street at 1.30 and seen nothing wrong either.

This second policeman returned at 1.45. He found Catherine lying close to the wall in the southwest corner of the square between the raised flower bed and the school gates. Her body had been hacked open from groin to breastbone and the contents ripped out 'like a pig in the market'. She had been torn to bits in less than ten minutes. The policeman who found her had never been more than 30 yards away.

He sprinted across to Kearley & Tonge's warehouse across the square. The night-watchman cautiously opened the door. 'For God's sake mate, come to my assistance. There's another woman cut to pieces.'

The night-watchman blew his whistle and went to fetch help. The policeman stood guard over the body, nervously shining his lamp around the square. But Jack the Ripper wasn't there any more. Clutching a piece of Catherine's bloody apron, he was already on his way to Goulston Street, back in the East End...

Did you know?

? 'The body was on its back, the head turned to left shoulder, the arms by the side of the body... The clothes drawn up above the abdomen, the thighs were naked... The bonnet was at the back of the head – great disfigurement of the face. The throat cut...The intestines were drawn out to a large extent and placed over the right shoulder... A piece about two feet was quite detached from the body and placed between the body and the left arm, apparently by design... The peritoneal lining was cut through on the left side and the kidney carefully taken out and removed... The womb was cut through horizontally leaving a stump of three quarters of an inch. The rest of the womb had been taken away... I believe the perpetrator of the act must have had considerable knowledge of the position of the organs in the abdominal cavity and the way of removing them... It required a great deal of knowledge to have removed the kidney and to know where it was placed. Such a knowledge might be possessed by one in the habit of cutting up animals.'

? Catherine was wearing a black cloth jacket, a black straw bonnet, and a dark green dress patterned with lilies and michaelmas daisies. In her pockets she had a handkerchief, comb, cigarette case, a tin box of tea and sugar, a blunt table knife, two clay pipes and a few pieces of soap.

? Some time between 2.20 and 2.55am, the missing piece of her blood-stained apron was dropped at the bottom of the staircase at 108–119 Wentworth Dwellings (still there on the corner of Goulston and Wentworth Streets). On the right-hand wall just inside the doorway, someone had recently written in chalk on the black brickwork: 'The Juwes are The men That Will not be Blamed for nothing'. The policeman in charge of the case had the words rubbed out just after 5am – before the handwriting could be photographed – in case they sparked a riot in a heavily Jewish area. 'It was just getting light. The public would be in the streets in a few minutes, in a neighbourhood very much crowded on Sunday mornings by Jewish vendors and Christian purchasers from all parts of London... The writing was on the jamb of the open archway or doorway visible to anybody in the street... I do not hesitate to say that if the writing had been left property would have been wrecked and lives would probably have been lost.'

HOW JACK THE RIPPER GOT HIS NAME

At first, the women's killer was known as the Whitechapel murderer. On September 25, however, a couple of weeks after the second murder, the head of the Central News Agency received a letter from the East End:

> Dear Boss,
>
> I keep on hearing the police have caught me but they wont fix me just yet. I have laughed when they look so clever and talk about being on the right track... I am down on whores and I shant quit ripping them till I do get buckled. Grand work the last job was. I gave the lady no time to squeal. I love my work and want to start again. You will soon hear of me with my funny little games. I saved some of the proper <u>red</u> stuff in a ginger beer bottle over the last job to write with but it went thick like glue and I cant use it. Red ink is fit enough I hope <u>ha ha</u>. The next job I do I shall clip the ladys ears off and send to the police officers just for jolly wouldnt you. Keep this letter back till I do a bit more work, then give it out straight. My knife's nice and sharp I want to get to work right away if I get a chance. Good luck.
>
> > yours truly
> >
> > Jack the Ripper.
>
> Dont mind me giving the trade name... They say I'm a doctor now <u>ha ha</u>

The letter was followed by a postcard stamped October 1, a few hours after the murders of Elizabeth Stride and Catherine Eddowes:

> I was not codding dear old Boss when I gave you the tip, you'll hear about saucy Jacky's work tomorrow, double event this time. Number One squealed a bit couldnt finish straight off. Had not time to get ears for police. Thanks for keeping last letter back till I got to work again.
>
> Jack the Ripper

The police then published both letters and the killer has been known as Jack the Ripper ever since.

? According to Masonic tradition, Hiram Abiff, the Masonic Grand Master who built Solomon's Temple, was murdered by three Jews. When caught, one of the Jews lamented: 'O that my left breast had been torn open and my heart and vitals taken from thence and thrown over my left shoulder' – disturbingly similar to the Ripper's victims. Was he a Mason?

? Sir Charles Warren, the policeman who ordered the words to be rubbed out, was heavily criticised for destroying such a significant clue. Why did he do it? Well, among other things, he was a very high-ranking Mason!

? Wentworth Dwellings stand on the east side of Goulston Street, on the corner with Wentworth Street. There are four staircase entries from Goulston Street, most now converted into tiny shops or sandwich bars. Jack the Ripper's stairwell was second from the left as you face the building, between Nos 44 and 46 Goulston Street. He dropped a piece of Catherine's apron just inside the door. It was stained with blood and 'faecal matter', and may have been used to carry her kidney and womb from Mitre Square.

? Two weeks after Catherine's murder, Mr Lusk, chairman of the newly formed Whitechapel Vigilance Committee, received a piece of human kidney through the post, accompanied by a letter 'From hell':

Mr Lusk – Sir, I send you half the Kidne I took from one woman

prasarved it for you tother piece I fried and ate it was very nise. I may send you the bloody knif that took it out if you only wate a whil longer.

Signed Catch me when you can Mishter Lusk.

The piece of kidney was examined. It might have been a medical student's prank. But he had gone to a lot of trouble if it was because the kidney was apparently a pretty good match for the one left in Catherine Eddowes' body.

5TH MURDER
Mary Jane Kelly – White's Row car park, Commercial Street (formerly 13 Miller's Court, off Dorset Street)

Dorset Street has disappeared under White's Row car park. The entrance to the street stood opposite the small green patch next to Christ Church. The site of Miller's Court is now occupied by the building just north of the car park

The last Ripper murder was the worst of all. There was very little left of Mary Jane Kelly by the time Jack the Ripper had finished with her.

She was different to his other victims. Only 25, better educated, a pleasant blue-eyed blonde who had been a nanny before falling on hard times. She didn't live in a doss-house, but rented her own room at Miller's Court. She had recently split with her boyfriend, who disliked what she did for a living. She was only doing it because he had lost his job.

In the early hours of November 9, Mary Jane was drunk and singing, lurching down Commercial Street asking people for money. She picked up a respectable-looking man of about 34, with a dark moustache, carrying a parcel in his left hand. 'All right, my dear,' she told him, as she took him back to her room. 'Come along. You'll be comfortable.'

In the middle of the night, several neighbours heard someone shrieking 'Oh murder!', but took no notice. Mary Jane wasn't found until just before 11 o'clock next morning, when the rent-collector peered through her window and nearly fainted at what he saw:

> The throat had been cut right across with a knife, nearly severing the head from the body. The abdomen had been partially ripped open, and both of the breasts had been cut from the body, the left arm, like the head, hung to the body by the skin only. The nose had been cut off, the forehead skinned, and the thighs down to the feet, stripped of the flesh...

> The entrails and other portions of the frame were missing, but the liver etc it is said were found placed between the feet of this poor victim. The flesh from the thighs and legs, together with the breasts and nose, had been placed by the murderer on the table, and one of the hands of the dead woman had been pushed into her stomach.

That was the end of Mary Jane Kelly, but it was also the end of Jack the Ripper. The country held its breath, waiting for another murder. So did the rest of the world, because he was internationally famous by now. But no more women were killed in the same frenzied manner. Mary Jane was the Ripper's last victim. He vanished after her death, disappearing as abruptly as he had arrived, and was never heard of again.

Did you know?

? 'About 2am I was coming by Thrawl Street, Commercial Street... I met the murdered woman Kelly and she said to me, Hutchinson will you lend me sixpence? I said I can't... She went away toward Thrawl Street. A man coming in the opposite direction to Kelly tapped her on the shoulder... He then placed his right hand around her shoulders. He had a kind of small parcel in his left hand with a kind of strap round it. I stood against the lamp of the Queen's Head public house and watched him... They both went into Dorset Street... They both then went up the court together... I stood there for about three quarters of an hour to see if they came out. They did not, so I went away.'

? The man's description: 'Slight moustache curled up each end and hair dark. Very surly looking. Dress, long dark coat, collar and cuffs trimmed astrakhan and a dark jacket under, light waistcoat, dark trousers, dark felt hat turned down in the middle, button boots and gaiters with white buttons, wore a very thick gold chain with linen collar, black tie with horseshoe pin, respectable appearance.'

? Miller's Court was teeming with people at the time of Mary Jane's murder, and so were all the other murder sites. There was no safety in numbers when Jack the Ripper was about. His ability to come and go undetected was one of the most terrifying things about him.

? One of the pubs where Mary Jane and the other women looked for customers was the Ten Bells, on the corner of Fournier and Commercial Streets. It was still there at the time of writing, although in danger of redevelopment.

The Ten Bells

SO WHO *WAS* JACK THE RIPPER?

No-one will ever know. He was never caught and the police never came close to identifying him beyond reasonable doubt. The feeling among criminal psychologists is that he almost certainly committed suicide after the last murder, because after what he did to Mary Jane Kelly there was nowhere else for him to go. It's what his kind of murderer usually does, if the police don't catch them first.

Crackpot theories have always abounded as to his identity – everybody from the Jews and the Freemasons to the royal family have been accused at one time or another. But the only certainty is that whoever he was, Jack the Ripper was clinically insane. He wouldn't have torn the women apart if he wasn't.

In February 1894, Sir Melville Macnaghten, then deputy head of Scotland Yard's Criminal Investigation Department, wrote a confidential seven-page memorandum on the Ripper case. He shared the psychiatrists' view that 'the murderer's brain gave way altogether after his awful glut in Miller's Court, and he immediately committed suicide, or, as a possible alternative, was found to be so hopelessly mad by his relations, that he was by them confined in some asylum.'

Macnaghten named three possible candidates, one of whom has always been a leading suspect in the case:

> A Mr M J Druitt, said to be a doctor and of good family, who disappeared at the time of the Miller's Court murder, and whose body (which was said to have been upwards of a month in the water) was found in the Thames on 31st Dec – or about 7 weeks after that murder. He was sexually insane and from private info I have little doubt but that his own family believed him to have been the murderer.

Montague John Druitt was 31 at the time. He had been educated at a well-known public school before reading Classics at Oxford. He may then have studied medicine for a year before switching to the law. But he failed as a lawyer and turned to schoolmastering instead, only to be sacked from his teaching job on December 1 1888 – just three weeks after the last Ripper murder. He killed himself a few days later by weighing his coat down with stones and throwing himself into the Thames.

Was Druitt insane? There was insanity in the family. His mother was in a lunatic asylum and Druitt left a suicide note saying he didn't want to go the same way. Is it possible that he caught syphilis from a prostitute, was driven mad as a consequence and sought violent revenge? Did he write any of the Ripper letters, disguising his language to conceal his education, and signing himself with his middle name? Nobody will ever know for certain, but one thing is beyond dispute – his own family didn't rule it out.

WHAT NOW?

The Whitechapel Art Gallery, next to Aldgate East Underground, is usually worth a look. David Hockney and Jackson Pollock have exhibited there in the past.

The Tower of London is 400 yards south of Mitre Square. The Royal Exchange (see page 190) is just under half a mile from Mitre Square, west along Leadenhall Street.

If you've had enough of Jack the Ripper land, your quickest escape is via the Underground at Liverpool Street railway station. The station is where the *Kindertransport* came in before World War II – trainloads of Jewish kids from Germany and Austria who would never see their parents again. The Underground was used as an air raid shelter during the war, home to many East Enders during the Blitz:

> Thousands upon thousands pushed their way into Liverpool Street Station, demanding to be let down to shelter. At first the authorities wouldn't agree to it and they called out the soldiers to bar the way… The people would not give up and would not disperse… A great yell went up and the gates were opened…

> Some people feel a certain nostalgia for those days, recall a poetic dream about the Blitz. They talk about those days as if they were a time of a true communal spirit. Not to me. It was the beginning of an era of utter terror, of fear and horror.

Nearest public lavatories Aldgate High Street, Whitechapel Underground, corner of Wentworth and Commercial Streets

⊖ Aldgate, Aldgate East, Liverpool Street station

WHERE TO EAT

Whitechapel is traditionally a neighbourhood for recent immigrants. The food used to be all Jewish. Now it is often Bangladeshi. Try the following:

Bengal Village 75 Brick Lane. Bangladeshi, of course.
Café Naz 46 Brick Lane. This one too.
Lahore Kebab House 2 Umberstone Street. Good kebabs and curry.
Arkansas Café Unit 12, Old Spitalfields Market. American barbecue, popular with US bankers from the City.
Herb & Spice 11a White's Row. Curry again.
Dirty Dick's 202 Bishopsgate. Atmospheric old English pub with barrel tables, popular with City workers in suits.

ENGLISH HERITAGE

English Heritage is the independent but government sponsored organisation responsible for the historic environment of England. Its aim is to protect England's unique architectural and archaeological heritage for the benefit and enjoyment of people now and in the future.

Properties

The most visible aspect of its work is the 400-plus sites and monuments in its care, most of which are open to the public, many of them free of charge. They are to be found all over England, and range from World Heritage Sites Stonehenge and Hadrian's Wall, through grand houses like Audley End and Osborne House – favourite home of Queen Victoria – to the ruins of great medieval abbeys and castles, megaliths and ruined chapels. From the castles of Pendennis and St Mawes at the tip of Cornwall, built by Henry VIII after his split from the Pope to counter the possibility of invasion by the forces of Catholic Europe, to Carlisle and Aydon Castles on the Scottish borders, much earlier fortifications against the ever-present threat from the marauding Scots, all of history is here. But not just history: the fact that our heritage is all around us and part of daily life is exemplified by Aydon Castle in its other guise as a working farm right up to 1966.

London properties

In and around London, English Heritage properties range from a length of the wall that protected Roman London, to the Jewel Tower, part of the original Palace of Westminster, and to the grandeur of Kenwood, standing in magnificent grounds beside Hampstead Heath, with its splendid Adam interiors now housing a fine art collection, including a Vermeer and a Rembrandt. Marble Hill House, Chiswick House and Ranger's House are all splendid buildings, and Rangers House now houses part of the amazing Wernher Collection of European art.

A different kind of experience is to be found at two of English Heritage's properties in south-east London. Eltham Palace was one of the major royal medieval palaces, used as a regular home by kings and queens from Edward I to Henry VIII, who grew up there. The magnificent Great Hall was built by Edward IV. But even more remarkable is the Art Deco home grafted into the medieval remains by Stephen and Virginia Courtauld in the 1930s. Their spectacular designs, which included a centrally-heated cage for their pet lemur, Mah-Jongg, have recently been completely restored. Another kind of experience again is to be found at Down House, home of the great Victorian scientist and creator of the Theory of Evolution, Charles Darwin. It was in his study here that he worked on the scientific theories that first scandalised and then revolutionised the world, culminating in the publication of the hugely significant *On the Origin of Species by Means of Natural Selection* in 1859.

Protecting the heritage

But English Heritage does much more than manage the historic properties in its care. As England's principal centre of expertise on all aspects of the historic environment, its advice leads to the protection of the best of the past – some of it surprising! As you look around you while following the walks in this book, you will see hundreds of buildings listed as being of vital historic importance, and therefore preserved for the future. The great buildings that saw history happening are of course on the lists; but so are scores of 'ordinary' buildings down the side streets, houses that were simply homes for generations of Londoners.

The thousands of protected historic monuments include the ruined edifices of England's great industrial past and of the conflicts of the twentieth century – symbols to many of poverty, exploitation and suffering, but nevertheless important as indelible records of huge swathes of history. Conservation areas range from the glorious Georgian terraces of Bath and Stamford through chocolate-box villages to streets of Victorian and Edwardian houses. There are 43 known and researched historic battlefields on the Battlefields Register and some 15,000 historic gardens on the Parks and Gardens Register. Every aspect of England's heritage is covered.

English Heritage supports archaeological work of all kinds, from traditional excavation through geophysical survey of buried remains to the detailed analysis of standing buildings. Archaeological scientists do ground-breaking research in dating methods, artefact conservation and the study of environmental remains such as human and animal bones, pollen and seeds. The Collections and Building Conservation teams carry out wide ranges of research and practical conservation work. The Education Service is internationally acclaimed for the work it does at all levels of formal education. The National Monuments Record houses over eleven million items… One could go on!

Membership and visits

There are currently around 470,000 members of English Heritage, people who support the organisation because they believe the membership fees are a tangible and direct way of supporting its work. Membership also gets them in free to English Heritage properties, and to most of the thousands of re-enactments that take place at the properties each year. Millions more visit English Heritage properties and re-enactments each year. Visitors from overseas can make the most of a trip to England by buying an Overseas Visitors Pass, which will allow them free entry to all the properties for a fixed period. Details of all the possibilities and advantages of joining English Heritage or visiting its sites can be obtained from English Heritage Membership Department, PO Box 570, Swindon SN2 2UR; telephone 0870 333 1181; e-mail members@english-heritage.org.uk

Go on – treat yourselves!

Index

Adams, John 5–6
Admiralty 8, 10
Albert, Prince 39
Andrews, Julie 111
Anne, Queen 20
Asquith, Herbert 9, 174
Asquith, Margot 9
Athenaeum Club 36
Austen, Jane 114, 149

Bach, Johann Christian 31, 36
Baird, John Logie 137–8
Ball, John 58
Banks, Sir Joseph 10, 130
Banqueting House 11–12
Barnardo, Dr 203
Bath, Knights of 27, 54
Beatles 129, 142, 151–2
Beatty, Admiral 89
Becket, St Thomas 24, 53–4
Beckett, Sam 178
Beerbohm Tree, Sir Herbert 39, 111
Beerbohm, Max 39, 173
Bell, Clive 180
Belloc, Hilaire 173
Berkeley Square 159
Blanc, Louis 178
Blood, Thomas 60–2, 77–8
Bloody Tower 49
Boehm, Mrs Edward 34
Boleyn, Anne 23, 47, 65–6,70, 74, 76–7
Bolingbroke, Lord 131—2
Boswell, James 29–30, 111–12, 130
Bourget, Paul 160
Bowie, David 129
Bragg, Sir William 137
Bridges, Sir John 48, 69
British Museum 175–8
Brontë sisters 191–2
Brooke, Rupert 178, 183
Browning, Robert 20
Brummell, Beau 33, 150
Brynner, Yul 111
Buchan, John 144
Buckingham Palace 31
Burke, Edmund 27, 104, 116, 130–1
Burlington House 149
Byron, Lord 148–9, 150, 153

Cabinet War Rooms 29
Cadogan Hotel 169–70
Café Royal 143
Calder, Ritchie 91–2
Campion, Edmund 57
Canaletto, Antonio 142–3
Canning, George 20,130
Carnaby Street 142
Caroline of Brunswick, Princess 5, 24
Carrington, Dora 174, 180
Caruso 111
Casanova, Giacomo 6, 30, 112, 135–6, 175
Caxton, William 16
Ceremony of the Keys 71
Chamberlain, Neville 9
Chaplin, Charlie 175
Chapman, Annie 201
Charles I 7, 8, 11, 12, 14, 41–2
Charles II 12, 20, 23, 51, 62, 110
Charles, Prince 90
Charterhouse 95
Chaucer, Geoffrey 16, 20, 27, 197
Cheshire Cheese 102–3
Chesterton, GK 103
Chopin, Frederic 148, 167, 188
Churchill, Sir Winston 9–10, 12–13, 29, 88–9, 174
Clapton, Eric 129
Clarence, Duke of 62–3
Clark, Petula 111
Clerkenwell Green 97
Clive, Lord 159
Coleridge, Samuel Taylor 117, 149
Collins, Joan 111
Collins, Wilkie 118, 178
Conan Doyle, Sir Arthur 103, 144, 178
Congreve, William 103, 132
Conrad, Joseph 178
Cook, Captain James 10–11
Courvoisier, Francois 99–100
Covent Garden market 112
Coward, Noel 111, 145, 166
Cranmer, Archbishop 23, 52, 187
Cromwell, Oliver 15, 27
Crown Jewels 60–2, 63–4
Culpepper, Thomas 67
Cumberland, Duke of 5

d'Arblay, Fanny Burney 160–1

Darwin, Charles 20, 36, 149, 150–1, 178
Davy, Humphrey 130
De Quincey, Thomas 117
Defore, Daniel 42
Dereham, Francis 67
Diaghilev, Sergei 174, 180
Dickens, Charles 20, 27, 36, 87, 98–101, 103,
    115, 118–19, 132, 178, 179, 185, 189, 192–3,
    196
Dighton, John 50
Disraeli, Benjamin 10, 36, 87, 149, 166, 178
Donne, John 89
Dostoevsky, Fyodor 40
Douglas, Lord Alfred 143–4, 145, 148, 170
Downing Street 8–10
Druitt, Montague John 208–9
Dryden, John 20, 131–2
Dudley, Lord Guildford 67, 69, 70, 72, 80–1,
    187
Duke of York's steps 37
Duval, Claude 113
Dylan, Bob 129, 142

Eaton Square 165
Eddowes, Catherine 203–4
Edward I 20, 24, 42, 49
Edward II 21–2
Edward III 20
Edward IV 16
Edward V 20, 21
Edward VI 20
Edward VII 32, 115, 145
Edward VIII 21
Edward the Confessor (St) 13, 19, 20, 21, 24–5
Edwards, Talbot 60
Eisenhower, Dwight 34, 89
Eliot, George 178
Eliot, T S 174, 178–9
Elizabeth (mother of Elizabeth II) 32
Elizabeth I 4, 8, 20, 23, 48–9, 69, 73, 74, 95, 104
Engels, Friedrich 139–40, 178
English Heritage 154
Essex, Earl of 69–71
Evelyn, John 7, 121, 195–6

Faraday, Michael 36, 149, 178
Farriner, Thomas 193–4
Fawkes, Guy 14, 16, 73–4
Ferdinand, Archduke 32
Fisher, (St) John 70, 73, 81
Flambard, Rannulf 54–6
Flamsteed, John 76, 121
Fleming, Ian 162–4
Forest, Miles 50
Fox, Charles James 20, 27, 130
Franklin, Benjamin 43, 94, 123–4
Froissart, Jean 14
Fry, Elizabeth 101

Gainsborough, Thomas 35
Garfunkel, Art 129, 203
Garrick, David 20, 27, 96, 110, 116–17, 130

Gaveston, Piers 21–2
George II 20, 26
George III, 5–6, 8, 23–4, 31, 110
George IV 5, 24, 34, 86, 110
Gerard, Father John 56–7, 58
Gibbon, Edward 27, 130
Gilbert, W S 178
Gladstone, William 10, 20, 37, 168
Globe, the 197
Goldsmith, Oliver 102–3, 130
Gonne, Maud 183
Gorky, Maxim 175–6
Gough Square 101–2
Granger, Stewart 111
Grant, Duncan 180
Grattan, Henry 20
Gregory, Lady 183
Greville, Charles 157, 189
Grey, Lady Jane 67–9, 70, 186–7
Gruffydd, Prince 56
Guildhall 188
Gwyn, Nell 36, 110, 113

Haggard, Sir Henry Rider 178
Haley, Bill 111
Hamilton, Emma, Lady 11, 28, 35, 86
Hampden, John 16
Handel, George Frederick 20, 27, 88, 155–7
Hanff, Helene 132–3
Hardy, Captain 86–7
Hardy, Thomas 20, 178
Harris, Frank 144
Harrison, George 152
Harrison, Rex 111
Hastings, Lord 64–5
Haymarket 39
Heine, Heinrich 124
Hendrix, Jimi 129, 155–6
Henry III 13, 20, 21, 28
Henry IV 14, 18, 25, 54
Henry V 18–19, 20, 25, 26, 28
Henry VI 13, 25, 26, 52–3
Henry VII 20, 26
Henry VIII 4, 23, 76–7
Herschel, William 119–20
Hess, Rudolph 75–6
Hogarth, William 97, 112, 117
Hogg, Thomas Jefferson 140–1
Holloway, Stanley 111
Holst, Gustav 178
Horse Guards Parade 8
Howard, Catherine 66–7, 70
Huxley, Aldous 178

Imworth, Richard 25
Irving, Henry 111
Irving, Washington 158, 178

Jacobs, Josef 62
Jagger, Mick 129, 136
James I 20
James II 7

James, Henry 160
Jeffreys, Judge 52
Jellicoe, Earl 89
Jerusalem Chamber 17, 18
Jewel Tower 16
Jinnah, Muhammad Ali 178
John, Augustus 173, 175
Johnson, Samuel 20, 27, 29, 96–7, 101–3, 111–12, 116, 129–30
Jones, Brian 129
Jonson, Ben 20
Jordan, Dora 168–9

Kelly, Gene 111
Kelly, Mary Jane 206–8
Keppel, Violet 164–5
Keynes, John Maynard 174, 180
Kingston, Sir William 47
Kipling, Rudyard 20, 122–3, 178
Krupskaya, Nadezhda Konstantinovna 98
Kumegusu, Minakata 178

Lamb, Lady Caroline 150
Lambeth Palace 16
Langtry, Lillie 111, 115, 145
Lawrence, DH 144, 174
Leigh, Vivien 165–6
Lenin, Vladimir Ilich 97–8, 175–7
Lennon, John 152
Lind, Jenny 39, 167
Livingstone, David 20
Lloyd George 9
Longfellow, Henry Wadsworth 103
Lopokova, Lydia 180
Lovat, Lord 82
Lutyens, Edwin 165

Macaulay, Lord 20, 36, 168
MacDonald, Ramsay 174
Magna Carta 184
Mahler, Gustav 108
Mansfield, Katherine 174
Mansion House 188
Marconi, Guglielmo 92–3
Martin Tower 60
Marx, Eleanor 135
Marx, Karl 139–40, 176–7, 185
Mary, Queen 4, 20, 47, 67
Mary, Queen of Scots 20
Mazzini, Giuseppe 178, 183–4
McCartney, Paul and Linda 152
Melbourne, Lord 25, 150
Melville, Herman 124–5, 149, 188
Mendelssohn, Felix 88–9, 148, 158
Metternich, Prince 166–7
Middle Temple Garden 105
Middle Temple Hall 104
Mill, John Stuart 36
Monmouth, Duke of 70, 82
Montfort, Simon de 27–8
Montgomery, Bernard 34
More, Sir Thomas 14, 46, 70, 72, 77, 80

Morrell, Lady Ottoline 173–4, 175
Morse, Samuel 178
Mosley, Sir Oswald 164
Mozart, Wolfgang Amadeus 31, 138–9, 164, 175, 190
Museum of London 93

Napoleon III 35
Nelson, Lord 11, 28, 85–7, 89, 120, 152, 154–5
Newgate Prison 98
Newton, Sir Isaac 20, 43, 62, 91, 121
Nichols, Mary Ann 200
Nicolson, Harold 41, 164–5
Nijinsky, Vaslav 111, 174
Nithsdale, Earl of 74–5
North, Lord 8
Nureyev, Rudolph 111

Old Palace Yard 15
Olivier, Laurence 165–6
Ono, Yoko 152
Orczy, Baroness 106
Orwell, George 144, 178, 179

Palmerston, Lord 20, 166
Parker Bowles, Camilla 90
Parliament, Houses of 12–13
Partridge, Ralph 180, 181
Pavlova, Anna 111
Penn, William 75
Pepys, Samuel 12, 26, 41–2, 83, 103–4, 121, 194–5
Percy, Major Henry 34
Peter the Great, Tsar 54, 62, 78
Picasso, Pablo 180
Pitney, Gene 136
Pitt, William the Elder 20, 34, 123–4
Pitt, William the Younger 10, 20, 33
Plekhanov, GV 178
Polidori, John 141
Pope, Alexander 103
Pound, Ezra 178, 183
Praz, Mario 178
Princes, two little 20, 49–51
Pym, John 16

Queensberry, Marquess of 143–4, 147–8, 169–70

Rains, Claud 111
Ralegh, Sir Walter 15–16, 51–2, 70
Rambert, Marie 111
Rattigan, Terence 166
Redgrave, Michael 166
Reynolds, Sir Joshua 27, 117, 129–30
Richard II 20, 22–3, 58, 93
Richard III 17, 25, 49–51, 53, 65
Richards, Keith 129, 136
Rimbaud, Arthur 135, 178
Ripper, Jack the 198–209
Rizal, Jose 178
Robeson, Paul 111

Rochford, Lady 67
Rogers, Ginger 111
Rolling Stones 128–9, 136, 142
Roosevelt, Eleanor 32
Roosevelt, Theodore 103
Ross, Robbie 169
Royal Academy of Arts 149–50
Royal Exchange 190
Royal Opera Arcade 37
Royal Opera House 108
Russell, Bertrand 173, 178
Rutherford, Ernest 20

Sackville-West, Vita 164–5
Salisbury, Countess of 66
Sanctuary, Westminster Abbey 17
Sargent, John Singer 160
Scott, Sir Walter 36, 149, 161
Shakespeare, William 26, 27, 104, 105, 188
Shaw, George Bernard 109, 113, 144, 178, 183
Shelley, Percy Bysshe 140–1, 176
Sheridan, Richard Brinsley 20, 114–5, 130, 153
Simon, Paul 129, 203
Smeaton, Mark 58
Smith, Adam 130
Somerset House 119–20
Soult, Marshal 188–9
Southey, Robert 149
Spector, Phil 136
Spencer, Lady Diana 27, 90
Spenser, Edmund 20, 27
St Bartholomew-the-Great church 93–4
St Dunstan's-in-the-West church 103–4
St James' Palace 4–7
St James' Park 29
St James' Square 34
St John's Gate 96
St Paul's Cathedral 85–92
St Paul's church, Covent Garden 113
St Sepulchre church 98–100
Starr, Ringo 152
Stein, Gertrude 178
Stephen, Adrian 180, 181
Stephen, Thoby 180
Stephen, Vanessa 179, 180, 181
Stewart, Rod 129
Stoker, Bram 178
Strachey, James 180
Strachey, Lytton 174, 175, 180, 181
Strachey, Oliver 180
Strauss, Richard 111
Straw, Jack 58
Stride, Elizabeth 202
Summersby, Kay 35

Taine, Hippolyte 178
Talleyrand, Prince 157–8
Tchaikovsky, Peter Ilich 144
Tennyson, Lord 20, 103
Thackeray, William Makepeace 20, 36, 95–6, 99–100, 103, 115, 167, 178
Thatcher, Margaret 10

Theatre Royal 110
Tower Green 64
Tower Hill scaffold 79–82
Tower of London 44–83
Trafalgar Square 40–1
Traitors' Gate 46–9
Trollope, Anthony 36, 178
Trotsky, Leon 98, 178
Turner, Reggie 169
Twain, Mark 103, 178
Tyler, Wat 58, 93–5, 97
Tylney, Elizabeth 68

Unknown Warrior 19

Valois, Catherine de 26
Van Buren, Martin 158–9
Verdi, Giuseppe 39
Verlaine, Paul 135
Victoria, Queen 25, 31, 39, 87, 158
Villeneuve, Admiral 87
Voltaire 103, 115, 190

Wagner, Richard 109, 133–5
Walewski, Count Alexandre 87
Wallace, Alfred Russel 150–1
Wallace, William 14, 49
Walpole, Horace 26
Walpole, Sir Robert 9
Waterloo Block 63–4
Watts, Charlie 129
Waugh, Evelyn 178
Weil, Simone 178
Wellington, Duke of 8, 10, 38, 39, 87, 89, 149–50, 157, 161, 166
Wells, HG 178
Wesley, John 96
Westminster Abbey 18–28
Westminster Hall 13–15
White Tower 53
White's Club 33
Who, The 142
Wilberforce, William 20, 167–8
Wilde, Oscar 39–40, 143–4, 145, 147–8, 169–70, 178
Wilhelm, Kaiser 32
William III 7, 20, 22
William IV 86, 168–9
William the Conqueror 20–21, 44, 53
Wilson, Harriette 37–8, 150
Woolf, Leonard 181
Woolf, Virginia 165, 174, 179–81
Wren, Sir Christopher 51, 89, 90–1, 121, 170, 196
Wyatt, Sir Thomas 4, 48, 59–60, 81
Wyman, Bill 129

Yat-Sen, Sun 178
Yeats, WB 103, 174, 182–3
York, Duke of 13

Zeta Jones, Catherine 111